FROM IDEAL TO ACTION

THE INNER NATURE OF A CATHOLIC SCHOOL TODAY

Edited by J.

before the last date shown

VERITAS

First published 1998 by
Veritas Publications
7-8 Lower Abbey Street
Dublin 1

Compilation copyright © J. Matthew Feheney 1998

ISBN 1 85390 318 3

**British Library Cataloguing
in Publication Data.
A catalogue record for
this book is available
from the British Library.**

Cover design by Barbara Croatto
Printed in the Republic of Ireland by Betaprint Ltd, Dublin

CONTENTS

INTRODUCTION

This volume is for the use of members of Catholic second-level school communities, including principals, teachers, parents, trustees and members of Boards of Management. I hope that it will stimulate and contribute to research on Catholic schools in Ireland, especially studies of the philosophy, theology and administrative policies that underpin such institutions.

The following pages concentrate exclusively on Catholic second-level schools, catering for students in the 12-18 age group, and do not deal with primary schools. The history, management and administration of primary schools, as well as the challenges facing them, are so different from those relating to second-level schools that the former would require a separate volume. To take but one feature, ownership: since 1975, all Catholic primary schools in Ireland are under the patronage of the local bishop, while the majority of Catholic second-level schools are under trusteeship of religious congregations.

Background

Catholic second-level schooling in modern times officially began in Ireland with the passing of the Relief Act of 1782, which allowed Catholics to teach and conduct schools without fear of prosecution. It took almost another hundred years, however, before the first Government grants became available to these schools. Initially this state aid, made possible by the Intermediate Education Act of 1878, was in the form of payment by results, with grants being awarded on a pro-rata basis, in direct relation to success rates in the Intermediate examinations. After 1924, capitation grants were paid to these schools, as well as incremental salaries to teachers. Since 1967, 90 per cent of capital expenditure (more in some cases) and all operational expenditure has been paid by the state.

In speaking of Catholic second-level schools, there is a

distinction to be made between those that are officially Catholic and those that, while in theory inter-denominational, are virtually Catholic because of the great preponderance of Catholics on the staff, on Boards of Management and in the student body. When discussing this matter at greater length in chapter 15, I have used the term *de jure* Catholic schools for the former category, and *de facto* Catholic schools for the latter. The *de jure*, or official, Catholic second-level schools are the 420-odd voluntary secondary schools catering for more than 200,000 students, aged 12-18, or 60 per cent of the total student enrolment in this age-group. Another 15 per cent of students attend 70-odd comprehensive and community schools that are virtually, or *de facto*, Catholic. The remaining quarter of the student population attend a fourth category of second-level school, i.e. the 246 vocational schools and community colleges, some of which might be said to be virtually Catholic and in most, if not all, of which there is a significant Catholic influence. The schools and colleges in this fourth category are under the control of thirty-eight Vocational Education Committees (Department of Education, 1995).

The use of the word 'inner' in the title of this book may require a word of explanation. It is best understood in the light of the distinction made by Gerald Grace in his article on the future of Catholic schools in England. Grace makes a distinction between analysis at surface level and at a deeper level. The surface-level characteristics of a Catholic school that might catch the attention of a potential or actual parent or member of the public might be: success in public examinations, attractive uniform, success in sporting and other extra-curricular activities, behaviour of students in public, public relations image, the nature of the buildings, and so on.

At a deeper level, however, the things that give a Catholic school its character are less obvious. They include: ethos, philosophy and mission statement of the school, approach to discipline, staff development, nature of leadership, relationships between members of staff, religious education programme, pastoral care programme, and so on. It is these 'inner' characteristics that ultimately determine the nature of a Catholic school, and it is with them that this volume is concerned.

What is a Catholic school?

Attempts to define a Catholic school can be made from two directions. The first approach is a juridical one based on Canon Law; the second seeks to identify elements characteristic of a Catholic school. Thus, for example, Canon 803 makes it clear that no school may bear the name Catholic except by the consent of the competent ecclesiastical authority; Canon 802 stipulates that the local bishop has a responsibility to ensure that schools with a 'Christian spirit' are established, while Canon 806 specifies the right of the bishop to 'watch over and inspect Catholic schools in his territory' and 'to issue directives concerning the general regulation of them'. Canon 795, on the other hand, is concerned with the nature of the education provided and reminds us that it 'must pay regard to the whole person, so that all may attain their eternal destiny and at the same time promote the common good of society. Children and young people are therefore to be cared for in such a way that their physical, moral and intellectual talents may develop in a harmonious manner, so that they may attain a greater sense of responsibility and a right use of freedom, and be formed to take an active part in social life' (CORI, 1996, 14).

Apart from Canon Law, the Church has made several statements over the past thirty years clarifying further the nature of a Catholic school. In 1965, the Vatican Council issued a Declaration on Christian Education, *Gravissimum Educationis*, which made clear that the religious dimension of a Catholic school is revealed in:

1. The specifically Christian view of the human person.
2. The climate of the school community.
3. The relationship fostered between faith and culture. (CORI, 1996, 16)

Since its Declaration on Christian Education (1965), the Catholic Church has issued three separate documents on the Catholic school: *The Catholic School* (1977), *Lay Catholics in Schools: Witnesses to Faith* (1982) and *The Religious Dimension of Education in a Catholic School* (1988). In addition to these, there was a separate document issued on catechesis, *Catechesi tradendae* (1982). A prominent theme running through the first three documents is that there is something distinctive in a Catholic school. What makes the Catholic school distinctive is its attempt to 'create for the school community a special atmosphere animated by the Gospel spirit of faith and charity' (*GE,* 8). The specific mission of the Catholic school is stated in unequivocal terms in the 1977 document *The Catholic School*: 'The specific mission of the Catholic school is a critical, systematic transmission of culture in the light of faith and… the integration of culture with faith and of faith with living' (*CS,* 1977, 49). The same document sees education as the development of the whole person '… since in Christ, the Perfect man, all human values find their fulfilment and unity' (*CS,* 1977, 35).

The theme of the need for integral formation of the human being is again underscored in the 1982 document, *Lay Catholics in Schools,* in the course of which it is stated that this comprises, 'the development of all the human faculties of the students, together with preparation for professional life, formation of ethical and social awareness, becoming aware of the transcendental and religious education' (*LCS,* 1982, 17).

The Religious Dimension of Education in a Catholic School declares that what makes the Catholic school distinctive is its religious dimension, which is to be found in the education climate, in the personal development of each student, in the relationship established between culture and the Gospel, and in the illumination of all knowledge with the light of faith (*RDECS,* 1988, 1).

Running through these statements is an emphasis on the peculiar culture that should be characteristic of a Catholic school. In brief, this culture is one that fosters and promotes religious faith.

In *Catechesi tradendae,* the integration of religious education with the rest of the curriculum in a Catholic school is emphasised:

> The special character of the Catholic school, the underlying reason for it, the reason why parents should prefer it, is precisely the quality of the religious instruction integrated with the education of the pupils. (*CT,* 1982, 69)

McLaughlin, however, alerts readers to the limitations of basing discussion of Catholic educational principles on phrases drawn from Church documents alone: 'they are not fully self-sufficient, but need to be understood by reference to the wider belief, tradition and practice of the Church, and in the light of *inter alia* sustained philosophical analysis... there are dangers in basing discussion of Catholic educational principles on phrases drawn from documents of this kind'. McLaughlin is quick to add, however, that these documents can provide a guide to the central features and elements of Catholic educational principles'. What I have tried to do here, therefore, is not to provide an exhaustive definition of a Catholic school, which would be impossible within the limits of this brief introduction, but, as it were, to give the 'central features and elements' so that they help to put the chapters that follow into perspective. Some of the contributors have also, though not at length (see Grace and Treston), touched on this topic.

Research in Catholic schools

Many of our readers will be aware of the renewed interest in Catholic schooling in the USA following the publication of the research of Professor Anthony Bryk and his team in *Catholic Schools and the Common Good* (Harvard, 1993). Bryk, however, is only one of a long line of distinguished academics who have subjected Catholic schools to extended critical inquiry. The results of their research has confirmed many of the things always claimed for Catholic schools: that they have an inspirational ideology, that they promote community, that they provide good pastoral care and that they generate 'social capital', a concept that is explored by McCann, Greeley and O'Keeffe in this volume.

In Australia, Marcellin Flynn has carried out pioneering research on the efficacy of Catholic schools, embodying his findings in several volumes (Flynn, 1985, 1993). In England, a recent publication by Dr James Arthur, *The Ebbing Tide* (1995), has aroused both interest and controversy and is referred to by several of our contributors (McCann, Grace, O'Keeffe, Feheney). More recently, McLaughlin, O'Keefe and O'Keeffe have edited a wide-ranging series of essays under the title, *The Contemporary*

Catholic School (Falmer, 1996), in the course of which the
themes, context, identity and diversity of Catholic schools are
explored by contributors from several disciplines within the field
of education. The present volume may best be understood within
this context of critical inquiry and research into Catholic schools
within the major English-speaking countries. We aim to review
the present position, envisage the future, in so far as this can be
done, and nudge interested parties to engage in pro-active
planning and, where necessary, reshape the Catholic school to
meet the challenges of a new millennium.

Themes
The chapters of this book are arranged under six different
themes. The first, Ethos, Values and Culture, is one that is very
prominent in the Vatican documents on Catholic schooling.
Joseph McCann approaches this theme from a theological
perspective, examining the implications of the crucifix in the
classroom. Having first examined the distinctiveness of
Catholicism, he goes on to consider the Church's educational
mission and the reality of Catholic schools. Tom O'Keeffe looks
at the operative goals of one Catholic school using the
expectations of members of the school community as an
expressive symbol, or indicator, of these. He reminds us that the
goals or objectives of a school do not exist 'out there' in some
mission statement or school prospectus: rather, goals exist only in
the minds of people and may be perceived quite differently by
students, parents and teachers. Expectations are, however, deep
yearnings of the human heart and may be regarded as an aspect
of the culture of the school in action.

The culture of schools also features prominently in Kevin
Williams' chapter on 'Religion, Culture and Schooling'. In the
course of the paper, he traces the Christian influence that has
permeated the Irish school system for the past seventy years,
evident at times even in publications emanating from the
Department of Education. Today, however, a Christian school
culture will not be found acceptable to everyone. Williams
touches on the delicate balance between openness, which is a
virtue, and a strong Christian ethos which nourishes both faith

and Christian praxis. He reminds readers of the vital role played by religious education in facilitating an integration of experience across the curriculum.

Under the theme of religious education, Kevin Treston, an Australian with experience of Catholic schools in several countries, including Ireland, looks at the school as an agent in evangelisation. Evangelisation is a recurring theme in literature on Catholic education and one that, perhaps, is not well understood. Treston reminds us that, for those actively involved in the Christian faith, evangelisation is an appeal to ongoing conversion, while for those who have withdrawn from practice, it is a call to reconciliation. Anne Looney, a practising catechist, reflects on some of the challenges facing religion teachers today, not least of which is survival. Catechists can sometimes be unwittingly exposed to the anger and frustration of parents in ideologically opposed camps: one group wanting a return to the good old days when the catechism was memorised and there were simple answers, while the other wants open discussion of complex moral issues. Looney looks at the new syllabus in religious education, which is about to be introduced to second-level schools, and draws attention to the challenge of striking a balance between the demands of catechesis on the one hand, and teaching the prescribed religious education programme on the other.

Pastoral care is an essential ingredient of a Catholic school, as the recent documents from Rome so clearly stress. It is also something for which Catholic schools are being complimented in the US at present. In my own chapter on pastoral care, I argue that it is not enough that pastoral care be implicit: it must also be explicit and be incorporated in a programme with a detailed syllabus, and sustained by a staff support structure. These latter assume added importance in view of the new demands in this area, especially the obligatory syllabus in Relationships and Sexuality Education and the recently published one in Civic, Social and Political Education. Frank Steele looks at school discipline, a topic that, like the poor, will always be with us. His approach to the subject is 'meditative', taking the form of a 'pilgrimage in meditation in search of the specifically Gospel roots of discipline in any school that would desire and labour to be Catholic, not just in name, but in spirit and truth'. In his view, discipline is intrinsically bound up with pastoral care, and the approach to it is a tangible expression of the ethos of the school.

Under the heading of contemporary challenges, Bernadette Flanagan tackles the issues relating to Christian feminism in a Catholic school. What she has to say applies not only to girls' schools but also, if not more so, to boys' schools. She suggests that the primary challenge which feminism poses to educational agencies is the necessity for them to create communities of learning where the reality of being men and women together in the world can be explored. This will, inevitably, include a review of the type of language used to describe God. Under this theme also, I have looked at a problem that is of increasing concern to principals and teachers, that is, the challenge of matching the curriculum to the talents and gifts of the students. Against the background of Howard Gardner's theory of multiple intelligences, I point out that, despite the existence of at least eight different intelligences, the two that are much favoured above the others are linguistic and logical-mathematical intelligences; not alone the curriculum, but also methods of teaching and assessment (including the most important examination at second level, the Leaving Certificate), give pride of place to these two intelligences. The fate of the students who are weak in these two areas, though generously gifted with other intelligences, are discussed in the chapter.

In recent years there has been a good deal of research into the nature of leadership and the ways in which leadership qualities can be promoted and utilised to their best advantage. Though this research was initially concerned with leadership in the world of business, the results are now being made available to people in the field of education. Catholic schools depend on a wide range of leaders, from trustees and members of Boards of Management, to principals and teachers. Teresa McCormack looks at the changing roles of trustees and Boards of Management. These bodies will be entrusted with new responsibilities when the provisions of the Government's White Paper on Education become law, something that is expected to happen sooner rather than later. McCormack stresses the need for both trustees and Boards to be pro-active if they are to discharge their duties adequately and influence the future development, not only of their own schools, but also of education in general in this country. To be pro-active, however, means being informed, confident and determined, and this requires training and development. Eileen Doyle takes a thorough look at this, tracing the growth of an awareness of the need for staff development and the emergence of structures to facilitate it. She notes that while individual professional needs continue to merit attention, the current focus in schools is on staff development. Collaboration between staff and Boards of Management can result in the best of two worlds: the promotion of a sense of community in the school and the development and tuning up of the professional expertise of the teachers.

David Tuohy and David Coghlan combine their complimentary expertises in education and management to chart a vision for Catholic schools, involving meaning, community and excellence. While pointing out the distinction between leadership and administration, they emphasise that these two roles are interdependent in the person of the school principal. They suggest that there will always be a concern with excellence in Catholic schools – that individuals develop their talents and that these talents bear fruit 'one hundred fold'. They also note that a more Christian approach is to ensure that achievements are norm-referenced, where all individuals try to reach a prescribed standard, rather than criterion-referenced, where success is judged in comparison to others. This question could well be the subject of a staff workshop.

Ultimately, however, school effectiveness is measured by the extent to which proclaimed goals are actually achieved. And this brings us back to the purpose of a Catholic school, something which several of the contributors remind us should be set out clearly in a school mission statement, reviewed regularly and amended to meet changing circumstances.

The future is both a safe and a dangerous topic on which to write. Emboldened, however, by T. S. Eliot's lines, 'Time present and time past/are both perhaps present in time future,/and time future contained in time past' (*Four Quartets*, 'Burnt Norton', I), Andrew Greeley, whose name is synonymous with Catholic education in the USA, tackles this topic in respect of Catholic schools in his own country. Greeley's chapter is both exciting and depressing: exciting because the latest research in the US, with its favourable reports of Catholic schools, confirms what he has been saying about Catholic education for more than thirty years; depressing because he feels that Catholic leaders in the US, especially his own priest colleagues, have largely ignored not only his own research findings, but also the good news about the success of Catholic schools. Gerald Grace, recently appointed director of the new Centre for Research and Development in Catholic Education at the Institute of Education, University of London, summarises the position of Catholic schools in England and Wales and outlines some of the challenges the future will bring. I myself do something similar for Irish schools, emphasising the need for pro-active planning to be supported by extensive staff development.

While the future of Catholic schools in Ireland and Britain is unlikely to be jeopardised by shortage of money, as is the case in the US, they face another and, perhaps, more sinister challenge there – the pervasive influence of market forces. Grace reminds us of Joseph O'Keefe's motto, 'No Margin, No Mission', indicating that Catholic schools will lose both their mission and their soul, if they concentrate on chasing the indicators of success promoted by market forces and turn their backs on the poor and marginalised. Though this temptation is not, in itself, new, its current packaging is much more attractive and beguiling than in the past.

I wish to express my thanks to our contributors for meeting deadlines, to my publisher, Veritas, especially Fiona Biggs, and to my colleague, Anne Fleischmann, for advice and support.

J. Matthew Feheney
Editor
Christian Leadership in Education Office (CLEO)
Mardyke House, Cork
15 August 1997

PART I

ETHOS

1
THE CRUCIFIX IN THE CLASSROOM: DISTINCTIVE SYMBOL OF A CATHOLIC SCHOOL

Joseph F. McCann CM

Introduction

Michael Paul Gallagher SJ in a recent book tells a story about standing in a Catholic church in India, with lots of statues and a life-sized crucifix, when a class of children with their teacher came in on a school tour. The class included Hindu and Muslim children. The Muslims were amazed at all the statues, but the Hindu youngsters were disturbed by the graphic image of the crucified Christ. Before long, Fr Gallagher found himself helping out the teacher, explaining the story of the passion, death and resurrection of Jesus, the Son of God, to a multi-faith class – and it struck him how distinctive Christianity is among other world religions (Gallagher, 1997, 68).

He might equally have been struck by how distinctive Catholicism is among other Christian denominations, for the crucifix is the single most powerful Catholic symbol. Not the cross, the Christian symbol *par excellence,* 'a stumbling-block and a scandal' though it may be, nor a picture or icon of the death of Jesus, but the crucifix with the statue of the naked body of Christ upon it, depicted realistically, after the western tradition.

The purpose of this paper is to elaborate a model of Catholic schooling in terms of school organisation, curriculum content and educational process, motivated by the insight that belief about the nature of God, human beings and the world makes a real difference in the way schools are organised and run. 'Crucifix in the Classroom' – the most distinctive visual clue of a Catholic school – is both its title and theme.

The paper will be divided into three parts: in Part One, the topic of Catholicity and its qualities will be discussed. Part Two will take up the Catholic Church's involvement in schools; Part Three will tackle the reality of Catholic schools. The conclusion will deal with the theological/educational questions that these considerations raise about Catholic schools in today's world. The paper pretends to no originality, but hopes to set in order a number of issues that Catholic (and Christian) theologians and educators need to address. While parts of the paper may apply to all Christian schools, its main focus is the distinctive reality of a Catholic school.

Part One: Catholicism and its distinctiveness

There are two kinds of definitions: essential definitions and operational definitions. Essential definitions attempt to pluck out the heart of the matter, to put in a form of words what makes something be what it is and not something else. Operational definitions are simpler and, in ways, more useful, because they aim only at a working description, isolating the features that distinguish the thing defined from other things. In other words, how you would know it if you met it in the street.

An essential definition of Catholicism includes many matters that all Christian churches hold in common. One could begin there, and progressively distinguish towards the specifically Roman Catholic religious culture, but brevity demands that a short-cut be taken. Let us begin, then, with an operational definition of Catholicism – a proposed list of qualities that pick this particular Christian tradition out from others.

Tom Groome (1993) suggests that Langdon Gilkey's description of Catholicism would be a good place to start. Gilkey named four characteristics which he took to be especially Catholic:

> A sense of the reality, importance and 'weight' of tradition and history...
>
> A sense of humanity and grace in the communal life of Catholics...
>
> A continuing experience... of the presence of God and of grace mediated through symbols to the entire course of ordinary human life...
>
> A drive toward rationality, the insistence that the divine mystery... be insofar as is possible penetrated, defended and explicated by the most acute rational reflection. (Gilkey, 1975, 17)

The first quality, the place of tradition in Catholic life, is obvious. Gilkey considered an appreciation of tradition and history an important source of strength to the Church, while quite aware that that tradition's authority had been undermined by modernity, and that it also ran the danger of stifling and suffocating needed change.

Gilkey comments on the second characteristic, the communal life of the Catholic Church, and remarks with surprise at the ability of the Catholic community, at its best, to display an understanding forgiveness for the weaknesses of human nature, despite the apparent rigidity of Catholic morality, especially in sexual matters.

The third characteristic is most evident simply by entering a Catholic Church, as in the case of the Indian children in Michael Paul Gallagher's story above. Catholics delight in symbols. At a more profound level, this delight manifests itself in a thoroughgoing sacramentality, a cherishing of ritual and sacred objects, involving experiences of all five senses (taste and smell and feel and sight and sound) as signs of grace. Gilkey is struck by three aspects of the Catholic use of symbols: the sense of transcendence constantly touching ordinary human life, the wide variety of symbolic communication used to convey the mystery, and the deeply felt and powerful religious significance of these means of grace for each stage of life. He also notes that relativism, liberalism and the critical stance of modern thought have shaken the certainty and disturbed the comfortable acceptance of the mysterious, the awesome and the transcendent, when captured in any other form than the abstractions of speculative thought.

The last characteristic is fundamental to the idea of education and schooling: Catholicism has always embraced reason and rationality, subjecting even the sacred truths of religion to the probing light of the human mind. The deepest Catholic faith sought to find its footing in understanding. But, Gilkey remarks, the Catholic devotion to rationality was combined with an acceptance of ecclesial authority and religious revelation, which seemed to outsiders to compel Catholics to enter on the enlightenment project, as it is called, not wholeheartedly, but with a certain hesitancy.

The four characteristics, rationality, symbolism, communal forgiveness and tradition, are of a piece. Christians take two contrasting positions concerning the Church. In the first position, the Church is both visible society and divine institution. In the other position, the Church is an invisible society, made up of people who, as individuals, are unknown, because it is the inward response of faith which makes the real Christian and not external membership in any visible group. Those holding the second position maintain that the Church as divine institution is independent of any earthly society. The first position holds that the Church as a society is of divine institution. Protestant and Reformation Christians generally take the second position; Episcopal and Catholic Christians (including the Orthodox and Roman Catholic Church) adopt the first (Cross and Livingstone, 1974, 'Church').

This has implications for the Church's approach to education. The Catholic theology of Church takes very seriously institutional and social arrangements as signs of God's presence. Catholic theologians caution that a theology of the Church must avoid repeating the historical heresies about the two natures of Christ, ignoring either human nature or divine nature. For instance, we should not reduce the Church's teaching to a simple handing on of a tradition in a fashion akin to other societies. For an unbeliever, Jesus Christ is a gifted human being, and the Church an exceptionally resilient organisation; for the faithful, Jesus is the Son of God made man, and the Church, the Body of Christ and Temple of the Spirit. This perspective is central to any understanding of the educational mission of the Church.

Part Two: The Catholic Church's educational mission

One of the ironies of the modern world is that religious terms are hijacked for baser purposes. A notable capture has been the word 'mission', now used for very worldly enterprises. Car-hire firms have 'mission statements' nowadays. 'Mission' (sending) is primarily a 'Church' word in common speech, indicating the works or activities of the Church, as in foreign missions, mission to the homeless, educational mission, etc. Common speech misses its theological reference to the 'Missio Dei', the sending by

God, not of the Church, but of the Son, Jesus Christ, from the heart of the Trinity to earth. In turn, the Son sends the disciples to teach all nations in the name of the Father, Son and Spirit, with the promise of his presence to the end of the age (Mt 28:18-20). The work of the Church, then, is part of the work of God. God is a sending God who sends the Son in the Spirit to 'sum up all things in Christ' (Ep 1:9). The unity of the human race under the rule of God's will is needed to enable the people of the world to become fully human and come to the perfect establishment of human life. The Church is sent to reconcile all human beings, to serve the world, and to inaugurate the Kingdom of God.

A pivotal idea, used by the Second Vatican Council, to convey the mission of the Church is 'koinonia' or 'communion'. 'The notion of koinonia includes a vertical dimension of divine life and gifts received by the Church, and a horizontal dimension in sharing this life and gifts with others' (O'Donnell, 1996, 140-43). Translations or renderings of koinonia include 'partnership', 'shared life', 'joint partaking', 'participation', or 'community'. As with 'mission', the words employed to explain 'communion' have a common meaning, which relate to the theological meaning but are not entirely coterminous with it. Those not conversant with the theology of the Church will render the task of creating community (koinonia) as democratisation, with little appreciation for the 'vertical dimension'. The problem with a too 'horizontal' view is that it can become stuck in the here and now, concerned only with membership, responding to human needs rather than to the will of God, elevating the local at the expense of the universal, concentrating on the earthly and visible at the expense of the spiritual and mystical, looking to Christians rather than to Christ.

The mission of the Church is part of the sweep of the Spirit through history into eternity, from the first Word of God's Creation to the final Word of God's Judgement, and centred on the person of the Word spoken in our midst through Jesus Christ. The Church gathers people in unity and mutual service for the transformation of the world in justice, and this is an insight that contemporary theology has rightly emphasised. But it is just as true that the Church is made by the gathering of the people of

God into the body of Christ through the Spirit in thanksgiving to the Father. Accordingly, the properly understood idea of koinonia, communion or community, is a powerful and multi-faceted one. It is probably, according to O'Donnell, the most favourable approach for Christians to renew their sense of Church and understand their theology. O'Donnell remarks that the understanding of koinonia must be squarely in the context of the Eucharistic celebration, 'the source and summit of Christian life and a principal manifestation of the Church'. He goes on to remark, however, that this understanding 'involves a deep appreciation of the meaning of the Eucharist, one that many people in the West may not yet have achieved' (O'Donnell, 1996, 142).

Koinonia, community or communion is both a reality and an aspiration for the Catholic Church. Catholics describe themselves as being 'in communion with God and with each other', vertically through the Spirit in Christ to the Father, horizontally in the Eucharist, with the bishop, between the bishops, and among the faithful. One way of establishing communion, encouraging communion, and enhancing communion is the bond of ecclesiastical unity. But the aspiration recognises that community is never perfect. So Catholics desire full community throughout the world and the whole of creation in Christ, and work to achieve it.

Thus an amount of common ground can be found between distinctive Catholic culture and Catholic schooling by employing the concepts of 'community' and 'mission', ideas linked in the farewell discourse of Jesus from John's Gospel: 'May they be one so that the world may believe' (Jn 17:21) Both ideas are also combined in the Great Commission, the final chapter of the Gospel according to Matthew, where the idea of 'community' is implied in the 'making of disciples' and 'mission' is contained in the command itself, 'Go... make... baptise... teach...'.

'All authority in heaven and on earth has been given to me. Go, therefore, make disciples of all nations; baptise them in the name of the Father and of the Son and of the Holy Spirit, and teach them to observe all the commands I gave you. And look, I am with you always, yes, to the end of time (Mt 28:18-20).

All Christians now generally share this approach to mission. But the history of Christian mission has gone through a number of distinct phases, each determined by different theological insights, and different factors of history, economics, opportunity and technology. David Bosch (1992) has identified a set of missionary objectives that have characterised Church mission through the centuries, some of which obviously share common threads with the ideas of Christian educators today:

1. A concern for discipleship (following Christ).
2. A priority for evangelising the poor.
3. The witness of a loving Church community.
4. Establishment of Christian institutions, such as hospitals and schools.
5. Respect for the personal response of faith to God's invitation.
6. Missions to heathen countries, for the love of God and neighbour.

The Catholic tradition has typically promoted numbers 3 and 4, 'witness of the Church community' and 'establishment of institutions', and these share obvious affinities with the qualities of Catholicism listed by Gilkey. Thus, the lines of the typical Catholic school emerge as an institution whose structures deliberately involve the participants in the liturgical, social, intellectual and aesthetic environment of the Church, for the formation of the individuals within it and the transformation of the wider society. For Catholicism does not turn its back on the world or on rational thought; on the contrary, through its theologians, philosophers and teachers, it incorporates (some say co-opts) culture in the service of faith.

A recent shift in the understanding of the nature of Church and mission in both Protestantism and Catholicism, converging on the understanding of mission as the *Missio Dei* (Mission of God), has resulted in a renewed attention to the rest of Bosch's mission objectives, notably numbers 1, 2 and 5, 'discipleship of Christ', 'priority for the poor' and 'respect for the personal response of faith'. Catholic educators are somewhat divided about the direction Catholic schools have been taking since the

Second Vatican Council. Is the function of a Catholic school to transmit Catholic values only to children from committed Catholic families in a Catholic community? Or can the Catholic school also prepare pupils (Catholics and others from different religions) in a Catholic religious atmosphere, with an emphasis on social justice, to be successful citizens in an open, pluralist and secular society? And can these objectives be combined in the one institution? (Murray, 1996).

On one side of the debate is John Haldane: '...the primary function of Catholic schools is to transmit Catholic truths and Catholic values. Everything else, no matter how important, is secondary to this' (Haldane, 1996). Another on the same side is James Arthur (1995) who claims that, in the UK, there are three models of Catholic schools: holistic schools (Catholics alone), dualist schools (secular educational programmes plus a voluntary Catholic religious programme), and pluralist schools (many faiths and cultures treated equally). Of these, Arthur asserts that the only truly Catholic school is the holistic one, and it is the only one to have clear support from Church teaching.

On the other side of the debate, Bernadette O'Keeffe (1992, 48) agrees with Arthur in that she identifies models of Catholic schooling: the 'bedrock' model (100 per cent Catholic), the joint school model (50 per cent Catholic, 50 per cent Anglican), the minimal risk model (up to 15 per cent non-Catholic admissions), the urban school model (a large proportion of non-Catholic students), but she differs from him in arguing for the multi-faith school as the way forward for Catholic schools.

The centrality of Trinitarian theology for the renewed understanding of Church has led to a rediscovery of the person, as an individual-in-community, autonomous yet relying on others, free yet interdependent. These ideas can be traced principally in the Second Vatican Council's documents and in various statements since then from the Sacred Congregation for Catholic Education: *The Catholic School* (1977), *Lay Catholics in Schools: Witnesses to Faith* (1982), *The Religious Dimension of Education in a Catholic School* (1988). Modern Catholic educational principles have reaffirmed the importance of holistic formation, of integration of disciplines, of the freedom of the individual person, of the development of the community, of insertion in the culture, and of society and nature, both as a sphere for action and as a source of knowledge (Murray, 1991, 20). For example, a report to the English Catholic Bishops enumerated four key elements that define a Catholic school:

> 'a perspective centred on faith in Christ as Saviour';
> 'a deep respect for the individuality and integrity of all human beings';
> 'a commitment to the pursuit of justice';
> 'the promotion of a sense of mission', which would enable individuals to 'renew the face of the earth'.
> (Report, 1981, 119-120)

Furthermore, recent Catholic official documents on education and schooling have maintained the obligation of Catholic educators to be open to and co-operative with other denominations and other religions for ecumenical action and interfaith dialogue (Lane, 1996, 129). Yet the thrust of the Catholic school has historically been to preserve the Catholic ethos and the transmission of Catholic doctrine. So the tension remains, a tension implicitly contained in the first command to mission: 'teach all nations all that I have commanded you.' Christian mission is not one of domination or absorption. Early Christian missionaries went to the Jews first and then to the Greeks, but they did not make the Greeks into Jews. Catholic schools seem destined to be pulled apart in the tension between 'teaching what Jesus commands' and the direction to teach 'all nations', and this tension in the Catholic classroom will continue to be 'crucial' in more senses than one.

Part Three: The reality of Catholic schools

Educators, along with other professionals in the human services, are accustomed to high levels of jargon and opaque terminology, as well as to unreal and vague rhetoric. Researchers tend to devalue stated aims and goals in favour of the actual, though unstated, reality. It comes as a surprise, therefore, to discover a new trend in American educational research. Recent surveys have found that American Catholic schools do abide by their mission statements, and that these commitments to ideological goals have a discernible effect on the education of the students. In particular, it is surprising to see documented in research, which has neither Church sponsorship nor association, the connection between effective and successful teaching and learning of poor inner-city children, with 'consensual, supportive and caring communities' (Cooper, 1996, 46).

The most famous example of such research is the study of Catholic high schools and their internal organisation by Anthony Bryk and his associates (Bryk *et al.*, 1993). The Bryk team found that Catholic high schools were marked by academic success. The research team discounted the factors of class or income or race, which are often alleged as reasons for the success of Catholic schools. They attributed the success of Catholic schools to four causes:

> focused academic attention;
> communal organisation;
> inspirational ideology;
> decentralised governance.

They found that the academic curricula of Catholic schools were narrower than in corresponding public schools, and that this emphasis on core subjects came from a common conviction as to the things young people ought to learn, which stemmed from a common belief regarding the nature of young people and their destiny. This led to a common education of mind and spirit, high teacher commitment, high pupil engagement, and an evident communal organisation that affected the school in many ways. The Catholic schools maximised face-to-face opportunities for meeting pupils, took for granted a teacher role that extended well beyond the classroom and the academic discipline, and assumed a collegial relationship among the teaching staff that was generally helped by the smaller size of the average Catholic schools.

Of particular interest for the current discussion is the team's conclusions on what they called 'inspirational ideology'. They identified the principles enunciated at the Second Vatican Council as decisive in creating a purpose for separate Catholic schools: 'The charter for Catholic schools shifted from protecting the faithful from a hostile Protestant majority to pursuing peace and social justice within an ecumenical and multicultural world' (Bryk *et al.,* 1996, 30). In terms of school organisation and curriculum, this ideology emerges with two important ideas: personalism and subsidiarity. Personalism is a commitment to humanity and humaneness in the common relationships inside the school, especially the relationships between staff members and students. The reason for promoting personalism is that it is a moral vision of how people should relate with each other in a just society. Subsidiarity requires that the school values human dignity and human effort, that efficiency is not the criterion for educational decisions, and that the school keeps things as small-scale as it can to enhance human relationships.

A further consequence of the 'inspirational ideology' was the peculiar strength of conviction attached to the subjects on the curriculum. As teachers, administrators, parents and even students shared a similar vision of what a human being should know and be able to do, and similar beliefs concerning human history and destiny, consensus was widespread and motivation high for a core set of subjects. In particular, the 'humanities' played a major part in the school's academic life. Equally, because this was a consensus around what all should know and achieve, there was considerable 'academic pressure' on students to cope and succeed. Accordingly, the situation was reached in which Catholic schools, even urban schools, had higher-than-expected academic standards and lower-than-expected drop-out rates. This phenomenon was the one that attracted the attention of secular educational researchers in the first place. The interesting aspect of student engagement in Catholic schools was that it was not attended by particularly excellent teaching and instruction! (Bryk *et al.,* 1993, 94).

There have been other evaluations of Catholic schools and schooling during the last thirty years since the Second Vatican Council. A 1997 report on twenty-seven Catholic second-level schools in poor city areas in the United Kingdom echoes the findings of the Bryk research. The UK Catholic schools are described as 'beacons of hope', as 'caring Christian communities', and an official inspector called one school, 'an oasis in a deprived area'. In this instance, however, the report highlighted the contrast between the atmosphere of personal and academic expectations of the community created in the school, with the demoralised and deprived community of the local neighbourhood (O'Keeffe, 1997).

Other American and Australian reports have investigated academic results in terms of adherence and faith in adult life in students educated in Catholic schools. Others, again, have looked at the climate and ethos inside the school (McDonagh, 1991, 47-80). The direction of the research has been towards underlining and reaffirming the secular value and academic credit of the education children have received in Catholic schools, and in locating an effective cause in the communal experience in which they have participated. James S. Coleman put this in a 'sound-bite': social capital. He wrote:

> The community that is created by and exists within the Church, a community that connects families to one another and to the school through the Church, is an important resource for children and young people as they move toward adulthood. This is not a common kind of conclusion to come from a secular scholar; it is, however, the conclusion that one is driven to by results of the research that I have carried out. (Coleman, 1989)

Bryk and his partners agree with Coleman's idea of social capital, with the qualification, 'we locate that capital in the relations among school professionals and with their parent communities' (Bryk *et al.*, 1996, 40). Capital of any kind is a resource whereby one can achieve other objectives. Education as human capital was a common idea in the 1960s. What is new about the notion of social capital is that it is attached not to any cognitive learning or technical skill that the individual student might have acquired, but to the actual experience of spending time in a community with a particular ethos. Research suggests that the experience of community based on expectations of rational discourse, mutual respect and personal responsibility, challenged by the awareness of world community and uncompromising moral commitment, allied to an acceptance of human failure with a deep optimism in rationality and humanity, founded on faith in God's creation of the world and in his providence over history, gives people the encouragement, confidence and humility to perform to the best of their abilities.

Conclusion

Observers agree that the distinguishing mark of a Catholic school is its intentional creation of community and its uninhibited use of signs, symbols and rituals – secular and sacred – to ensure that community happens (Lesko, 1988). A notable feature of Catholic-school community is that it is not dependent on its neighbourhood (though local people can be involved) but on the institutional Church itself. It is the Church, after all, which endows the school community with its particular edge, its ideological motivation, its social dimension, its global awareness, its moral emphasis, its religious conviction, and the sense of eternal consequences for temporal affairs charges its communal activities with meaning.

But this raises a question. Catholicism and the Catholic school are caught between two impulses: a commitment to the power of reason and a respect for human thought and learning, and an appreciation of sign, symbol and image, in particular the sign of Christ's presence in the Church community – two of the characteristics picked out by Gilkey. Respect for human reason and learning implicates Catholic education and Catholic schooling in the ways of the world and the commerce of culture, for the Catholic teacher must stand in the marketplace of ideas along with all the rest. On the other hand, Catholicism holds fast to the appreciation of sign, symbol and sacrament, indeed also to the special nature of certain times, places, objects, actions, words and people which are caught up in the revelation of God. This aspect of Catholic education and the Catholic school runs counter to contemporary culture and is accorded no value in the currency of the world. What, then, happens to the Catholic school when the culture empties mystery from symbol, when the unity of the Church community is challenged by individualism, and when the authority of the Church community is questioned by personal autonomy? Catholicism is a particular statement of the Christian tradition, distinctive especially in its 'institutionality', and so questions around the organisation of the school and its relationship to the Church are the more pointed.

Scripture scholars see the beginnings of the Church at the foot of the cross of Jesus, as the disciple whom Jesus loved accepts the mother of Jesus into his home as his mother also (Jn 19:25), as the Son prays to the Father (Lk 23:46), as all people are drawn to the Son (Jn 12:32), as even the Gentile centurion recognises the Son of God (Mt 27:54; Mk 15:39), and as Jesus hands over the Spirit (Jn 19:30). But there were others at the Cross, who were, indeed, drawn to the place, but not converted by the events there, or, at least, not at that time: a passer-by on the highway, Pharisees and scribes, two thieves and several soldiers are all identified as being present. Only one thief and the centurion respond with faith. But even the centurion, in the Gospel according to Luke, is more cautious in his statement of recognition, and more obviously a man of his culture (Lk 23:47).

In his public ministry, Jesus seems sometimes to interact with people, and even works miracles for them, without requiring that they become formal disciples. It seems to be the same at the cross of Jesus, where those of deep faith, wavering faith, implicit faith, and no faith, come together, drawn indeed by the mission of God made man in Jesus Christ, but do not enjoy a faith experience. Might the mission of God not be the same in the Catholic classroom where Jesus still hangs upon the cross, a stumbling block for the Jews and foolishness for the Gentiles? (I Cor 1:23).

2

VALUES IN A CHRISTIAN SCHOOL: THE CASE OF ST XAVIOUR'S

Tom O'Keeffe

Introduction

This paper is condensed from a longer study which examined the operative goals of a Catholic voluntary secondary school for boys in a city in the south of the Irish Republic. In the interests of confidentiality, we have used a fictitious name, St Xaviour's College, for the school in question. In real life, it has an enrolment of about 700 (all boys), is now about fifty years in existence, has a history of academic and sporting successes, and has a largely male staff.

The methodology used for an evaluation of the goals of St Xaviour's involved an examination of one of the expressive symbols of the school: the expectations of its students, teachers and parents. The goals or objectives of a school do not exist 'out there' in some mission statement, school prospectus or statement of philosophy (though these latter may contain an attempt to express them or to suggest them). Rather, goals exist only in the minds of people and may be perceived quite differently by students, parents and teachers. Expectations are not just hopes or idle fantasies: they represent the deep yearnings of the human heart. In this sense they provide an indicator of the student, parent and teacher perceptions of the function or mission of the school. We are dealing here with the basic underlying assumptions of the school community, what we might call their culture in action.

The expectations of the school community of St Xaviour's College were explored with the aid of a forty-item questionnaire to Leaving Certificate students, their parents and their teachers. The range of questions embraced the full human and personal development of students, while focussing in particular on five expectation dimensions, clusters or factors, namely, vocational, academic, personal, social and religious development. Tensions and balances between the expectations of the three groups were examined and the question of congruence raised, that is, the congruence between the operative goals of St Xaviour's as an actual Catholic school, and the ideal Catholic school as envisaged in Church documents, especially as encapsulated in the Address of Pope John Paul II to the English Bishops on 26 March 1992:

> The Catholic school is a witness to the truth that genuine education seeks to do more than simply impart knowledge, or train people to perform an economically productive task. All education worthy of the name seeks to bring forth as it were a full person, a person in whom moral excellence is no less developed than are theoretical or productive abilities.

Design and method of study

This is a comparative study analogous to one carried out in Australia by Marcellin Flynn among Year 12 students in Catholic schools in New South Wales in 1972, 1982 and 1992 (Flynn, 1985, 1993). For purposes of validation and comparison, I have used Flynn's questionnaire and submitted my findings to the same statistical procedures, including factor analysis. My sample involved 141 Leaving Certificate students, average age eighteen, 141 homes and 48 teachers. Since this study is modelled on the well-known Australian one, the reader will note that I occasionally refer to the latter for purposes of comparison when analysing my results. The entire study, of which this paper is part, is available from the Christian Leadership in Education Office (CLEO), Cork, which provided supervision for the study when it was carried out in 1996.

Goals

The content of the goals of a school can be classified into three: instrumental, expressive and organisational. But the relationship between these three types is not static: there is an inherent tendency for them to compete with and displace one another; for example, cultural activities (expressive goals) may tend to be squeezed out by academic pressures (instrumental goals). This dynamic applies, too, to the way goals are viewed or evaluated both within and without the school (Lambert *et al.*, 1970, 16).

We must always bear in mind that schools, as social organisations, are open systems, in constant interaction with their many environments. All school boundaries, both internal and external, are highly porous. Having porous external boundaries means that it is not possible for the school to be isolated from sources of influence in the wider cultural and social environment in which it is located. Hence the goals that the schools pursue are not always consciously chosen. They are the result of a complex of pressures which bear on the school from within and without.

Students, parents and teachers, as shown in the study, can and do evaluate goals differently, as, indeed, can other elements of the wider society. Latent conflicts are, therefore, built into the goal system of schools (Lambert *et al.*, 1970, 44). Indeed, we can say that endemic conflict between goals is a chief dynamic of the school society.

There exists, therefore, in the school community a dynamic tension which can produce displacement and cause dysfunction. Severe dysfunction can lead to non-attainment of the basic goals a school or society strives to attain. It can be argued, on the other hand, that some tension, creative tension, and balance between quite different expectations is healthy, and can promote change or morale, or even bring about some unintended attainment.

In the light of these considerations I shall explore the implications and context of the different expectations of students, parents and teachers concerning St Xaviour's College. To this end I provide a visual comparison of these clusters of expectations in Figure 2.1. These expectations embrace the full human and personal development of students, while focussing in particular on vocational, academic, personal, social and religious development.

*   *   *

Figure 2.1. *Comparison of the expectations of students, parents and teachers of St Xaviour's College, 1996*

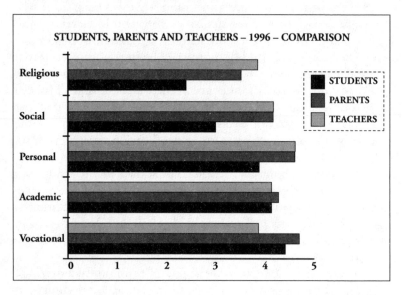

Vocational Development: employment, careers, third-level opportunities

Underlying the expectations of St Xaviour's College Leaving Certificate students is a very deep concern about employment. Strong indications of this preoccupation were found in the open-ended responses. As they prepare for the Leaving Certificate, and to leave school, they face the prospect of having no job, or of not being able to enter their chosen career or profession. Their highest expectation, therefore, is vocational, 'that St Xaviour's should prepare them well for future careers, employment and third-level places'. In this they mirror the expectations of their Australian counterparts of 1982 and 1992 (Flynn, 1993, 166).

Parents not only share, but, on the mean score, outstrip their sons' concern for vocational preparation to help them to cope with life after leaving school.

This fear of and concern regarding unemployment is understandable and explicable. Ireland has become fully integrated into the economic life of Europe at a time when western society is beset by major problems. These problems are largely those created by massive unemployment, and, as Dr Liam Ryan points out in his commentary on the European Value Systems Study, they affect Ireland to an extreme degree because of the peculiar structure of our population, where the numbers annually coming on the job market double the numbers of those retiring; an imbalance that will last until the end of the century (Fogarty *et al.,* 1984, 103).

This analysis is further underscored by Christopher Whelan, in *Values and Social Change in Ireland* (Whelan, C. (Ed.), 1994) – a study of the findings of the 1990 European Value Systems Study for Ireland, plus a comparative study with the 1981 survey, indicating value changes over the 1980s in Ireland. At the beginning of the 1990s, as Whelan states, the class structure contains a substantial number of positions that are viable only in so far as they are underwritten by state welfare programmes and from which, given present economic circumstances, there appears to be no escape. Such positions currently account for more than one quarter of what 'is ironically termed the gainfully occupied labour force' (Whelan, 16).

Long-term unemployment has now become not the curse of the few, but the fate of the many, and as in a more relaxed age, nothing quite focussed the mind as impending execution, so, to-day, nothing quite changes one's construction of reality, one's perception of educational goals in our case, as impending permanent unemployment.

If such is the emphasis of students and their parents on vocational development, the teachers, on the other hand, consider vocational preparation as much less important. In fact, they consider it among the least important aspects of their task as educators. This does not mean that teachers are out of touch with the real-life situation or the needs of their students – the high priority of a mean of 4.21 out of a possible 5, their second highest, which they attach to academic development, is surely a proof of this. They recognise the tension with regard to the goal of education – whether it should be geared towards preparation for a job or towards the development of the person. In a world where jobs and skills can become quickly obsolete, it would be foolish to think that education can focus simply on the needs of the economy. At the same time, in a country plagued with unemployment, it would be foolish to think that one could prepare students for adult life without helping them to acquire the qualifications and skills which they will need in order to get a job.

This tension can be properly resolved only if one begins from a vision of the human person that views employment as only one of the areas in which a person can contribute to the good of others, and can develop his or her potential. Thus, I believe that the teachers in St Xaviour's College provide a creative and necessary balance which maintains that preparation for future employment and careers is best served by the all-round personal development of the student.

Academic development: Leaving Certificate, third-level education

The fulfilment of the above vocational expectations of students depends largely on their academic achievement in the Leaving Certificate examination. The Leaving Certificate is seen as a 'gateway' to employment or to further education. It is not in the least surprising, therefore, that the students make academic development their second highest priority, in keeping, yet again, with the Australian findings of 1982 and 1992 (Flynn, 1993, 166).

Teachers, too, place great emphasis on academic learning, and, like their students, make it their second priority. Though parents balance the academic development by placing it third to vocational and personal development, they, none the less, accord it great importance. They rate it with a mean of 4.33, as compared with 4.21 from the teachers.

If we juxtapose the very high rating accorded to academic development – as opposed to that accorded to social development, for example – with the policy of 'streaming' in St Xaviour's, we get a glimpse of how the requirements of academic success and the 'points system' may be dominating our curriculum to the detriment of such significant and worthy goals as the promotion of civic virtues. There may be evidence here of some goal displacement.

Personal development: character, personality, independence and initiative

The teachers of St Xaviour's give highest priority to the personal development of their Leaving Certificate students, in line once again with their Australian counterparts (Flynn, 1985, 103; 1993, 177). They see that education is at the service of the integral development of the person, and maintain that students are best prepared for their future lives and careers by assisting them to understand themselves, develop their character and personality, and foster within themselves qualities of independence and initiative. Parents, while placing personal development second to vocational development, give it, nonetheless, equal support to the teachers – a mean score of 4.43.

These findings or trends are remarkably close to the Australian parents' and teachers' scores and expectations in the 1982 and 1992 surveys (Flynn, 1993, 171, 176). The St Xaviour's students, like those in the Australian studies of 1982 and 1992 (Flynn, 1993, 166), place personal development in third place. In the short-term, at least, they see life in terms of jobs, careers and academic achievement; a point of view one can readily appreciate. Yet the overall picture here is one of balance, where a healthy creative tension exists between the expectations of these three groups of stakeholders.

Social development: community, civic affairs, the needs of others

The next expectation of students is social development. Like all people, they can only achieve a sense of personal identity in the context of their society. Writers such as Bernard Lonergan, Viktor Frankl and others consider that human persons are constituted by meaning and relationships. Taking into account the historical situation, human persons find fulfilment and meaning to the extent that they are open to self-transcendence in relationships with others.

Leaving Cert. students in St Xaviour's, however, consider social development to be much less pressing than the more urgent demands of the Leaving Certificate, vocational needs and personal development. Viewed graphically in Figure 2.1, the drop is very obvious, from 3.71 on the personal development scale to 2.95 on the social development scale. Though this trend is in line with the ranking of the Australian students' survey in 1982 and 1992, and understandable at this stage in the students' development, there is little room for complacency in a Catholic school where the senior students rank the expectation that St Xaviour's should 'encourage students to be concerned for the needs of others' among the fifteen lowest of their operative goals, in twenty-seventh place out of forty. And this at a time when we hear constantly about the social conscience of youth!

Both parents and teachers are in exact agreement (4.14 and 4.15 on the Means' scale) concerning the importance of the social development of students. They stress the importance for students to be concerned for the needs of others, and provide that creative balance.

It is interesting to note that the social expectations or goals of 'helping students to understand the society in which they live' and of 'encouraging students to take part in local and civic affairs' are included by all three groups among the fifteen lowest expectations of St Xaviour's. This fact underscores the criticisms by the priest/sociologist Dr Mícheál Mac Gréil SJ, in his address to the Annual General Meeting of the Association of Principals and Vice-Principals of Community and Comprehensive Schools in Galway in October 1993, concerning the neglect by the Irish education system and Irish educationists of the social dimension of education. The vision of these educationists, he concludes, and this may well apply to St Xaviour's school community, 'is one of upward and outward mobility'. They (the educationists) are strongly personalistic and individualistic, and, in this currently strong personalistic and individualistic environment,

> a social emphasis would be seen as possibly restrictive, provincial and parochial. Students, however, live in the real world of families, neighbourhoods, communities, voluntary groups and social concerns.
> (Mac Gréil, 1994, 189)

The personal development aspects of education, as well as the technological aspects, need the antidote of the social aspects. (MacGreil, 1994, 189). Without the social aspect, schools, St Xaviour's among them, may well be akin to a three-legged stool trying to stand on two legs.

Religious development: faith, liturgy, religious education, integration

Religious expectations are by far the lowest concern of the Leaving Certificate students at St Xaviour's. This picture reflects fairly closely Marcellin Flynn's findings in his Australian surveys of 1982 and 1992, where he notes a decline in religious attitudes and values over that decade (Flynn, 1993, 166, 172, 177, 181). Religious aspects of life appear much less important than careers and vocational preparation, exams, personal development and social concerns. At the level of the students' operative goals there does not appear to be that integration of the religious and academic that is central to the Church's vision of education (*Catholic School*, a.49). Some balance, however, is being provided by the teachers, and to a lesser extent the parents, in the importance they assign to the Christian community and faith environment aspects of school life.

Though these trends may not be at all surprising to those involved in the current Irish educational scene (Hogan, 1985, 418, for example), there is, nonetheless, cause for concern. Pressures from the Leaving Certificate appear to be distorting some goals of St Xaviour's as a Catholic school. We hear frequently and stridently of the ethos of academic competitiveness as a major feature of school life in Ireland today— the points system of entry to third-level education, and concern about employment, to which I have already referred. Though in their analysis of the 1990 European Values Survey, Whelan *et al.* found that unemployment is negatively associated with church attendance, rituals and ceremonies, they concluded that this is due to the impact it has on an individual's self-esteem rather than to the estrangement of significant segments of the people from Catholicism *per se* (Whelan *et al.*, 1994, 26-27).

These pressures alone cannot, I believe, be responsible for the level of apathy towards religious development noted in this study.

Other wider, more universal and well-documented trends are obviously at work. These trends are linked to the whole process of global individualisation – a process in which values, beliefs, attitudes and behaviour are increasingly based on personal choice, and are less dependent on tradition or social institutions, a process in which 'values are no longer dominated by institutional religion, but are based on personal choice... (where) self-development and personal happiness are leading principles for individual action' (Ester *et al.,* 1994, 7). Yet in this whole analysis we must bear in mind the cautionary words of Andrew Greeley, the American priest/sociologist, against using words like 'modernisation', 'secularisation', 'rationalisation' and so on, trippingly, as though they are 'proven social energies whose nature and triumph are beyond question' (Greeley, 1994, 133). In this whole area one must be wary of the 'good old days' fallacy, the assumption that there was a time and a place when humans were more devout, more orthodox, more open to religious control than they are now. Recent research in the social history of religion in pre-modern Europe, according to Greeley, suggests that the 'Ages of Faith' could more appropriately be called the 'Ages of Superstition and Magic'. The peasant farmers in Europe were not, by contemporary standards, particularly devout, orthodox or moral. The same thing can be said of Ireland before the advent of Cardinal Paul Cullen (Greeley, 1994, 133).

Nevertheless, the challenge posed by the confusion of young people, a confusion diagnosed by Bernadette MacMahon in a study carried out among 15-17-year-olds in Dublin city and county between 1978 and 1980, and confirmed in more recent studies (MacMahon, 1987), cannot be ignored. A central finding of that study was 'a substantial degree of uncertainty among pupils with regard to the main beliefs of the Catholic faith'. The overall picture was seen by her as indicating a pervasive uncertainty, which was more marked among boys than girls. While it was accepted that the problem of adolescents' 'crises of faith' is a familiar one, it was also seen that it calls for an enlightened response (MacMahon, 1987, 21). The fact that, in 1984, a quarter of the Irish people who believe in God are not sure of what sort of God they believe in (Fogarty *et al.,* 1984, 91), a fact reiterated in the 1994 study of the European Values Systems Study by Whelan *et al.* (1994, 35), suggests that the level of knowledge among adults may be contributing to the confusion and apathy among young people.

In the light of the findings in the study, and in the above context, it is obvious that the St Xaviour's school community faces a challenge. The central challenge, I believe, is one of enlightenment: to bring the whole school community, students, parents and teachers, to an appreciation of their current state and of their strengths and resources as a Catholic school. I have looked at the current situation through one small window, the window of expectations, and have found creative tension, goal conflict and evidence of some goal displacement. Our strength and resources lie in the very metaphor we use – and try our best to live, though with mixed results – to describe St Xaviour's, namely, a community.

Community: social capital

Following the research of James Coleman and Thomas Hoffer in the United States (Coleman *et al.*, 1987), the community dimension of Catholic schools has increasingly come to be interpreted as the social capital of those schools. Just as physical capital exists in a school in the form of buildings, playing fields and various amenities, there also exists human capital and social capital. Social capital is comprised of the network of relationships surrounding a person. That network involves one's family and the broader community of adults of which the family may be part. This social network is found in Catholic schools which combine with the Church and the parish to form a supportive enclave of adults who, with the children, are united around a system of shared beliefs and values about the nature and role of education. In contrast, state schools tend to be pluralistic, and lack the unification around central values that is a feature of Catholic schools. Indeed, Coleman and Hoffer conclude that:

> religious organisations are among the few remaining organisations in society, beyond the family, that cross generations. Thus, they are among the few in which the

MARINO INSTITUTE OF EDUCATION

social capital of the adult community is available to children and youth. (Coleman *et al.*, 1987, 37)

Coleman and Hoffer found that the community of families which comprise religiously-based schools produced a rich social capital, which resulted in better academic performance, especially for the disadvantaged who most need and are most likely to lack social capital from their own families (Coleman *et al.*, 1987, 16).

In *The Catholic Myth, the Behaviour and Beliefs of American Catholics*, Andrew Greeley, in the light of his own research and that of James Coleman, confirms that 'it is precisely the community-forming component of Catholic education which makes [Catholic schools] effective' (1990, 178). John Clare, the education editor of *The Daily Telegraph*, commenting on the report of HM's Chief Inspector, cited the self-same reasons for the outstanding success of Catholic schools in Britain. Two factors are principally responsible: the schools' ethos and the support that the pupils receive at home. He goes on to say:

> Catholicism, it seems safe to assume, is not incidental to either. By ensuring that teachers and parents share – or at least strongly sympathise with - the same rigorous system of beliefs and values, it creates the ideal conditions for an effective education. (*The Tablet*, 10 February 1996, 172)

Not only are Catholic schools an integral part of the parish life that surrounds them, but they are also bonded to a world-wide Church which has a rich tradition of beliefs and underlying values, reflected, expounded upon and celebrated in symbols, rituals, myths and ceremonies. This intricate network of relationships – reflecting common traditions, beliefs, values and expectations – is responsible for the rich social capital of Catholic schools, and in turn, has a very supportive, positive and powerful effect on students who attend these schools.

School ethos
School ethos, the very soul, as it were, of social capital, though shown by the research just mentioned and other works to be

crucial to the effectiveness of a school, has been suspected of being some kind of cover for clerical control in Ireland. Pluralism in this country suffers from the numerical imbalance of religious groupings. It is easier for Jews or Presbyterians than Catholics to maintain a distinctive school ethos. Catholic schools are sometimes seen almost as a state system, and, consequently, are resented if they try to assert a religious character (Andrews, 1994, 155).

The religious label of a school is not always an adequate expression of its character. One has to explore the variety of reasons for which schools are chosen. Catholic parents may choose Protestant primary schools for their small class sizes. Non-believers may choose a Brothers' school or a convent school for their pastoral care or good results. Teachers may seek employment at a Catholic school, not because they have any particular commitment to the religious ethos of that school (they may even resent being questioned at an interview about their religious commitment), but because it is convenient to their home or offers well-regulated work.

On the other hand, some schools are effectively what they set out to be, are congruent with their goals, namely a community of study, worship, beliefs and morality, not forgetting the sinners; a gospel school which shares its wisdom – adults with young people and young people with adults; a community which goes beyond the mere imparting of knowledge and becomes a place where young and old, students, parents and teachers can grow, be hurt and healed, learn to play as well as to work, experience friendship and the belonging that is possible only in such a community (cf. Lane, 1991, 18).

However imperfect the efforts in a school to iron out the wrinkles of goal conflict or goal displacement, however imperfect the efforts to make the rhetoric a reality, however imperfect the efforts to incarnate shared values and beliefs in a school, they are better than no attempt at all. In the absence of any explicit philosophy, the gap will be filled by the consumerist values of the market-place.

All these efforts have to be firmly rooted in social capital and in a collaborative model of school management, where the special role of parents is acknowledged. As our expectations relating to parental involvement in St Xaviour's bear out, and as stated in the OECD Report:

> In the main, parents have left the business of education to the schools, believing that the schools know best. For their part, managers, principals and teachers have scarcely encouraged the intervention of parents. (OECD Report, 1991, 58)

The Catholic school, however, regards (even if it does not always manifest this attitude) the family as the basic unit in society. Even more than this,

> The Christian family is at the heart of the Church's mission to exemplify God's love for his children – more especially in the impersonal and neutral life which is currently fostered by an isolationist, individualistic civil society. (Buetow, 1988, 153)

As Coleman and Hoffer (1987) have shown, the network of close relationships among family, school and Church found in Catholic communities provides a real source of social capital for the young people embedded in those communities. Accordingly, a collaborative framework of school management which taps into and reflects that rich network can only work to further enhance the quality of education. Therein lie both the challenge to and the strength of the St Xaviour's school community.

Everything, however, comes at a price, even social capital. And it would be easy for St Xaviour's, as, I feel, it is easy in the whole Irish Catholic school scene, to overlook the extent to which we live on another form of capital, our religious capital. As the results of my brief audit show, we may well be overdrawn in this department. The words of the British Chief Rabbi, Jonathan Sachs, are apposite for both Ireland and St Xaviour's, especially in the light of our findings in the area of religious expectations:

> Living, as we have done, by the inherited habits of an essentially religious way of life, we have come to underestimate the religious faith needed to sustain them. (Sachs, 1991, 83)

3

RELIGION, CULTURE AND SCHOOLING

Kevin Williams

Throughout the history of civilisation, religion, culture and schooling have been related. This relationship is to be found in the Jewish and Islamic traditions as well as within Christianity. In the Western tradition, in both the monastic foundations of early Christian Ireland and in the cathedral schools of medieval Europe, the pursuit of learning and praise of God went together. To understand and to spread the Word of God were conceived as inseparable aspects of the Christian's mission. At the time of the Reformation, on much of the European continent, Catholic and Protestant rulers assumed for themselves the *auctoritas docendi*, which had hitherto been exercised by the papacy. These rulers envisaged the authority to rule, to 'command for truth', and to educate as intimately linked, and they used their newly appropriated authority to develop an educational infrastructure that would serve to promote a uniform cultural and religious identity among their inhabitants. The characterisation by John Knox of the city of Geneva under the rule of Calvin as a 'school' (see Oakeshott, 1975, 285) dramatically reflects the tendency to combine the educational and catechetical remits of governance. In the nineteenth century one of the most famous (or perhaps notorious) statements of the role of religion in schooling is conveyed in the words of Sir James Graham after the strike movements of 1842 (the Plug Riots): 'the police and soldiers have done their duty, the time is arrived when moral and religious instruction must go forth to reclaim the people from the error of their ways' (cited in Johnson, 1976, 50). Significantly, the system of public schooling which developed in nineteenth-century Britain was built up largely by the individual churches.

Somewhat ironically, part of the impulse behind the system of publicly sponsored schooling, which was introduced into Ireland in 1831, was to separate religious from secular instruction. Awareness of the potential for social disharmony deriving from the conflation of religious with cultural identity led to the attempt to introduce multi-denominational schooling. The aim of the architects of the system of national education was therefore to prevent religion becoming an obstacle to the forging of a shared identity on the part of the inhabitants. The Stanley Letter sought to limit the remit of the state to secular learning and to assign responsibility for catechesis to the respective Churches. The attempt, in the words of Lord Stanley, to 'unite in one system children of different creeds' (Hyland and Milne, 1987, 100-101) was strenuously resisted by all the Churches, with the result that education in practice assumed a denominational character. On the foundation of the Irish state in 1922, a system of educational administration was already in place through which the government could realise its aim of promoting cultural nationalism. In the light of the salience of religion in Irish culture, this also involved the continuation and strengthening of a connection between religion and education.

The Catholic Church in particular found itself dealing with a government that was sympathetic to its educational project. The educational documents of the Irish state provide a very clear statement of an almost ideal conception of how religion and culture can fuse in the formation of citizens. Here is not the place to examine these documents in detail (see Williams 1997a, 1997b), but the relationship between religious and civic education is worth considering. The Introduction to *Memorandum V. 40*, published in 1942, proposes the 'integration' of religion with national culture as 'a task calling for the co-operative efforts of all teachers' in order to provide within the school a 'unity' which would reflect that of the 'good home' where 'tradition, faith, work and recreation blend naturally and easily with one another' (Department of Education, 1942).[1] According to the document, '[s]ocial education is closely associated with religious instruction' . . . [in] the right formation of citizens . . .'(ibid.). This conjunction of religious with civic/social formation is also pronounced in the treatment of civics, which first appeared in the version of *Rules and Programme for Secondary Schools* published in 1966. Affirming the relationship between religious education and civics, the document states that civics is not to be regarded as a substitute for religious and moral training nor for that training in character formation and general behaviour which is an essential objective of all education, but rather... as the complement and extension of such training. (Department of Education, 1986/87 edition, 165)

The relationship between religion and civic education is also evident in the 'Notes on the Teaching of Civics' published in the same year.

It is not difficult to see the importance of co-ordinating civics with religious instruction... It would not be very effective for the civics teacher to discuss with his pupils the political and social duties of the citizen unless the moral principles underlying those duties had already been dealt with in the religious instruction class. (Department of Education, 1966)

Recent Government documents on education mark a move away from the certainties of earlier times (see Williams 1997a, 1997b). The Green Paper on Education of 1992 (Government of Ireland, 1992) is neutral, even negative, towards the place of religion in Irish education. Although the White Paper of 1995 (Government of Ireland, 1995) takes a more positive view of the relationship between religion, culture and education, there is no return to the language and tone of previous documents.

Ireland has not been unique in conferring a Christian character on its public schools. In Germany, recent legal action on the presence of crucifixes in classrooms of state schools in Bavaria demonstrates how deeply felt is the commitment of Bavarian citizens to maintaining the explicitly Catholic identity of their schools. Nor are policy makers in Ireland alone in finding the relationship between religion and the culture of the public school problematic. The relationship between Christianity and public schooling in the UK has been a complex and controversial feature of the Education Reform Act of 1988. Throughout the Western world the status of religious schools in secular states is a sensitive issue, arousing in France, for example, typical *passion française* (Coutty 1997).[2] Yet even in Ireland, as we have seen, the secular *Zeitgeist* has come to influence the state's treatment of the relationship between religion, culture and schooling. The relationship between culture and Christianity in Irish schools, which had seemed natural and unproblematic, now requires closer definition and articulation. The attempt to provide such a definition may help us to understand what is meant by a Christian school. But first let us consider the relationship between religion and the culture of schools.

Religion and the culture of schools

Every social organisation, political party, hospital, sports body or school has its own culture or ethos in the sense of a dominant, pervading spirit or character. When people speak of school spirit, they are referring to an important aspect of the culture or ethos of a school. The still fashionable term 'hidden curriculum' also captures some of what is meant by this ethos or culture. Although rarely to the fore of the consciousness of teachers and pupils, the culture or ethos of a school is often perceptible to visitors. Sometimes it is suggested in the prominence given to symbols – to symbols of religious practice or to other symbols – of patriotism/nationalism, of sporting, artistic and academic endeavour, of civic and community involvement. Although impalpable, ethos is none the less real. When most of what we have learned at school has dropped into the deep well of human forgetfulness, a sense of the ethos of the school we attended remains part of our consciousness. This is not surprising, as the ethos of a school touches the quality of our lives and can constitute an important element in the fabric of our very identity.

Positive moral values can form part of the living ethos of any school that purports to be a genuinely educational institution. As a repository of humane and civilising values, every school should act as a countervailing force to dehumanising influences within the wider society, and can even serve as the conscience of that society. Every school should also offer to pupils and staff an arena of human fellowship and mutual support, as well as of cultural enrichment. Commitment to proper educational values can make of the school an oasis of humanity or a place apart from the 'getting and spending' (Wordsworth, 'The World Is Too Much with Us') of the world outside. In such a school, young people enjoy an opportunity to be children, secure for a while from the world outside the classroom, where the demands of a precocious adulthood urge themselves so insistently upon them.

But what is distinctive of a Christian school is that, as a matter of policy, it aims to foster in young people a commitment to the message of the Gospel and reinforces this as part of the school's ethos. A Christian school points young people to the ultimate values and purposes of human life and introduces them to a quality of life which lies always beyond the mere fact of life (Whitehead, 1926, 80). Note, however, that many positive educational values are neither peculiar to, nor the monopoly of, Christian schools. A sense that education is not merely a matter of academic success, and even a concern for the disadvantaged, may be part of the vision of a Christian school, but these values and commitments must not be represented as if they defined its character. Likewise, we should note that mission statements about Christian or Catholic ethos which do not extend beyond platitudes about developing 'the whole person' or 'rounded persons', say little that anyone could possibly disagree with. For example, if we try to unpack the term 'rounded persons', we shall discover that believers and non-believers will differ greatly in what they are prepared to count as 'rounded'. The problem is less with the aspiration but rather with how the human development implied is to be interpreted.[3] After all, who would be against the development of persons who are 'rounded', at least in the metaphorical sense? It is time to accept that a Christian school culture will not be found acceptable by everyone.

Anodyne platitudes fail to get to the heart of the matter in the way that some of the earlier Irish documents do. What ultimately distinguishes a Christian school is a conviction that the aim of education is

> to develop, with the assistance of God's grace, the whole man with all his faculties, natural and supernatural, so that he may realise his duties and responsibilities as a member

of society, that he may contribute effectively to the welfare of his fellow man, and by so doing attain the end designed for him by his Creator (Department of Education, 1942). Underlying this conviction is a belief that

> [e]ach human being is created in God's image. He has a life to lead and a soul to be saved. Education is, therefore, concerned not only with life but with the purpose of life. And, since all men are equal in the eyes of God, each is entitled to an equal chance of obtaining optimum personal fulfilment (Department of Education 1971, 12).

Some readers may be put off by the rather old-fashioned and regrettably sexist language of these statements. But a Christian school that is clear-sighted about its *telos* does not have to be intolerant, ungenerous and illiberal in its culture. One of the most distinctive features of the culture of a Catholic school should be its openness.

Openness and school culture

To understand what is meant by this openness we must distinguish between different kinds of school culture, closed and open. A closed school culture is one that sets limits to what is permissible to think and say, and where the cultivation of intellectual autonomy on the part of pupils is discouraged. Indeed, secular or non-denominational schools that exclude any expression of religious belief from the school can also be said to set limits to the autonomous development of children. In as far as they seek to preclude the development of religious belief, these schools can likewise be characterised as closed. By contrast, an open school culture respects the freedom of pupils and encourages intellectual autonomy. The open Christian school actually seeks to promote the development of the autonomous individual. Indeed, if institutions are to count as being properly educational, they must foster a critical, inquiring spirit, consistent with the development of intellectual autonomy. Schools are informed by an authentic Christian ethos must offer genuine openness as well as stability (McLaughlin, 1987, 73-83). Where a Christian ethos operates with a proper respect for human freedom, young people are given an opportunity to share in a heritage which they are ultimately free to accept or reject. A Christian ethos actually expands the horizon of human freedom and, where it does not, we are no longer dealing with genuine religion but with some distortion of it.

There is no incompatibility between being autonomous and participating in the Christian tradition. After all, live traditions allow for, and accommodate, modification, adaptation and change as a matter of course. Such traditions are to be conceived as fluid and vibrant rather than as rigid and fixed. At the heart of every liberal tradition there must lie a freedom and an inventiveness. After all, where a situation is genuinely novel and without precedent (as, for example, with new developments in fertility treatment), it is to the resources of our tradition that we must turn in framing our response. As participants in a living tradition, we have recourse to resources that allow us to cope with changing circumstances. and our familiarity with these resources enables us to respond to new situations.

These views are perfectly consistent with those expressed in the Vatican document, *The Religious Dimension of Education in a Catholic School: Guidelines for Reflection and Renewal.* The authors of this document ask that critical thinking be encouraged in young people (Congregation for Catholic Education, 1988, 24, 29, 53) and that they be made active participants in their own education (ibid., 15, 18-19, 54-6). In accordance with this spirit of openness, a Catholic school, subject to certain conditions (see Williams 1995), must be prepared to welcome the children of parents of different religious persuasions and those of non-believing parents in a spirit of Christian generosity. The Vatican Congregation has an open attitude towards the presence in Catholic schools of pupils who are non-believers (ibid., 5, 57-8) as well as of baptised young people who have ceased to practise their religion (ibid., 8-10, 40-1).

In the next section, I wish to consider the relationship between Christianity and the cultural heritage that is to be found in the school curriculum.

Christianity and the school curriculum

The religious response to life is a disposition composed of beliefs, convictions, attitudes and feelings concerning the human person and her or his destiny. Religion provides a way of apprehending the world which informs the whole life of believers and provides the spring of moral commitments to act in ways that are consistent with realising this ultimate destiny. Woven into the stuff of how we conceive of human life and its purposes, religious faith shapes significantly the culture that is incorporated into the school's curriculum. Christianity is not simply the placing of an icing of additional, spiritual values on a neutral cake of culture. It is not that there is a Christian mathematics, science, geography or history, but rather that Christians conceive of these and of other areas of the curriculum as the response of the human mind to different aspects of God's creation. Let us consider this conception of the school curriculum in more detail.

The great metaphysical questions regarding creation, and humankind's nature and purpose, which can arise in teaching science or geography, are also religious questions. Consideration of the influence of religion on human affairs arises in the study of history. Religion informs views about human moral responsibility which are addressed in teaching literature, just as it does questions about human sexuality which arise in teaching biology and home economics and, indeed, the moral issues which arise in such subjects as business studies or technology. The teaching of practical subjects can also acquire a religious dimension (Williams, 1994). This derives from the Christian understanding of human action as participation in the creative activity of God – an understanding that is rooted in the great monastic, notably Benedictine, tradition of Christendom, the monasteries of which have always been places of labour as well as of learning. Where the teaching of practical subjects is animated by such a view, this teaching involves *pari passu* communicating an aspect of the religious response to the world. With regard to personal, social and health education, and relationships and sexuality education, there obviously exists a peculiarly Christian vision of human, physical, psychological and spiritual well-being which will inform the approach taken to these areas.

The Christian heritage is central to so many of the achievements of Western culture. Religious faith has inspired many great works of art – of painting, sculpture, music and literature. Many of the poems studied in Irish schools have religious themes. For instance, 'I see His blood upon the rose', by Joseph Plunkett, is an evocation of the pervasive presence of God, through Jesus Christ, in the world of nature. The famous lines by Joyce Kilmer – 'I think that I shall never see/a poem lovely as a tree… Poems are made by fools like me/But only God can make a tree' – express a sense of reverent wonder at the bounty of God's creation. Teaching young people to respond to such poems as Milton's 'Paradise Lost', 'The Collar' by Herbert, 'Batter my heart three-person'd God' by Donne or 'God's Grandeur' by Hopkins, means teaching them to enter more deeply into their Christian heritage.

Of course, religious belief itself is rooted in a rich cultural context and the study of the great sacred texts contributes to the cultivation of general cultural literacy. Besides alerting us to the action of God in human life, the Jewish and Christian Scriptures are great repositories of our cultural heritage. The Old and New Testaments are part of the literary and moral capital of Western civilisation (see Williams, 1992). But the study of Scripture is not merely a cultural engagement, and I shall conclude with some comments on the place of religious education in the Catholic school.

The role of religious education

My concern in this conclusion is with religion of a catechetical character rather than with the study of religious beliefs, which is most appropriately described as the sociology of religion. This is a perfectly legitimate aspect of the school curriculum but must not be confused with denominationally-specific religious education. There is absolutely nothing illiberal in affirming the particular need for and value of catechesis if conducted with respect for the principles of openness discussed previously. It is hard to see how we can actually teach religion without initiating children into a particular religion, just as we cannot teach sport without actually teaching children to play a specific game, or teach music without teaching an individual musical instrument.

It is unrealistic to expect that a programme of religious education which is not denominationally specific can initiate young people into the lived and living experience of a religious tradition.

Religious education plays a vital role in facilitating an integration of experience across the curriculum. One reason for the centrality of religious education within the school curriculum derives from its concern with human experience itself. The young person's own experience lies at the heart of what takes place in religion class in a way that does not occur, for example, in the study of physics or of accountancy. As a principle of pedagogic procedure, the student's own experience can be drawn upon in a way that is not possible in such subjects as physics or accountancy. The student's own experience is therefore relevant to religious education in a very special manner.

Reference to the place of experience in religious education does not mean that religion becomes a version of personal and social development. Although religious faith has implications for moral education, and for full personal development, its primary concern is with the spiritual realm of human experience and with deepening the response of young people to the action of God in their lives. Accordingly, it concentrates on subject-matter that is explicitly and directly theological, rather than on material that would find a more appropriate place in programmes of personal and social development. The same point applies to themes relating to justice – justice is a legitimate Christian concern, but it should not dominate religion class. In any case, the issue of income distribution on a national and international scale is treated in other subjects, for example, civics, geography, economics and the business subjects, home economics, history and economic history. The primary purpose of religious education must be to the fore of the minds of Christian educators. This purpose coincides with that of the Catholic school: it is to enable young people to grow in awareness of and sensitivity to the transcendent action of God in their lives.

PART II

RELIGIOUS EDUCATION

4

THE SCHOOL AS AN AGENT IN EVANGELISATION

Kevin Treston

The title of this chapter is provocative. Various roles of the Christian school, such as a community of learning, an agent for cultural socialisation, a centre for pastoral care, may sit more comfortably with people of a post-modern consciousness. The word 'evangelisation' may conjure up images of tele-evangelists, indoctrination, colonising by European missionaries and the imposition of dogmas on hapless students trapped in religion classes.

I propose that the role of the Christian school as an agent of evangelisation is a valid one in our contemporary world. To support the proposal, I will engage in three discourses. The first discourse is about a modern understanding of evangelisation, the second discourse concerns a culture and Church in rapid transition, and the third discourse is about the nature of the Christian school. By examining how each discourse interacts with the others, I will then explore how the role of the Christian school as an agent of evangelisation may be realised in practice.

At the outset, one must acknowledge the difficulty of using evangelisation as a role for the Christian school in cases where students are increasingly drawn from a multi-faith, pluralistic and even atheistic culture. An additional reservation is related to a knowledge of the story of Christian evangelisation, a story replete with examples of both success and oppressive proselytism.

Discourse on evangelisation

The injunction of Christ to 'Go therefore and make disciples of all nations' (Mt 28:19) appears to be a straightforward directive. Yet, the story of Christian missionary activity illustrates how complex the implementation of this injunction has been. Despite its problems, two thousand years of evangelisation have seen Christian communities established in every corner of the globe and in most cultures. What then is meant by 'evangelisation'?

Arbuckle describes evangelisation as 'the actual proclamation, by word and example, of the Good News of Christ to the nations' (Arbuckle, 1990, 9). In the prophetic apostolic exhortation *Evangelii nuntiandi* (1975), Pope Paul VI wrote: 'the task of evangelisation is to be regarded as the Church's specific grace and calling and the activity most fully expressive of [its] real nature. The Church exists in order to evangelise'(14). If evangelisation is at the heart of the energy of the Church's mission, then all structures of the Church are constituted for the purpose of evangelisation, proclaiming, celebrating and serving the dream of Jesus, the reign of God (Sobrino, 1985, 257).

During the twentieth century, dramatic global cultural changes have given a new impetus to evangelisation. The rapid transmission of Western technological culture, with its rampant materialism, has disseminated a world view that is essentially post-Christian and pagan. A new approach to evangelisation is called for when a culture has discarded its Christian heritage. The emergence of states in Africa and Asia has challenged the relevance of the historical marriage between Christianity and Europe and insisted on honouring the principle of inculturation. Those involved in promoting evangelisation have to relinquish the dream of establishing a new 'Christendom', whereby nations are bonded by the unity of the universal Church. In hindsight, one may wonder if the price of the first conversion of Europe was too high. By harnessing the Gospel to positions of power and privilege, the Church tried to form Christian empires with state churches. All too often, the Gospel was compromised and prostituted by politics and economics. The shadow side of the Church story is a sombre reminder of how easily the ideals of evangelisation are perverted by religious ideology.

A contemporary understanding of evangelisation suggests that its scope is very broad. Avery Dulles reminds us that, prior to Vatican Two, the term 'evangelisation' was seldom used by Catholics, and when it was, it was used in a missionary context (Dulles, 1995, 397). Evangelisation has different emphases for people in different circumstances. For people who are actively involved in their Christian faith, evangelisation is an appeal to ongoing conversion. For those who have withdrawn from the practice of their Christian faith, it is a call to reconciliation. For those of no religious faith, evangelisation is an invitation to accept the Good News. Those who are broken by the forces of oppression may experience evangelisation as a sign of hope for society and culture. Evangelisation aspires to transform cultural values (*Becoming a more Evangelising Parish*, 1994, 2-3). This description of the scope of evangelisation alerts us to its multi-purpose character. Those who are initiating evangelisation need to discern which is the more appropriate approach. For example, in the Catholic school, members of the school community would probably be represented by each of the groups of people identified above and include the whole spectrum of religiosity, even a few not of the Christian faith.

The scope of evangelisation suggests a variety of possible approaches to its implementation. One action for evangelisation would be *proclamation,* which would include such activities as giving witness to the spirit of Christ, religious education programmes, worship and prayer. Another manifestation of evangelisation would be *dialogue,* where we seek to discover God's presence in the world through conversations and interactions with diverse groups of people and institutions. A third approach would be *inculturation,* which would affirm Gospel values already present in the culture and continually promote values that enhance the dignity of humankind and planetary health. A fourth expression would be *liberation,* where justice is upheld and oppressive structures are combated. In reality, the various approaches often merge as actions that ground the dream of Jesus, the reign of God, in everyday life. For example, in the Catholic school, the members of the school would aspire to be a learning community that nurtures its people in holistic values with 'life in abundance' (Jn 10:10).

If a Catholic school is to fulfil a role as an agent of evangelisation, then certain principles of authentic evangelisation must be respected. From the description of a contemporary understanding of evangelisation, I propose the following principles:

- Freedom of conscience and respect for the integrity of each person is an imperative. Both Paul VI and John Paul II teach that the Church proposes the truth of the Gospel but imposes nothing (*Redemptoris missio*, 39).

- The primary goal of the school as a community of learning is esteemed.

- Those initiating the process of evangelisation seek to be witnesses to the Good News.

- Presumptive religious language is avoided.

- The culture of the school reflects Gospel values.

- Members of the school community (staff, students, parents, those in governance) work co-operatively to achieve the mission and goals of the school.

- An atmosphere of respect for multi-faith and multi-culture prevails.

- Approaches to evangelisation are modified according to the levels of readiness, ethnicity and religious culture of the school.

- The provision of a comprehensive religious programme empowers students to make informed choices about religious traditions.

- The spirit of evangelisation is first experienced by the quality of relationships and pastoral care rather than religious rhetoric.

These principles of evangelisation as applied to a Christian school provide a reference point for an exploration of the school as an agent for evangelisation. Before we pursue this theme, we need to enter into the second discourse, a discourse about a culture and Church in transition.

Discourse on a culture and Church in transition

Contemporary social commentators tend to agree that our world is on the threshold of a new era of consciousness. An Irish priest and social psychologist, Diarmuid O'Murchu, writes: 'We are, therefore, in an in-between period, a time of transition. It is an exciting space, but a very disturbing one. The old securities are gone; the new possibilities are still vague, fudgy and, to say the least, ambiguous. The challenge facing all of us is to name what's going on, connect with its energy, and to enhance its positive driving force to carry us into a new future '(O'Murchu, 1995, 9). A brief analysis of some features of this cultural phenomenon will highlight the context of evangelisation and the role of the Catholic school.

Technology and the information explosion

Computers, e-mail, satellite communications and media link the world as never before. Mobile phones are a symbol of the global accessibility of people to contact each other through technology. Commercial media generates a global culture based on a consumer ethic. Images of the good life are promoted through commercial advertising. Life styles, ethics, fashions, relationships and values often reflect instant gratification and addictive materialism.

Technology also brings enormous benefits in the sharing of information and in scientific applications to commerce, medicine, agriculture, health, entertainment and communications. Unless the Church continually evaluates its mode of communication by utilising modern technology, the Christian metanarrative of God's revelation through Jesus can appear dull in contrast to the persuasive presentations of modern media. The Christian tradition of discernment will expose those values espoused by the media which denigrate the dignity of people and planetary health.

Movement from the industrial to the ecological era

During the last two centuries, a basic symbol or metaphor of western society has been the machine, which governs the world like a global engineer. In the latter part of the twentieth century, a holistic understanding has rediscovered the world as an organic whole. The interdependence of all life forms constitutes a vast network of relationships in mutual co-operation. The emergence of the ecological era has many strands of energy, including earth-care ethics, a critique of the ideology of capitalism and the rise of feminine consciousness (Tarnas, 1991, 422).

Fragmentation of human relations

Although the family remains a vital source for nurturing values, there is evidence to demonstrate that family patterns are being radically altered (*Sydney Morning Herald,* 29 January 1997, Agenda 9). Economic necessity and social expectations are forcing many parents to work longer hours with less quality time for their children. Dysfunctional family patterns have a ripple effect in society by widening the circle of alienation and social dislocation. The spectre of unemployment generates anxiety among young adults. The widening gap between rich and poor is a blight on the life styles of affluent western countries. To balance this rather pessimistic picture, there are also many happy people in our society, who celebrate life and share satisfying relationships.

Contemporary philosophies of education

The philosophies of pragmatism and empiricism are very influential in constructing meaning systems in western societies. Pragmatism highlights the priority of experience over abstract truth and emphasises the value of relevance. Pragmatism and empiricism both have a functional view of knowledge (Buetow, 1988, 28). Utilitarian philosophies with their offshoots of capitalism, Marxism and economic rationalism, pose enormous threats to the goals of a Christian school. Not only do they construct meaning systems that conflict with the vision of God for humanity, but they canonise market-driven forces of economic efficiency. The school's curriculum is evaluated in terms of its effectiveness in contributing to national productivity. Pressures on schools from governments to restructure and be more accountable to national economic growth restrict the creativity of the school in the scope of its curriculum (Knight,

1992). When a climate of economic rationalism is endorsed, a more liberal appreciation of learning is discarded.

Habermas, a modern German philosopher, proposes that there are two basic realms of social reality, the 'system' and the 'lifeworld' (Habermas, 1987, 171). The 'system' refers to the complex processes that emerge in human productivity, for example, law, finance, commerce, military, politics. 'Lifeworld' describes the myths, symbols and communal stories that energise the people. The steady increase of state and Church bureaucracies challenges Christian schools to ensure that the 'lifeworld' story of Jesus and the reign of God is the axis around which the energies of the school rotate.

Church in transition

During the twentieth century, the Church's philosophical and theological foundations have shifted from its Platonic and Aristotelian frame of reference to one that is situated within a dynamic and evolving consciousness of world history. Christian theology is in ferment as it seeks to bring the lens of faith to a new cosmology and to initiate serious conversations with science and social sciences, especially physics, psychology, sociology and anthropology. The starting point for the three contemporary theologies of liberation, creation and feminism, is the human condition in the cosmos, rather than academic speculations in the security of monasteries (Ó Murchú, 1997, 14).

The evangelising activity of the Church now is confronted with the daunting task of modifying its approach to correspond to a new paradigm of consciousness. The European character of Christianity, in its structures, law, doctrinal formulations, worship and ethics, is being reshaped to validate the Jesus story in multi-cultural Christian communities. The moral disorder of excluding women from mainstream Church leadership is slowly being rectified. The decline in clergy numbers and emerging lay leadership are stimulating a revival of the primal tradition of ministry, as well as demanding radical new pastoral structures for Church communities.

In the ecological era, the quest for salvation by humans is now understood in the wider context of salvation for the cosmos.

Multi-faith conversations enrich our appreciation of the mystery of God's revelation as well as uncover the wisdoms of God's Spirit in creation. Christians are encouraged to deepen their knowledge of their own tradition and celebrate it within an awareness of God's providential care of all creation.

The Christian school somehow has to straddle the world views of all the stakeholders – students, staff, parents, pastoral workers and those in governance – and encourage the formulation of a common mission statement with a consensus on basic goals. With both Church and society moving to new uncharted frontiers, the school needs to live in courageous uncertainty. The massive decline in affiliation to the liturgical Church, as well as growing paganism, suggest that increasing numbers of children enrolling in Catholic schools come from homes with little or no religious culture. The collapse of a Catholic sub-culture has diminished opportunities for religious socialisation. Teachers in Catholic schools report a significant increment in 'folk' Catholics and a veritable wasteland of religious knowledge and practice. Another movement in the composition of students in Catholic schools is the desire of parents of other religious traditions, or none, to enrol their children in Catholic schools because of the perceived ethical and pastoral care services available there. Other factors, such as the esteemed academic standing of a school and its discipline, are frequently cited as reasons for enrolment (Flynn, 1993, 169).

To explain how the Christian school may fulfil the role of evanglisation, I will engage in the third discourse about the nature of the Christian school, and then allow each of the three discourses to interact with each other. The third discourse will be explored from two angles: firstly, the ethos of the Christian school, and, secondly, how its evangelising role may be manifested.

Discourse on the Christian school

Essential features of a Christian school
The most obvious feature of a Christian school, not always

articulated, is that its goals should be aligned with the educational mission of the Church. Foundational Christian beliefs and practices such as Trinity, Christology, human dignity, justice and the common good, rationality and learning, reconciliation, community and sacramentality, all constitute themes that speak of the special character of a Christian school. Although my descriptions of the essential features of the Christian school will be drawn from a Catholic tradition, many of those so designated would be common to schools with an explicitly 'Christian' character. However, there would be some significant theological divergences from fundamentalist Christian schools. Theologically, the educational endeavours of the Christian school should be an integral dimension of the teaching (kerygmatic) role of the whole Christian community. In practice, at least in many western countries, the Christian school has minimal contact with the parish, especially the second-level schools.

Let us consider, then, the essential elements of a Christian school.

Spirituality
Does the school conduct its learning within a world view that assumes the spiritual essence of people? Spirituality is the search for ultimate meaning. A religious understanding of life connects us to the profound mystery of God within us and the world. A basic purpose of a Christian school is to invite its members to learn within a meaning system that affirms them as people who are loved by God and transformed by grace in Christ. Spirituality infuses the whole curriculum and utterly rejects the dualism of separating 'secular' subjects from 'religious' ones. Likewise, it repudiates a closed system of religious indoctrination.

Sacramentality
Sacramentality is the celebration of God's presence in creation. A Catholic perspective on creation celebrates the divine creativity in every facet of the cosmos, in the evolution of history and in the earth community. The beautiful hymn in praise of creation (Gen 1) is a kind of symphony for each phase of creation with the blessing of the Creator, 'God saw that it was good'. This feature

of the Christian school encourages students to be enthusiastic stewards of earth care and to oppose a galloping technology which threatens to debase the earth by a wanton abuse of its resources. Sacramentality provokes our imagination to wonder at the mystery of the myriad forms, colours and interrelatedness of creation.

Trinity and community

The Christian image and metaphor of God is Trinity. God as Trinity is the one God who generates life (God as Father and Mother), who is passionately involved in the human condition and in creation (God as Son), who is the energising power of love (God as Spirit). God as Trinity reveals God's nature as sexual, communal, relational and loving. Thus, we who are created in the image of God are relational by nature. A Christian school would emphasise the school as a reconciling community with a network of pastoral care. A culture of co-operation and mutuality would encourage a real partnership between students, staff, parents and other stakeholders.

Jesus and the reign of God

The person of Jesus and his desire for a new world order, the reign of God, is the reference point for core values in the school. Christ is 'the image of the invisible God; the first born of all creation' (Col 1:15). Jesus is both Redeemer who reconciles us and creation with God, and Reminder who shows us whom we might become. The vision of the Christian school proposes values that overturn our comfortable assumptions about our priorities and addictions (Treston, 1992, 9). The school community regularly reviews its policies and direction to align them with the values of the intended new world order of the reign of God.

Christian anthropology

A Christian anthropology proposes that people are both blessed and broken, capable of sin but essentially good through the graciousness of a loving God. As ethical beings, we can make choices for good and evil. A holistic understanding of human nature affirms the oneness of our being and encourages us to embrace life with enthusiasm (Groome, 1996, 110). A summation of the essence of Christian anthropology is the saying of Jesus, 'I have come that they may have life and have it abundantly' (Jn 10:10). This theme of 'life in abundance' will flow through the whole curriculum as a positive attitude to one's body, to the nurturing of physical, psychological, academic and spiritual well-being. The kind of education a school offers cannot be decided until it has first agreed on its understanding of human nature.

A learning community
Schools are constituted to promote learning. Holistic learning implies that the curriculum is liberal in its scope as well as forming students for active citizenship. The principle of rationality insists that we have been given a reason to inquire and extend the boundaries of knowledge for ourselves and for humankind. Learning is intended to provoke the imagination to reconstruct images of how we might live more harmoniously in creation. Because the Christian school is part of a wider national educational network of schools, the curriculum is shaped by influences that do not necessarily sit comfortably with the ideals of curriculum for a Christian school. Because governments carry the public purse, there is little alternative for Christian schools than to make the best of a flawed philosophical situation.

Justice and the common good
According to Luke's gospel, Jesus commenced his ministry with a dramatic statement about his mission of liberation (Lk 4:18). Matthew's Gospel concludes the fifth sermon with a vivid picture of the Last Judgment, where the criterion of holiness is the quality of justice (Mt 25:46). The principle of common good enjoins women and men to strive for justice and peace and combat aberrations to human dignity. A just school endeavours to raise consciousness about issues of justice, empower its members to be skilled in promoting justice, and be just in its curriculum.

Sharing the Christian story

The explicitly Christian identity of a school is of particular significance in a post-modern climate of relativism. The cultural tendency to be suspicious of schools that proclaim their Christian character reflects a moral relativism of rejecting the validity of any metanarratives, such as Christianity. The ecumenical movement and a growing sensitivity to multi-faith situations also add a note of uncertainty to the prospect of sharing the Christian story. However, it is a matter of integrity for the school to uphold its essential character, not only by its Christian culture and learning environment, but by a comprehensive religious education programme and opportunities for spiritual development. Sharing its story is an invitation to participate in a 2000-year-old heritage of spirituality and wisdom. In an ideal scenario, this sharing would happen in a partnership between the local church, parents, students and staff of the Christian school.

Focus

The description of the features of a Christian school provides a reference point for describing the evangelising role of the Christian school. Now, let us bring together the three discourses to illuminate this evangelising role.

Evangelising and the school

The discourses on evangelisation, society and Church in transition and the nature of the Christian school enable us to identify aspects of a Christian role in an evangelising role. My approach to this is to propose two models of Catholic schools and then discuss how evangelisation is experienced in both. A model does not describe the actual operation of the school but rather presents a lens to describe the general configuration of its rationale, philosophy and curriculum. As previously indicated, I have chosen schools from a Catholic tradition to illustrate the issue of evangelisation. One model is the 'traditional Catholic school', the other is the 'transforming Catholic school'.

The traditional Catholic school

In the traditional Catholic school the great majority of its staff, students and parents are Catholic, with a significant level of affiliation to the worshipping Church. In the traditional Catholic school, Catholic liturgical services and public devotions are celebrated by all students. The religious education programme is explicitly Catholic in its orientation and has a catechetical flavour. This model of school has often been historically associated with religious congregations, and it developed rapidly in the nineteenth century to parallel the emergence of the national education systems. The goal of this model of school is succinctly stated by John Haldane, a professor of philosophy at the University of St Andrews: 'The primary function of Catholic schools, therefore, is to provide forms of education through which the essential doctrines and devotions of Catholicism are transmitted (Haldane, 1996, 133). The traditional Catholic school, especially the primary school, was (is?) considered an essential dimension of the parish. Its ecclesiology mirrored a view of Church that was more orientated towards an institutional model than a community promoting the reign of God in the world. Evangelisation in the traditional Catholic school would seek to deepen the faith commitment of its members, as well as faithfully communicate the Catholic tradition.

The validity of this model of school has increasingly been questioned in view of the demise of a Catholic sub-culture and the dramatic shift in religiosity (or lack of it) in the student population. There was an uneasiness about a catechetical mode of religious education as a possible breach of religious freedom. Further questions were raised about its degree of congruence with the theology of the Second Vatican Council, which encouraged a spirit of openness towards the modern world and favoured dialogue and service for the good of humankind. Perhaps there will always be a place for the traditional Catholic school, but I would question its universal application as a model for Catholic schools in contemporary culture and in a changing church.

The transforming Catholic school

The transforming Catholic school has an explicitly Catholic character which invites members to experience what the Gospel means by participation in the culture of the school. Although there will be a pluralism of beliefs in such a school, the Catholic ethos is promoted but never imposed. The religious education programme for Catholic students is conducted in a spirit of inquiry and openness (Crawford and Rossiter, 1988, 71). All students are required to engage in the religious education programme according to their levels of religious readiness and faith affiliations. The multi-faith stances of the students are honoured in theory and practice in the curriculum (Dwyer, 1993, 95).

The transforming Catholic school is an agent for evangelisation by conducting learning within a religious vision of the world. It seeks to invite its people to *live* the Gospel and respect how God's revelation has embraced all creation. The evangelising school aspires to transform values in the community which affirm the dignity of people and our earth. A climate of solidarity with the community and a desire to work co-operatively with all those of good will towards justice, endorses the school's commitment to service (Lane, 1991, 7). Through its contribution to the wider educational scene, its relationships in the community and its influence with parents, the transforming Catholic school offers a vision of Christ for everyone. For many students, the face of Christ in the school is the only face of Christ they will encounter, or, at least, the only encounter with Christ that makes any sense to them.

Conducting learning in transforming Catholic schools is a more complicated task than that of traditional Catholic schools. The ethos boundaries of the transforming Catholic school are much more fluid and a great deal of flexibility is required to respond creatively to the multi-faith and multi-cultural environment. The climate of invitation to the pluralism of the school is a challenge to complex scheduling. The danger of minimalism is ever present. Administrators can become so aware of respecting the cultural and religious pluralism, that the ethos and religious thrust of the school may be reduced to the lowest common denominator. A disturbing trend is for the marginalised to perceive that they are not welcome in Catholic schools (see, for example, Johnston and Chesterton, 1994).

The effectiveness of transforming Catholic schools depends on a number of factors. One critical concern is the availability and formation of staff who are committed to the ideals and mission of the school. Another challenge is upholding the Gospel value base of the school against an intrusive and oppressive consumerism. A further problem is developing a consensus about the identity of the transforming Catholic school among the stakeholders, such as pastors, parents, students, staff and people in governance. If, for example, pastors still judge the school by how many students attend Mass on Sunday, then they will inevitably suffer a great disquiet about the worth of such a school. The relentless pressures from educational agencies and the impact of economic rationalism, tend to dictate policies and philosophies that may conflict with the vision and mission of the school.

I do not wish to end on a pessimistic note. My work in many schools in several countries has confirmed me in the value of a Catholic school as an agent for evangelisation. The fruits of the Second Vatican Council, the professional expertise of Christian educators, as well as their discernment of a changing Church and world, give cause for hope that the model and operation of Catholic schools will offer a vision for education that is transforming in its power to realise the spirit of Christ. By ongoing conversations and discourses on evangelisation, culture, Church and the nature of the Christian school, we will discover together the way forward for Catholic schools.

5

TEACHING RELIGION TO YOUNG PEOPLE TODAY

Anne Looney

Frank McCourt was once asked to write a composition for religion class on what it would be like if our Lord had grown up in Limerick, which had the Arch Confraternity of the Holy Family and was the holiest city in Ireland. He duly completed his task. He called his essay, 'Jesus and the Weather', and it went as follows:

> Anytime Jesus got hungry all he had to do was walk up the road to a fig tree or an orange tree and have his fill. If he wanted a pint he would wave His hand over a big glass and there was the pint. Or He could visit Mary Magdalene and her sister, Martha, and He'd get his feet washed and dried with Mary Magdalene's hair while Martha washed the dishes, which I don't think is fair. Why should she have to wash the dishes while her sister sits out there chatting away with Our Lord? It's a good thing Jesus decided to be born Jewish in that warm place because if he was born in Limerick he'd catch the consumption and be dead in a month and there wouldn't be any Communion or Confirmation and we wouldn't have to learn the catechism and write compositions about Him. The End. (McCourt, 1996, 206)

I doubt if the young McCourt was aware of the dialectic he was exploding in his brief diatribe. While his enculturation problem was a rather superficial one, it nonetheless points to the significance of the relationship between religion and culture for religious education. For the teacher, in this case the hapless Mr O'Dea, the failure of the imaginative and symbolic leap and ensuing hermeneutic dialogue between the religious tradition and the contemporary cultural context, can be frustrating. While there may be those who would consider that the young McCourt had in fact established a critical hermeneutic of his own in his composition, such an outcome had no place in the classroom of the catechism! Nevertheless, his brief but controversial composition should live forever in the annals of religious education in Ireland as an early indicator of the cracks emerging in the previously well-cemented relationship between Irish religion and Irish culture. In recent years those early cracks have become something of a chasm. The greatest challenge facing teachers of religion today is the demise of a culturally supported belief system.

In practical terms, this means that an ever increasing number of Irish people live their lives with only fleeting contact with formal, organised religion. In this regard they are following the well-trodden path of their fellow Europeans. What distinguishes the Irish journey towards non-belonging from its continental counterpart is the point of departure. Writing in 1968, Karl Rahner was prompted to differentiate this country from the rest of Europe:

> If in Ireland there is no 'lost working class', if even in the cities ninety per cent of the people fill the churches on Sundays, if there are so many vocations to the priesthood that other countries can share in this rich blessing, if Ireland is still making a contribution to mission work abroad which is far beyond the average for the originally Christian countries – then this is proof sufficient that in Ireland the Church is still the Church of the people, and not of a minority group in a pluralist society. (Rahner 1968, 9)

Rahner goes on to note that difficulties will arise as Ireland becomes increasingly developed and industrialised, but he is confident these will be overcome, 'for the Irish are still a Christian people' (Rahner, 1968, 9). Rahner was right in one regard. In 1968, the Irish were still a Christian, predominantly Catholic, people. Such monocultures were rare in the western world. It was the identification of faith and nationality in Ireland that has made the shift seem so sudden and so dramatic. Urban and suburban Ireland are rapidly becoming places of what Michael Paul Gallagher refers to as 'religious non-belonging'. He describes cultural unbelief as 'non-dogmatic atheism' and as 'an inherited confusion, a distance from roots, an unaggressive puzzlement about religious practices and their language, before Church religion and mediation'. It is an 'undramatic limbo of disinterest and non-belonging' (Gallagher, 1997, 20). While there are parts of rural Ireland that continue to manifest some of the characteristics of cultural Catholicism, the trend, especially in the religious practice and affiliation of the young, is downwards. Rahner noted that the Irish Church had not suffered the loss of the working classes, as had the rest of Europe in the sixties. In the nineties the Irish church is now suffering the loss of at least one generation and is well on its way to losing the second.

All of these changes have been well documented and statistically supported elsewhere. For the purpose of this exploration it is vital that the teacher of religion is located in this cultural context; for when this context is considered, then the dilemma of the classroom becomes apparent. While some religious commentators debate the hostility of some of the agencies of culture – the media, for example – towards religion and the Churches, religious education professionals must face something quite apart from hostility. The results of a 1991 survey of post-primary religion teachers in Ireland points to an RE classroom quite different from that of Mr O'Dea! Under the heading of 'Practical Experiences of Teaching Religious Education', in response to the question, 'Why do you think the class was worthwhile for the pupils?', the most frequently cited response (56.7 per cent) was that it was interesting and relevant. Only 17 per cent of the responses said that the lesson was worthwhile because it was a learning experience, and a mere 9.7 per cent gave contributing to spiritual development as a criterion of worthwhileness (Weafer, Hanley, 1991, 46). An effective RE lesson, according to the responses to this survey, is one which arouses interest, catches the attention of the students and is relevant to something outside the classroom. Handing on the faith is not mentioned. Church or religious practice is glaringly absent. The key to successful RE in an age of religious inertia appears to be in getting the students interested in the first place.

Teachers of religious education in Britain have identified several characteristics of an effective teacher. Firstly, an effective teacher is able to establish good rapport with pupils and has 'charisma'. An effective teacher is good at organising and 'is a survivor'. An effective teacher is open and enthusiastic, has strong religious faith, has qualifications and experience, keeps in touch with other subjects on the curriculum, and has a sense of humour! (Watson, 1993, 143).

These insights of Irish and British teachers would be deeply upsetting to the author of a letter published in *The Irish Times* of 1 July 1997. The author is grinding in her criticism of the process of teaching religion to young people today. Hers is not a lone voice, for such pleas appear from time to time in the letter pages of newspapers and in religious periodicals. Writing in response to the introduction of Relationships and Sexuality Education programmes in schools, she bemoans the passing of the Catechism from the classroom and its replacement by what she refers to as 'a type of golden syrup theology'. She continues:

> If religious knowledge was properly taught, there would be no need to have any of these Godless programmes.[1] Chastity and purity, right and wrong, the old Catechism and the New Catechism of the Catholic Church, the Ten Commandments and the Bible, all need to be taught and made central to the religious knowledge education programme.

Indeed! Include not going to Mass on Sunday being a sin, pre-marital sex being a really big sin and not obeying your parents the biggest sin of all and, for some people, religious education would be restored to its former glory. For it must surely be the golden syrup of theology that has been the undoing of many a God-fearing child. Too much sweetness, too much God-is-love-ness and not enough hellfire and damnation; too much freedom of conscience and not enough moral authority; too many paraliturgies and not enough sodalities – no wonder today's young person is adrift on a great tide of religious inertia. Those who express such concerns about the current teaching of RE and offer such remedies, do so out of a genuine and sincere belief that religion needs to be taught in black and white terms – good and evil, heaven and hell, sin and redemption – forgetting that we no longer live in a black and white world. For the world where the methodology of the catechism made sense – the world of certain questions as well as certain answers – is gone forever. Those who call for a back-to-basics approach to the teaching of religion see 'cultural atheism' as the consequence, rather than the context, of contemporary religious education. Presumably, they see a return to 'old' RE as the key to a return to the 'old' culture. But there can be no going back.

Just as there are those who call for a return to the old classroom, there are those who call for the abandonment of the classroom as the focus of religious education, especially when RE is viewed in catechetical terms. Catechesis is a ministry of the whole Church – the process by which members of the Church are led to maturity of faith. The classroom has a function only as a part of that process, with the parish community and home playing equally significant roles. But where 'parish community' and 'Catholic home' are non-existent, then classroom catechesis becomes difficult, if not impossible. There is no trinity of ministry supporting the development of mature faith. What is taught in the classroom may be contradicted in the community, or even in the home – not explicitly, but in the tacit acceptance or wholehearted support of mores and codes of behaviour at odds with the ideals of the kingdom of God expounded in the classroom. Meaningful liturgy, even if experienced in the classroom or in the school, may not be found in the parish community.

It has been remarked that the sacrament of Confirmation, the end of the process of initiation into the Catholic community, has become a sacrament of departure from the local parish. Increasingly, students no longer grow towards mature faith; they grow out of faith. Dermot Lane, describing religious education in the context of handing on the Christian tradition, ascribes a threefold aim for RE. Firstly, it seeks to awaken an experience and knowledge of God; secondly, it seeks to foster a maturity of faith; thirdly, setting RE firmly in the context of catechetical ministry, Fr Lane proposes that it should seek to promote 'an explicit discipleship of Christ for the sake of the Kingdom of God' (Lane, 1986, 160). It is worth noting Fr Lane's suggestion that all processes of handing on the Christian tradition must transform our understanding of human existence. Consequently, RE must, he argues, dialogue with the living tradition of Christianity and, at the same time, become involved in the transformation of society. The RE he describes is dynamic, culturally engaged, but profoundly ecclesial. In the context of classrooms where an increasing number of students are untouched, or at least unmoved, by ecclesia, is such an aspiration for RE a realistic one? Indeed, if the ethos of a Catholic school is seen as arising from its living contact with a living community of faith, we have to ask, whither this ethos when that living community of faith is struggling to survive?[2]

In England, where most school-based RE has evolved without the benefit of the catechetical genus, words like 'experience' and 'commitment' have until recently been noticeably absent from any debate about religious education in schools. Writing in 1985, John Sealey maintains that religious education which calls for any sort of engagement, commitment or involvement is not compatible with the curriculum goals of other subjects. 'RE, therefore, may be seen like education as a whole, as a second order process, with the aim of bringing pupils to a knowledge and understanding of religion' (Sealey, 1985, 83). Challenging the plea from John Hull for the restoration of common school worship, Sealey argues that such 'first order' experiences should have no place in curricular RE. Viewed from this perspective – as the knowledge and understanding of religion – community and cultural context becomes irrelevant to the RE enterprise. The religiously educated person is neither a believer nor one who brings a religious perspective to the great questions, but one whose general education has included the study of religion (Sealey, 1985, 30). Recent debate in Britain around the question of school worship and the place and purpose of RE in the curriculum has led to the revision of syllabuses. The

Education Reform Act (1988) and the Education Act (1993) set out the principles for reform. All locally agreed syllabuses must reflect the fact that the religious traditions in Great Britain are in the main Christian, whilst taking account of the teaching and practices of the other principal religions represented in that country. The consultation document for GCSE Religious Studies in Northern Ireland proposes that a course in Religious Studies should enable students to:

- stimulate an interest in and enthusiasm for the study of religion;
- develop a knowledge and understanding of at least one living religion;
- identify and promote exploration of, and reflection upon, questions about the meaning and purpose of life;
- consider religious and, where appropriate, other responses to moral issues;
- develop skills relevant to the study of religions;
- develop contexts within their work to explore and reflect on the content and issues of the cross curricular themes as appropriate. (CCEA, 1994, 1)

Unlike some other syllabuses in the UK, the Northern Ireland syllabus deals with Christianity only.

In contrast, the aims of religious and moral education in Scotland – where curriculum and structures are drawn up independently of the rest of the UK – envisage a closer engagement with religion. The aims of religious and moral education are to help pupils:

- develop a knowledge and understanding of Christianity and other world religions and recognise religion as an important expression of human experience;
- appreciate moral values such as honesty, liberty, justice and concern for others;
- investigate and understand the questions and answers that religions can offer about the nature and meaning of life;
- develop their own beliefs, attitudes, moral values and

practices through a process of personal search, discovery and critical evaluation (Scottish Office Education Dept, 1992, 2).

The rationale for religious and moral education arises from the vision of the person and his/her development rather than from the requirements of a liberal education to include the study of religion.

> Education is about the development of the whole person. Religious and Moral Education deals with the development of the person in relation to self-awareness, relationships with others, and the realm of beliefs, values and practices which go to make up a religious outlook on life. As such, it makes an important contribution to the personal and social development of pupils. (Scottish Office Education Dept, 1992, 1)

The vision of RE in Scotland is quite different from that in Northern Ireland. It arises out of the need to contribute to the holistic development of the individual. It asserts that just as the intellectual, social and aesthetic development of the person should be the focus of the education process, so too should his/her religious development. There is no mention of 'an explicit discipleship of Christ for the sake of the Kingdom of God' (Lane, 1986, 160). For this, as has been suggested already, is an aim proper to ecclesia rather than to education. The Scottish Catholic Education Commission which offers guidelines for religious and moral education in Catholic schools, amends the aims outlined above to mention the Roman Catholic tradition as the main focus of study. But commitment or affiliation to any community of faith is not mentioned as an educational aim.

The recent initiative of the National Council for Curriculum and Assessment to prepare RE syllabuses for assessment and certification is, together with the cultural change in the RE classroom, the most significant development in RE in Ireland in recent years. Proposed legislative change means that, for the first time, RE may be included in the range of subjects offered for assessment in the Junior and Leaving Certificates. The consultation process undertaken by the NCCA has led to the preparation of draft syllabuses and assessment proposals. The rationale for these makes it clear that it is the Scottish model rather than the English one which is being followed here. The holistic development of the individual is at the heart of the rationale for the inclusion of RE in the curriculum;

> While it is the concern of the whole curriculum built around the principles of knowledge, understanding, skills and attitudes, to promote personal growth and to facilitate the spiritual development of students, Religious Education is well placed to provide students with opportunities for reflection on human experience as well as for understanding and interpretation of that experience. Such opportunities encourage the students' participation in their own conscious and critical development. (NCCA, 1987, 4)

While the syllabuses do seek to 'contribute to the spiritual and moral development of the student' (NCCA, 1987, 3), commitment to any community of faith is not mentioned. In fact, it is explicitly excluded from the procedures for assessment and certification. The redrafts make it clear that students' participation or non-participation in any Church or community of faith will not be subject to assessment for purposes of national certification.

Does a Catholic school that decides to opt for the new RE syllabus thus opt out of a commitment to offer young people opportunities for the development of mature faith? Is choosing the assessment option in RE a sort of 'catechetical surrender' to cultural forces? Is it a tacit admission that 'handing on the faith' has been an impossible task? In the rationale introducing the syllabus in Scotland, the Scottish Catholic Education Council makes it clear that faith formation is the responsibility of the Catholic school. Such schools are responsible for a 'continuing process of faith formation which promotes an active prayer life and participation in sacramental activity'. The shift in responsibility is clear. Faith formation is the responsibility of the whole school. Handing on the faith is not a solo exercise for the beleaguered RE teacher but the role of the whole school community. 'Whole school' has become something of a cliché in contemporary educational debate. Discipline problems, bullying, health promotion, drugs awareness – all must be addressed in a 'whole school' context. For the Catholic school struggling to establish an identity in the new cultural context, whole school cannot be a mere glib slogan. For it may be that when living communities of faith are vanishing from the cultural horizon, Catholic schools will be called to be the locus of encounter with Gospel values. It may be that, more than ever, such schools are seen as embodying the Christian message. Faith formation is a task proper to the ecclesia rather than to the classroom. But for an ever growing number of students, the Catholic school may be the only ecclesia they ever encounter.

For those involved in teaching religion to young people today, these are challenging times. Cultural change, new initiatives in education and the changing role of the Catholic schools all have implications for the work of the religious educator. Mr O'Dea aside, religious educators, in their creative approaches, local curricular initiatives and imaginative use of limited resources, have shown themselves ready for the challenge ahead.

PART III

PASTORAL CARE

6

PASTORAL CARE IN A CATHOLIC SCHOOL TODAY

J. Matthew Feheney

Introduction

I propose here to examine the role of pastoral care in a Catholic school and will argue that the two belong together, both by definition and because of the nature of the challenge of Christian education today. After some clarifications and distinctions, I will examine the advantages of a group approach, in which the young people themselves are involved in their own pastoral care and development. Having explored the implications of this approach, I will then go on to look at the type of staff development and support structures this will require. I make a sharp distinction between a pastoral care programme and a syllabus for pastoral care, looking at the ingredients of each and making suggestions as to how Department of Education programmes, such as Relationships and Sexuality Education, can be accommodated within a comprehensive pastoral care syllabus.

Because of the special focus of this book, I am concentrating on pastoral care in post-primary schools in Ireland, of which there are some 768 registered with the Department of Education. These are classified into four categories: 445 voluntary secondary, of which the vast majority are Catholic; sixteen comprehensive schools; sixty-one community schools; and 246 vocational schools and community colleges, under thirty-eight local education authorities. (Department of Education, 1995).

Catholic schools, by definition, are involved in pastoral care because they are committed to the education of the whole person. A document issued by Rome stresses the holistic nature of the Catholic school:

> The Catholic school is committed to the development of the whole person, since in Christ, the Perfect Man, all human values find their fulfilment and unity. (*The Catholic School,* 1977, 35)

More recently, Cardinal Hume said much the same thing in different words and in greater detail:

> Education, in its broadest sense, is concerned with life-long inner growth, with the achieving of personal wholeness and integrity, with the development to the utmost of personal gifts and creativity.... It is one of the teachers' tasks to help develop their pupils' ability to form relationships and to be part of a living and loving community.... That part of the teacher's job is highly skilled, vitally important and sometimes lost sight of. One of the secrets here is to recognise that a school is not an institution, but a community. (Hume, 1977, 14, 17)

That the Catholic school can in reality, as well as in theory, be a learning community is confirmed by significant recent research from the US. Non-Catholic researchers, notably Anthony Bryk and his team from the University of Chicago, in the course of an extensive research project over several years, found that Catholic schools were notably successful in transforming themselves from educational institutions into communities of learning that promoted the pastoral care of their students (Bryk, 1996, 28).

After extensive research and analysis, Bryk found that this sense of community in US Catholic high schools, especially those in poor and run-down areas, was fostered by three distinct features. The first was an extensive array of school activities which provided numerous opportunities for face-to-face interaction and shared experiences among adults and students. Second were a set of formal organisational features that enabled the school community. Foremost here was an extended role for teachers, especially in activities that promoted and facilitated practical pastoral care. Thirdly, and crucial for communal school organisation, were a set of shared beliefs about what students should learn, about proper norms of instruction and about how people should relate to one another (ibid., 28-9).

Bryk, using a term first coined by Coleman, concludes that 'Catholic schools benefit from a network of supportive social relations, characterised by trust, that constitute a form of *social capital'*. He sees this *social capital* located 'in the reactions among school professionals and with their parent communities' (ibid, 34, 40). Andrew Greeley has discussed this matter at greater length in chapter 13.

By way of summary, therefore, we can say that Catholic education everywhere is, by definition – and in some places, notably in US inner cities, in practice – characterised by pastoral care. But can we say that Irish post-primary schools display a corresponding degree of pastoral care for their students? The answer, I fear, is partly yes and partly no.

Though post-primary schools in Ireland have a long history of informal caring for their pupils, the formal introduction of pastoral care in many of them has been quite recent. Before that, pastoral care was largely implicit in most Irish post-primary schools, as it still is in some. Few schools have either an explicit syllabus or an organised structure to support pastoral care. This is not to say that individual teachers do not display an active concern for their students. Nor does it belittle the role of form tutors, who attend to administrative tasks and sometimes assume responsibility for class discipline. Some schools even have year heads. The main problem, however, is the absence of both a formalised programme and an organisational structure to support it. At best the arrangement is uneven, at worst hit-and-miss, if not random and inadequate. When it comes to putting structures in place in a school, we must not forget the wise words of a great pioneer in pastoral care, Michael Marland, 'it is a truism of school planning that what you want to happen must be institutionalised' (Marland, 1974, 11).

If Irish voluntary secondary schools have one general organisational weakness, it is the paucity, in many cases the absence, of educational support structures, other than the teacher in the classroom. In these schools, which constitute a majority of all post-primary schools, there is no adequate middle management, a deficiency for which, arguably, the teacher union is no less to blame than the Department of Education (Leader & Boldt, 1994, 99). This lack of adequate structure extends right through the school, affecting the area of pastoral care as much, if not more, than other areas. There is little time available for formal planning, less for monitoring and review. It is, therefore, impossible at present to put Marland's advice concerning roles, duties and responsibilities into operation: 'The role of each person, spheres of responsibility and the links between them need careful planning as a total system, if the individual pupil is to have the care needed and if the school is to be a well-knit community' (Marland, 1974, 79).

The UK model
Most Irish teachers at post-primary level are aware of the concern for pastoral care in the United Kingdom, a concern that began in the early 1970s. Though the education of the 'whole person' was the rationale underlying it, many would say that it was the arrival of the large comprehensive schools which speeded up its introduction (Griffiths and Sherman, 1991, 6). The pastoral care system sought to make manageable the caring for large numbers of students, up to one thousand or more, by dividing them into year groups, under year heads, who, in turn, were under the supervision of a second vice-principal, who was also head of pastoral care. Each class or tutorial group had its own class or form tutor, who was also a subject teacher. There was additional remuneration for the head of year post, which involved administration as well as supervision, but not for the class tutor. In some schools, for pastoral purposes, classes were divided vertically into houses, each house having students from the highest class down to the lowest. Where this obtained, there were house heads instead of year heads.

The development of a pastoral system was a significant step in promoting the social, personal and emotional development of students. Subject teachers now had an additional resource and, gradually, not only the personal problems of students but also matters of discipline, under-performance and poor attendance came to be part of the brief of the class tutor. Hamblin described pastoral care in the UK as being 'concerned with skills and feelings… about respect for the individual and the transmission of values as well as provision of skills' (Hamblin). This sometimes led to a split between the academic and pastoral aspects of education, but where the system was working well, the two supported and complemented one another. When, we speak of a pastoral care system, therefore, the one we have in mind structurally resembles the UK system, with each class having its own class tutor/teacher and each year having a head of year, under a senior member of staff.

While the model of pastoral care that most Irish teachers are familiar with is the UK model, this is not to say that it is an exclusively English invention. Most countries these days have a section of their post-primary curriculum covering material that would come under the heading of pastoral care, though its title on the school timetable may vary from place to place. Often the title of the course is something analogous to social, personal and health education. In the English-speaking world, however, the term pastoral care is well established, can act as an umbrella title for all these programmes, and, despite its drawbacks, has much to commend it. It suggests an active concern and care for the students that embraces not only the imparting of helpful information but also the seeking out of the absentee and the rehabilitation of the offender.

The term pastoral care has a very obvious biblical and religious ring to it. It conjures up the image of a shepherd and his sheep, something frequently encountered in the Bible. Thus the prophet Ezekiel presents God as a shepherd watching over and caring for his people: 'As a shepherd keeps all his flock in view... so shall I keep my sheep in view. I shall rescue them from wherever they have been scattered during the mist and darkness' (Ezk 34:12).

All this is not to say that the image of shepherd-sheep is very meaningful to young people in post-primary schools today. Few people in Ireland are familiar with shepherds caring for sheep, but the image is, nevertheless, embedded in the popular imagination and it will be hard to find a better term than pastoral care for what we have in mind. Moreover, it is true to say that the name given to the subject is often indicative not only of the content but also of the underlying philosophical approach to the subject. In this paper I will be arguing that pastoral care is pre-eminently suitable for a Christian school: it embodies a vision going beyond the imparting of information to caring for the individual and promoting a Christian community.

The what and why of pastoral care

There is obviously more than one definition of pastoral care, but for present purposes I am defining pastoral care as 'the integration of the academic, social, emotional and religious education of our students so that an atmosphere of care obtains in the school community'. Pastoral care should constitute a significant attempt at putting the school mission statement into effect.

The statement of philosophy of most schools, and the mission statement, where it exists, includes a concern for the all-round development of the students. This, as Button (1986, 11) points out, has been implicit rather than explicit in the programmes and syllabuses of most schools in the past. But certain changes in the students, the society they come from and the school itself now require that this care and concern be made explicit. One of these changes has to do with the increasing fragility and vulnerability of the students.

A growing number of our students are virtually at risk: at risk from drink, freely available drugs, anxiety about unemployment, fear of failing examinations, fear of rejection. The school curriculum has become more and more examination-oriented. Competitiveness is built into the system at second level, with those at the top being rewarded with selection for further education while those at the bottom are considered failures. The society from which these students come is also fragile. There is a steady increase in social problems: drug abuse, drink abuse, violence, child abuse and breakdown of family life. There is also widespread ambivalence in society, especially in respect of moral standards and business ethics, and significant, though less widespread, ambivalence towards paramilitary violence.

The expectations of society with regard to what the school should provide for students have also changed, as Treston (1989, 7) points out. Various personalist psychologies, including developmental psychology (Maslow, Rogers), depth psychology (Freud, Jung, Erikson) have influenced education to be more concerned with individual growth. The concept of 'holistic' education is no longer confined to the writings of psychologists: one finds the word being used increasingly by school principals and members of Boards of Management. It is reasonable to assume that the more widespread use of this term is indicative that something more explicit and effective is being sought to facilitate the integration of the academic with the social, emotional and religious development of young people.

Another feature of today's post-primary school population is the fact that a significant number of the students are reluctant, even resentful, scholars. Over the years the strategy for post-primary education has changed: we have gone from a minority of academically able and willing volunteers to a whole-age cohort. This enormous change has taken place without the necessary accompanying change in the nature and range of the educational provision. This is not to say that the whole-age cohort does not have the right to a second-level education to meet their differing needs. It merely highlights a long-standing complaint that the second-level curriculum has not been adapted sufficiently to cater for the wide variety of talents of the students now attending our schools. Our curriculum continues to be excessively examination-oriented and academically weighted.

Recent research has shown the complex nature of human intelligence and it is now recognised that there are at least eight different and distinct types of human intelligence (Gardner, 1984, 1995). The average post-primary school makes little or no attempt to cater for all eight types. Arising out of the unsuitability of much of the curriculum for those students who are not gifted with linguistic and logical-mathematical intelligence, is a certain amount of what we might call dysfunctionalism. One of the ways this manifests itself is in disruption, which is sometimes a result of inability to cope with studies. The more successful the pastoral care in the school, the more it will be picking up the products of this dysfunctionalism. If the work of the class teacher in pastoral care sessions is likely to be so critical, time will have to be allocated for it. We recommend one period per week. If the pastoral care class proves successful, its beneficial effects will spill over onto other aspects of school life. An unsettled student will find it impossible to give his/her full attention to study. A low self-esteem can impede progress, and poor class spirit can destroy co-operation and peer support.

Study skills are an invaluable academic tool which are well worth teaching and learning.

There will be a new level of accountability within schools in the future. Schools will have to draw up school plans and report on how they were implemented. This will inevitably lead to a demand for congruence between the admirable aspirations outlined in the mission statement and what actually happens 'on the ground'. For, while most schools purport to cater for the intellectual, physical, social, emotional and spiritual education of their students, few can point to a structure that facilitates this. A well-planned pastoral care system, on the other hand, provides a practical means of tackling this task.

Before we move on, it may be well to clarify the distinction between pastoral care and counselling. There are three stages of depth in pastoral-caring ministries: pastoral care, pastoral counselling and pastoral psychotherapy. While the first two occur within the school, the third is a specialist ministry not normally done within the school and not directly concerning us in this paper. A simple way to distinguish between pastoral care and pastoral counselling is that while the latter takes place within a one-to-one relationship, the former is generally a class activity directed towards the immediate needs of a group of students. Pastoral care can be accomplished by many who have basic training in that area. Ideally, in pastoral care, the teacher accompanies the students through bad as well as good times, using the human skills of listening, relating and judicious intervention. Counselling, on the other hand, is a one-to-one relationship that requires appropriate time and space, normally a special counselling room.

Group approach to pastoral care

Some writers (Button, 1986, 11) consider peer friendship to be at the core of healthy social growth, and many young people who are at odds with their peers seem to be in difficulties with regard to other aspects of life also. A supportive group of peers is, therefore, one of the most useful benefits a pastoral care class can give a student. The involvement of the students themselves in their own pastoral care is a strategy, the efficacy of which is confirmed by theory as well as experience. Hamblin says that 'involvement of the students is crucial. Failure to make pastoral activities a joint enterprise between students and tutors deprives us of what may be the most potent agency for achieving pastoral aims' (Hamblin, 1993, 44).

The group is also the preferred channel in which to conduct pastoral care classes, and open discussion is an ideal, though not necessarily easy medium. Good communication is essential for any useful interactions to occur within the group, and the most basic and valuable communication skills have to do with listening. Personal attitudes and feelings can come in the way of receiving a message, and young people must learn to distinguish between messages that are verbalised and those that are communicated by body language. There are many amusing games and activities that may be used to explore these areas, including relaying a simple whispered message along a row of students and discovering how the message has become confused and garbled in the process. One of the great advantages of such an activity is that the experience may later be recalled and cited as an instance of the ease with which messages can be misunderstood. If this can happen with verbal messages, how much more does it apply to messages involving the interpretation of motives and meanings?

Decision-making will inevitably come up within the group context. The different styles of decision-making can be explored and discussed, including decisions made by authority, by majority, by minority and by consensus. Decision-making by consensus will be the more interesting and most complex of the lot (Feheney, 1994a, 133). It will require the group to listen carefully to each opinion, attempt to understand the different views, and wait while members of the group search slowly and patiently for a formula that will meet the shifting requirements of the group. Students will have to be reminded of the distinction between compromise and consensus, and how atypical the latter is in decision-making in commercial, public and political affairs. Moving from a system where authority is vested in the teacher to one in which responsibility is entrusted to the group, can be a slow and painful process and can pose a major challenge to the skill of the individual teacher brave enough to attempt it.

There will inevitably be some conflict arising in any situation involving groups, and teachers have to be prepared to deal with it. This conflict should be addressed and resolved rather than allowed to build up or smoulder underground. Learning to deal with conflict situations and resolving them constructively is a major part of the personal and social development area.

It must not be forgotten that all this effort in group work is aimed at developing a powerful and effective instrument in pastoral care. It is calculated to move the students from a dependent frame of mind to one of independence and personal responsibility. All this, however, can only take place within an environment that facilitates empowerment and personal development. And it goes without saying that some teachers can feel threatened by the development of such attitudes in students, howsoever educational they be.

In a school environment that facilitates and promotes the empowerment of students, the pastoral team may also need to revise their definition of an ideal pupil, the relationship between staff and pupils and even the dynamics of the learning situation. A passive and overly conforming student is not necessarily a 'good' student. Likewise, the student who feels alienated or who fails to see the significance of school rules, is not necessarily a recalcitrant one. It could be argued that commitment to a cause, however seemingly insignificant, can lead to responsible attitudes in later life. Moreover, mistakes by individual students should be considered within the context of general effort. After all, mistakes are made by active students, and active participation is a desirable trait in any student's character and personality.

Staff development
While the cultivation of group skills and group processes can pose a significant challenge for the class teacher, the development of the students will be an even more significant achievement. Moving from a teacher-directed class style to a collaborative group model will require the use of interactive skills by the students. These skills are fostered by creative learning techniques such as role play, creative drama and discussion methods. The teacher wishing to try out these techniques may require some

specific training and preparation in creative teaching and group skills. Fortunately, once a nucleus in the staff of any school develops these skills, these members can form a resource training group within the school to develop the skills of other interested teachers. In this type of situation, Button has some sound advice about setting up in-school structures to facilitate staff development and nurturing a climate to support it: 'The training of teachers should not be so much about the skills of individual teachers, but rather about evolving a developmental programme for the school staff as a whole' (Button, 1980, 79).

It is unlikely that a school that cannot manage the pastoral care of the staff will be able to manage it successfully in the case of the students. The first and most perceptive expression of the pastoral care of staff is the quality of the interpersonal relationships between members of the staff. The staff must learn to communicate effectively and relax together. The bonding that class teachers seek to promote in their classes must first be experienced in the staffroom. This bonding is unlikely to happen of its own accord: it must be planned and worked at. It includes the personal and professional growth and development of each member.

Treston (1989, 43) reminds us that effective pastoral care has to be nourished by a suitable spirituality. He sees spirituality not as an extra dimension but as being of the very essence of what care is. This is the spirituality that involves a search for God in the everyday things of life. We are here talking about such basic things as helping students to find meaning in their lives; to cope with bereavement and family breakdown; to help them grieve during their significant losses; to help them discover joy in creating and in new-found friends, as well as the excitement of new ideas and the mysteries of intimacy. Each student will be encouraged to draw from the riches of his/her own religious tradition.

Programme and syllabus

I make an important distinction here between a pastoral care programme and a pastoral care syllabus. The programme is the wider of the two. It means the sum total of personnel, structures and efforts being made by the school community to provide a suitable atmosphere of care within which the all-round education of the students can take place. The list, in addition to a syllabus, includes the school climate, the teaching staff and ancillary staff, the discipline system, the guidance counsellor/careers teacher, the school chaplain, staff-student relationships, liaison with parents and the local community, school ethos, values and policies. All these exist to help the students, and each one has its own special part to play in today's post-primary school.

The term 'pastoral care syllabus', on the other hand, is used to describe the explicit programme taught in class either by the class tutor/teacher or a team of teachers. Elsewhere, I have recommended that this syllabus include relationships, sexuality education, communication, self-esteem, school and school-related topics, society and social relationships, study skills, the body, health and hygiene, environment, recreation and leisure, personal development, personal and social skills, attitudes and values, substance abuse, the world of work (Feheney, 1994b, 8). Ideally, this syllabus will cover the entire five or six years of post-primary school, with different sections being covered to an appropriate depth with different classes each year.

Hitherto, not only the content of a pastoral care syllabus, but also the decision even to have such a syllabus, was entirely at the discretion of the individual school. Now, however, the Department of Education has decreed that certain sections of the syllabus suggested above must be taught in every post-primary school. The sections in question are those covered by a) Relationships and Sexuality Education (popularly known as RSE) and b) Civic, Social and Political Education (hereafter abbreviated to CSPE). The Department of Education has planned that Relationships and Sexuality Education or RSE would begin in every post-primary school in September 1997. To this end, two members of staff in each school have received some training, the extent of which is considered inadequate by some teachers' unions (ASTI, 1997). The Department of Education also hopes that each school will draw up its own syllabus in RSE and will establish an advisory committee with parent representatives. Despite the efforts of Niamh Bhreathnach, former Minister of Education, to involve many interested parties, including parent groups, in a wide consultation process preceding the introduction of the RSE programme (Doyle, 1997), there are still considerable fears and misgivings about its introduction. On the part of teachers, these fears have to do mainly with the adequacy of training being provided to deliver the programme, but, in the case of parent groups, there are misgivings about the content of the programme. There is, however, a provision that allows parents to withdraw their children from the programme, but schools see this as creating an additional problem in so far as any children withdrawn by parents will have to be supervised separately and this would mean extra demands on what is already a tight staffing provision.

It should also be pointed out that the new RSE programme is, in turn, only a part of a larger programme entitled Social, Personal and Health Education, generally abbreviated to SPHE (Egan, 1994, 11). This latter (SPHE) programme would, obviously form part of a comprehensive pastoral care programme, which could also include at least some parts of the new Civic, Social and Political Education (CSPE) programme. The CSPE is replacing an older civics education programme, originally drawn up by the Department of Education, but which, in the absence of revision and updating, was allowed to become obsolete.

A report of an expert advisory group on Relationships and Sexuality Education in 1994 recommended that 'Social, Personal and Health Education programmes need to be a core part of the curriculum right through primary and post-primary schooling' (Egan, 1994, 13). The report also felt that the syllabus should be a spiral one, extending in scope each year and revisiting the topics in deeper ways which would be appropriate to the age and stage of development of the students. In the primary-school sector it was felt that the class teacher was the best placed to implement the school-based element of the programme. Delivery at post-primary level would be by means of a timetabled core, with, where appropriate, cross-curricular links. At second level it was also envisaged that a variety of models could be used for the delivery of the programme. In some schools the programme would be delivered by a class tutor, whereas in others it would be delivered by a specialist teacher or team. The subject would be timetabled on a weekly basis and provision would be made for cross-curricular links.

In summary, we might say that, while in the past many schools had no special time allocated to pastoral care, they will, in the future, be obliged to timetable RSE, either separately or as part of the more comprehensive SPHE, and the teachers will, moreover, be required both to teach RSE and to prepare students to answer questions on this subject in their Junior Certificate examination. An obvious way to meet this requirement would be to allocate one period per week to pastoral care, during which both SPHE and the portion of it known as RSE could be taught. A small number of post-primary schools are already moving in this direction, but many of the others are still far from such an arrangement.

When it comes to drawing up a syllabus for pastoral care, teachers should be encouraged not to be totally dependent on an externally produced programme, no matter how attractive the latter may appear. This is not to say that externally produced programmes should not be used as a starting point, because, in the absence of experience in drawing up school programmes and with limited time at their disposal, teachers need a model on which to start, after which it is only a small step to making adaptations to meet the special needs of their own students. Later, with experience, some of them will hopefully go on to produce their own syllabus, incorporating the RSE component as specified by the Department of Education.

It would obviously be important for schools with a Christian ethos and commitment to situate the teaching of Relationships and Sexuality Education within a religious context. This is not to suggest, however, that it should be made the sole responsibility of the religious education teachers, much less thrown in their 'lap'.

Conclusion

In conclusion, we may say that the coming years give promise of heralding considerable innovations in post-primary schools in the general area of pastoral care. These innovations have, for the most part, however, been forced upon the schools, because, as a group, they have not been pro-active in the area of pastoral care, but have waited until changes were thrust upon them by the Department of Education. The new developments will be mostly in the area of social, personal and health education, with a special emphasis on relationships, sexuality, civic, social and political education. I have argued here in favour of each school developing a comprehensive pastoral care syllabus, which will not only cover these areas but will also include such topics as study skills, values and attitudes, decision-making, together with career and vocation choices. In other words, a pastoral care syllabus, being in theory a necessary ingredient of a caring Catholic school, should be so constructed and delivered that it can act as an umbrella course for those portions of social, personal, health, civic and political education prescribed by the Department of Education at post-primary level.

The period ahead is one of the most exciting times in Irish education for years. There is new draft legislation in education, new educational technology, new staff development opportunities, new courses of study for teachers. For people of vision, there are new and exciting challenges, new opportunities for leadership, especially Christian leadership, in education. Yes, there are many challenges and possibilities. But there are also risks. In a spirit of Christian hope, let us gladly take those risks. For, without risks, there will be no new ground broken or new trails pioneered.

In a way, pastoral care is not difficult: the main ingredient is love, continually expressed through affirmation, cheerful interest and concern. This contributes powerfully towards a happy atmosphere in school. John McGahern recently described the effect on him, as a teenager, of this interest and concern in a small country secondary school in the early 1950s:

> I look back on those five years as the beginning of an adventure that has not stopped. Each day I cycled towards Carrick was an anticipation of delights. The fear and drudgery of school disappeared: without realizing it, through the pleasures of the mind, I was beginning to

know and to love the world. The Brothers took me in, set me down, and gave me tools. I look back on my time there with nothing but gratitude, as years of luck and privilege, and, above all, of grace, actual grace. (McGahern, 1996, 135)

7

DISCIPLINE IN THE CHRISTIAN SCHOOL

Frank J. Steele

Christian schools in general, Catholic schools in particular, are held in very high regard across the globe because of their effectiveness in establishing and maintaining the highest standards in virtually every aspect of school life. Public opinion – which does not always follow or reflect academic investigation and professional analysis, but which, in this matter, appears to be supported by both – would maintain that the effectiveness associated with these schools derives, in large part, from their capacity to inculcate in those in their care a sense of respect for self and for others, and would further maintain that this respect is cultivated especially by means of proper emphasis on discipline.

To outline matters in this fashion is not to claim that all is well in all Catholic schools. There are Catholic schools that fail to establish and/or maintain acceptable standards of teaching and learning. In the matter of discipline, in particular, there is enough objective evidence to suggest that, if not as often or as widely as some might claim, there were still instances of Catholic schools in which the regime was unnecessarily and unacceptably harsh, and, alas, as the scandals of recent times on more than one continent have so sadly demonstrated, there have been instances of Catholic schools in which the regime was both brutal and sinful, to the appalling and abiding detriment of 'the least of these (cf. Mt 25:40)', whose status and predicament gave them first and greatest claim, particularly in Christian institutes, on understanding, support, protection and love.

Human error, weakness and even viciousness have, on occasion, blighted Catholic schools, and no good, moral or religious purpose is served by ignoring or denying that this has been the case. None is served either, though, by refusing to note and acknowledge that, today as yesterday, at home and abroad, parents of all sorts and conditions, including non-Catholics and non-Christians, vote, as it were, with their children's feet, and, by open preference and free choice, entrust the welfare of those they love to schools in the Catholic tradition, and do this precisely because they rightly anticipate that in such schools the very highest standards of academic performance, certainly, but also, and especially, of correct behaviour will be required of all without qualification or exception.

That much recognised, and done so in justice, it must also be acknowledged that it is not always the case that parental confidence and preference relates immediately, primarily, or, indeed, at all, to the specifically Catholic in the educational programme of the Catholic school. Furthermore, it must also be admitted that, especially in the 'first world', but also in all parts of the world that accept and absorb its values, it is not always entirely clear whether parents in general, middle-class parents in particular, accept the specifically Catholic values of the Catholic school, or whether the Catholic school accommodates its values to those of the parents, which may be, not just other than, but sometimes antithetical to and even destructive of those of the Gospel.

In the matter of discipline, it is not always clear whether the Catholic school itself is thinking and doing anything distinctively Catholic when it espouses and inculcates a set of values conducive to self-respect, mutual respect, and the good order which arises from, and issues in, both. It is, indeed, not always clear whether that which the Catholic school champions and fosters in the name and in the interests of discipline is particularly Christian at all, or is, in any way that matters *sub specie aeternitatis*, different to that which might be accepted and developed in a school that is purely humanist and secular in its origins, beliefs, practices and objectives.

What is attempted here, therefore, is a pilgrimage in meditation in search of the specifically Gospel roots of discipline in any school that would desire and labour to be Catholic, not just in name, but 'in spirit and truth (cf. Jn 4:23)'. This quest, it must be emphasised, is meditative. What is offered here is certainly offered tentatively and diffidently, but is still offered unambiguously and unapologetically, as an exercise in, and for, *lectio divina*. The contents of this paper are shared as seed and fruit of a continuing *ruminatio* of the Scriptures, of a prayerful digestion and appropriation of the Word of God, conducted sometimes 'in a mirror, dimly', sometimes 'face to face' (cf. I Co 13:12), always with a sense of provisionality, of depths unplumbed, of heights unreached, but always, too, with a yearning to know, understand, apply and live that which, in the matter of Christian education in general, and, here and now, of discipline in the Christian school in particular, 'the Spirit says to the churches' (Rv 2:7).

It's about Christ

Whatever else it may or may not be about, discipline in the Christian school must be about Christ. Fundamentally and definitively, it must be about, not Dewey or Marx, not Apollos or Paul (cf. I Co 3:4ff.), not Ignatius, John-Baptist or Don Bosco, not Nano, Catherine, Margaret or Edmund, not you, me, them or us, but about Christ, about him who is the Way, the Truth, the Life (Jn 14:6), who is the only '... name under heaven given among men by which we must be saved....'(Acts 4:12). We may, like Paul, refer to the altar dedicated, 'To an unknown god', in order to proclaim 'the Lord of heaven and earth' (cf. Acts 17:22ff). We may, as the Fathers put it, despoil the Egyptians (cf. Ex 12:35-36), i.e., appropriate, Christianise, mobilise the 'heathen', the 'secular', the 'profane', the arts and the sciences, all forms and products of human experience and expertise, all that reflects and fosters the Good, the True, the Beautiful, Prudence, Justice, Fortitude and Temperance, in our service of youth for the sake of the Gospel. But we may not, and we must not, confuse or conflate the categories. The Lord of creation is, indeed, present and, to some extent, discernible, and even accessible, in all that he has made, but his final, conclusive and saving self-revelation is in Christ Jesus (cf. Heb 1:1ff). Christ is Lord and Saviour (cf., e.g., Ph 2:5-11). It is he – a Person, it must be remembered, and not a law or a thesis or a programme – who is 'the first-born of all creation... the beginning, the first-born from the dead' (Col 1:15, 18), the Second Adam (cf. Rm 5:4), the Heavenly Man (cf.

I Co 15:42ff), the living heart, the defining core, the means to, and the measure of, humanity, the progenitor and the paradigm of what it is to be human, and, therefore, the centre and circumference of Christian culture, education, schooling and discipline. It is only through Christ, with him and in him, that those involved in the formation and education of youth for the sake of the Gospel can find their *raison d'être*, can discover the parameters and the constituents, the ends and the means, of that which is specifically and definitively Christian in who they are and in what they do.

The Christ who is 'a cornerstone chosen and precious (I P 2:6), the only foundation (cf. I Co 3:11) of the Christian school, and, particularly, of discipline in the Christian school, is – in respect of the ends of discipline – the Word in whom all things were made (Jn 1:3). He is the Logos in whom God speaks the fullness and the truth of all created things, visible and invisible. He is the Word in whom is uttered the complete, authentic reality about each and every one of us, and the extent to which we correspond in thought, word and deed to this Word is the extent to which we are truly our own most real and authentic selves. This Word is uttered in the creating and sustaining Fiat of the Father (cf. Gn 1:3), and is fulfilled in the Amen of the Son (cf. Rv 3:14). It is, precisely, participation in, and union with, this Word, this 'Yes' of Christ, which is the objective of discipline in the Christian home and in the Christian school, where, in 'the glorious liberty of the children of God' (Rm 8:21), the young are taught and trained to respond freely and positively in the Spirit to the invitation to be, and become, their own most authentic selves, that is issued in the Fiat of the Father, that is encountered in every human circumstance and choice, and that is answered in the free and faithful Amen of the Son.

In his ontological, universal Amen in the Spirit to the Father, Christ is the template of humanity, the law of our inmost being, the rule of every life, and the definitive task of Christian formation is the formation of Christ (cf. Ga 4:19) in each of the young, so that they may come to join in the Great Amen that is Christ. The aim of discipline, in the Christian home and in the Christian school, is to establish and maintain the conditions in which, in the Spirit, those in our care may best learn to say – in the spirit of adoption and not of slavery (cf. Rm 8:12-17) – '... let it be to me according to your word' (Lk 1:38), and grow 'in wisdom and in stature, and in favour with God and man (ibid. 2:52), and come, at last, to maturity, 'to the measure of the stature of the fulness of Christ' (Ep 4:13).

The Christ who is the 'head of the corner' of discipline in the Christian school is – in respect of the means of discipline – the same Master who teaches his disciples that authority must not be exercised among them as it is among the Gentiles, '... but whoever would be great among you must be your servant, and whoever would be first among you must be your slave; even as the Son of Man came not to be served but to serve....' (Mt 20:25-28). He is the rabbi who, 'knowing that the Father has given all things into his hands', washes the feet of his disciples, and, in so doing, says to them, 'If I then, your Lord and Teacher, have washed your feet, you also ought to wash one another's feet' (Jn 13:14). He is, in effect, the Christ who teaches, by deed as well as by word, that, in any Christian community, wherever and whenever authority is given, it is always given, not for power, but for service, and that those who, in any Christian community, are set over others, are so set, not for their own sake, but for the sake of those entrusted to their care.

This teaching, indeed, constitutes a constant, a universal and an absolute principle of life in Christ. It may very well be a principle honoured more in the breach than in the observance. Notwithstanding that, it is still a principle rooted, validated and vindicated in Christ himself, in his precept and in his practice, and it is, therefore, one with which all who exercise authority in the Christian school must struggle, in prayer and in practice, until, by the *via negativa* and, if needs be, the *via crucis,* they come to attain the always difficult equilibrium between the claims of authority and of service, and come, in any event, to use everything to do with discipline as a means of Christ-like *diakonia* of those whom a loving but jealous Providence has set in their care.

*   *   *

It's about Christ in me

This kind of authority does not come easily or readily to fallen nature. It is, in fact, difficult to understand and more difficult still to practise. Its exercise requires that we 'repent, and believe in the Gospel' (Mk 1:15). It requires that we be led by the Spirit into the desert (cf., e.g., Mt 4:1 ff), there in the searing, healing light of the Truth of God's Word to initiate in self-examination a process of *metanoia*, of transformation in Christ, of the formation of Christ in us. For it is only when that mind is in us that was in Christ Jesus (cf. Ph 2:5ff) that we will be able to experience that *kenosis*, that 'self-emptying', without which it is impossible to set oneself at the service of others for the sake of Christ and of his Gospel. This *metanoia*, this repentance, this conversion, is, precisely, a process, and it is lifelong. What is in view is no occasional or external change but a radical 're-turning' of the person towards God in the very depths of the heart. What is in view is the 're-formation' of the self in grace, so that the 'graven image' (cf. Ex 20:4-6), the caricature, the lampoon, we make of ourselves when, in pride, we 'idolise' ourselves, is re-made to the pattern of Christ, who is himself the *eikon* of the invisible God (Col 1:15), in whom all things are restored and re-created.

This process of conversion must be, not just personal, but institutional and structural. It must involve and envelop, not just the people who do things in the name of discipline in the Christian school, but what is done and how it is done. The burning, cleansing light of God's Truth must target policies and procedures, all who implement them, and all that is done in implementing them. This does *not* mean there will be no such mechanisms in the Christian school. Conversion in Christ is never that easy. It means that, like all corporate entities, the Christian school will have its policies and procedures, its rules and regulations, its ways and means of doing what must be done to inspire the young to accept the challenge of their own most authentic selves. It means, though, that in the Christian school, all of these ways and means and ends are ever under scrutiny, and given that authority is involved, and given that authority, especially when used by ostensibly good people for ostensibly good ends, is, as it were, a perennial occasion of sin, they will be rigorously scrutinised, in the light of a 'hermeneutic of suspicion', and the spirit that inspires them, both in conception and in implementation, will itself be subjected to a continuous process of testing and discernment to ensure it is not vitiated.

This constant examen of conscience, personal first, then structural and institutional, is a *sine qua non* of the process of conversion that must accompany and inform all things to do with discipline in the Christian school. It must be so lest, through any misuse or abuse of authority – not excluding such misuse and abuse associated with an emphasis on 'self-emptying', which fosters and reflects, not the genuine and necessary Gospel value of Christ-like obedience, but the insidious and pernicious Anti-Christ-like authoritarianism that has sometimes bedevilled the exercise of power amongst Christians – those in charge of 'little ones' incur the awful fate of those who scandalise them (cf. Mt 18:5-10).

It's about Christ in you

If it is to be, precisely, a *diakonia*, a mode of service for the sake of the Gospel, discipline in the Christian school must be a service to Christ. It must derive from, and be conditioned by, a profound conviction that what is done to the least of his is done to himself (cf. Mt 25:31-46). Those who are set in authority over the young in the Christian school must work and pray daily for the vision of a Simeon and of an Anna (cf. Lk 2:25-38) who, amidst the hustle and the bustle of the crowds, the wear and tear of the day, could discern in a child 'a light for revelation to the Gentiles' (ibid., 32), 'the redemption of Jerusalem' (ibid., 38). To discern Christ in the young, especially in the occasionally fraught environment of the school, is never an easy or a simple task. Indeed, there are times when, because of the complications that invest the mind and the heart, only the eyes of faith will be able to detect, especially – though not, of course, exclusively – in the school-resistant and teacher-defiant working-class male teenager, the lineaments of the face of Christ. However, if discipline in the Christian school is to be itself Christian, if the interpersonal encounters that are the very stuff of disciplinary experiences on all sides in every school are not to degenerate into something actually anti-Christian, it is imperative that those who exercise authority seek in constant prayer and meditation a 'vision', as it were, like that in which Peter, James and John saw Christ transfigured, and heard the voice from the cloud, and knew that this was the Son, with whom the Father was well-pleased (cf. Mt 17:1-8). In each of those who cross our paths in the Christian school, the God and Father of our Lord Jesus Christ has, as we noted, uttered the Word that is his Beloved Son, and, in each of them, we may discern with the eyes of faith the image of Christ, and hear with the ears of the heart the voice from the cloud which identifies the Son and bids us 'listen to him' (Mt 17:5). It must be emphasised that we treat here of nothing superficial or sentimental.

The daily circumstances in which we will need the 'vision' are very far indeed from being either. They are precisely the circumstances in which our evangelical convictions are most immediately and most strongly challenged and tested. They are the circumstances that easily lead to cynicism, to scepticism, to agnosticism, as it were, not about God as such, but about that which Scripture and Tradition teach us about the presence of God in the 'Other'. They are, therefore, the circumstances which, if not suffused with faith, hope and love, if not illuminated with the radiance of 'Tabor', will become, in every sense, graceless, and will issue in an effective 'godlessness' which will, imperceptibly but inevitably, and long before it is realised, undermine from within the moral entitlement of the school to the designation of Christian.

It's about Christ in us

The best environment in which to foster the kinds and modes of discipline appropriate in the Christian school is one in which the specifically communal nature of such a school is recognised and cultivated. Like the Christian home, the Christian school is meant to be a *koinonia*, a fellowship of believers grounded in unity of heart and soul (cf. Ac 4:32). As the Christian home is a 'church', an assembled community formed, convoked and sustained by the Lord, so too is the Christian school an *ekklesia* of the People of God, called and held together, not by chance, but by Providence, not for human or temporal ends, but for ends eternal and divine. As in the 'domestic church', so too in that which may, without impropriety, be called the 'scholastic church', the motivation and mechanism for the convergence and cohesion of those who comprise the community is participation in, and adherence to, the Lord (cf. I P 2:4 ff.). This, of course, is the Lord who empties himself of all dignities and who washes the feet of his servants. This is the Teacher who tells his disciples that they are not to be called Rabbi because they are, in fact, always co-disciples (cf. Mt 23:8). This is the Rabbi who blesses his Father because he has imparted divine knowledge to those who are most like pupils, and withheld that same knowledge from those who are most like teachers (cf. Mt 11:25). This is the heir to the sapiential traditions of the 'fathers' who, in calling all to learn of him (Mt 11: 28-30), invokes the child-like and woman-like language of Holy Wisdom (cf., e.g., Pr 8:22-33, Si 24:1-22). This, therefore, is the Master who inverts, subverts but, really, converts, all relationships in the Christian community in general, in the Christian school in particular.

What, indeed, is to become of the constitutive and definitive interaction between teacher and taught in the Christian school when, in the doctrine and example of Jesus, '... you are all brethren' (Mt 23:8), all fellow-pupils, as it were, at the feet of the one and only Master, the Christ (cf. Mt 23:10)? At the very least, that encounter must be radically transformed in the knowledge that we serve a God who announces, 'I will destroy the wisdom of the wise, and the cleverness of the clever I will thwart' (I Cor 1:19, Is 29:14). That transformation will be furthered in our recollection of the example of the teaching and remonstrating Christ who, on the road to Emmaus (Lk 24:1-35), instructed and corrected the two disciples, but, so very far from over-powering either their minds by argument or their wills by chastisement, with a truly divine courtesy and respect for their autonomy, 'appeared to be going further' (ibid., 24:28). In the Christian school, therefore, whilst there will and must be counselling, correction and, indeed, chastisement, discipline must be exercised and suffused with an irradicable and positive regard for the freedom under God of every single conscience.

Conclusion

In this paper, we have but sketched the broad outline of a meditative, scriptural approach to discipline in the Christian school. We have but initiated a pilgrimage of thought and prayer to the heart of the mystery of Christ in the school. We have indicated, not yet a destination, but a direction, and we can but hope that stronger and wiser men and women will push on along the highway, especially in the light of that which the various founding charisms of the religious institutes given to the education of youth for the sake of the Gospel tell us of discipline in, as it were, a pedagogy for the Kingdom. We have left unsaid virtually anything about discipline *in se*. In that regard, what is offered here are variations on a theme, with the theme as a given, something – necessarily, if not wisely, perhaps – understood.

Some there may be who might consider that Christ is already at the heart of our schools, and that the whole effort is, therefore, redundant. We need, however, to sing a 'new song' to the Lord (cf., e.g., Ps 33:3), and, for that, we need in our schools a Christ who is something more than 'muzak'. There is no room, of course, for that proprietorial sense that might regard all to do with Christian, Catholic education as the sole preserve of any one sector or kind of school amongst the range of those extant. Some may, indeed, have Abraham for their father, but the Lord of History is able to raise up children to Abraham by the most unlikely means and in the most unlikely circumstances (cf. Mt 3: 8-9). In these changing times, especially in the sphere of education and particularly in Ireland, in these challenging, confusing and, therefore, grace-filled times, it falls to all who serve the Lord of History in the schools to be prepared to go to meet him, bearing in their hands the lamp of faith, of hope, above all, though, of love (cf. Mt 25:1-13).

PART IV

CONTEMPORARY CHALLENGES

8

CHILDREN OF A LESSER GOD

J. Matthew Feheney FPM

It is a disturbing fact that a significant proportion of our children either fail, or leave school before reaching, the Leaving Certificate examination each year, many of them after as many as twelve years of schooling. I will suggest here that these 'failures' are not only due to family and social factors, or to the failure of these children to make the best use of their time in school, but also due to inappropriate methods of teaching, curricula and the nature of the Leaving Certificate itself. In this paper I will then go on to outline one alternative way of describing and assessing intelligence, before suggesting that this approach would better suit the needs of some children, as well as being in keeping with a Christian vision of life. I will also argue that it would be more conducive to enabling the students acquire a healthy self-image and achieve fulfilment in later life. Finally, I will mention briefly some of the attempts made to broaden the curriculum and change the approach to teaching, learning and assessment in second-level schools. I have chosen the above title for the paper because I feel that it captures some of the inadequacy and frustration which some of these alternatively-gifted children feel when they encounter failure at school, especially at second level.

Introduction

Problem of excessive failures
The *Early School Leavers Provision* Report shows that, during the years 1992 to 1994, on average, one third of all students in the age cohort left school 'educationally disadvantaged in the context of labour market conditions' (ESF, 1996, vi). Of this total, a small percentage (about 1,000) dropped out after primary school and did not go on to second level school at all. About 4,000,

though going on to second level, left without any qualification, while twice that number left school after three years with the Junior Certificate as their only qualification. Another 2,700 had completed a vocational preparation and training (VPTP) programme in addition to their Junior Certificate, while 5,500 completed the senior cycle during each of these years but failed to achieve the five subject passes which would have enabled them to obtain a full Leaving Certificate (ESF, 1996, v-vi). Though the above report stresses the loss to the Irish economy of the educational under-performance of so many young people, the loss for the young people themselves, in terms of self-esteem, self-confidence and personal fulfilment, is even more serious and long term.

Why do so many fail to complete second-level schooling successfully? The answer, while complex, would include one or more of the following reasons: lack the necessary intelligence; failure of individual students to apply themselves to their studies with sufficient diligence; family problems; personal and social problems; failure of the school or teachers to prepare students adequately. In this paper, I would like to concentrate on another set of reasons, which, though not the only ones, require highlighting at this period of our educational history. I will suggest that the programme of studies, the teaching approach and methodology and the method of final assessment at second level are too narrow and constricted to suit the wide range of abilities of all our children.

What is intelligence?
What is defined as intelligence has enormous influence on what is seen as legitimate knowledge in schools. If one or two forms of ability are given precedence over others, selection will happen on the basis of performance in these areas. Furthermore, if a form of ability is not recognised, then the knowledge related to it need not be included in the curriculum at all.

Though much has been written in the past about the nature of intelligence, there is more research being done on the topic today than ever before. In an attempt to measure intelligence, traditional intelligence tests have focused largely on the measurement of people's ability to engage in abstract reasoning. This has resulted in intelligence being equated with abstract reasoning, and, consequently, being measured accordingly. The emphasis on linguistic and logical capacities in intelligence, aptitude and achievement tests has been, and still is, predominant.

By defining intelligence in narrow linguistic and logical terms, we ensure that many children will not be regarded as particularly intelligent. Such a narrow view of intelligence tends to condemn those who do not possess these abilities to failure at school. This has inevitable implications for students' self-esteem and sense of identity (Hannon & Shorthall, 1991, 7). Moreover, a narrow definition of intelligence helps justify practices such as streaming and banding in schools and makes ability-grouping seem natural and desirable. The notion of fixed ability also exonerates teachers and educators because students are made to feel that failure is the result of a personal weakness on their part. In contrast to the fixed IQ which, in the past, people were believed to possess, contemporary brain-mind researchers believe that, with the appropriate stimuli, intelligence can be increased all through life and the only limits to our intelligence are self-made and are related to our beliefs about what is possible (Lazear, 1991, xiv).

Theory of multiple intelligences
Over the past four decades, traditional notions of intelligence and standardised tests have been scrutinised from a number of perspectives. Assumptions on which the testing edifice was based have been gradually undermined by work in developmental, cognitive and educational psychology. In the 1960s, Piaget's view that children pass through a number of qualitatively different stages called sensori-motor, pre-operational, concrete operational and formal operational held sway. By the 1970s, however, this view of universal development was being questioned by many investigators. Gardner became convinced that the Piagetian view of intellect was inadequate. He and his colleagues in Project Zero at Harvard University found that the achievement of developmental milestones in one domain was largely

independent of development in the other domains. Piaget's theory was also contradicted by research on the abilities of people who had suffered brain damage. Gardner found that functioning in other areas could remain largely unaffected (Gardner *et al*, 1996, 204).

The theory that ability varies across domains opened the way for considerable doubts about our traditional understanding of intelligence. Gardner suggested that intelligence is not a single entity but, instead, takes multiple forms. Problem-solving is recognised as a crucial component of each intelligence. To identify a list of various intelligences, evidence from several sources was consulted and only intelligences that satisfied a majority of the criteria were selected as *bona fide* intelligences (Gardner, 1983). In addition to satisfying these criteria, each intelligence had to have a core operation (or set of operations) and be capable of being encoded in a symbol system. Gardner emphasises that 'except in the rarest case, intelligences work in combination' (Gardner, 1990, vi). He defines intelligence as 'the ability to solve problems or fashion products that are of consequence in a particular cultural setting or community' (Gardner *et al*, 1996, 203).

Gardner believes that intelligence is best seen as a quality of human behaviour – not a mental quality. He says its definition will vary between cultures and between historical periods. As intelligence is the product of experience, one needs to be given the opportunity to develop it. All human beings possess each intelligence to varying degrees: we are born with an intelligence profile which he describes as a 'bio-psychological potential' and we use this set of abilities in different ways. To date, Gardner has identified eight distinct intelligences (Shores, 1995), each of which will be outlined briefly in the next section.

Eight gateways to knowledge

Logical-mathematical intelligence
The core operations of this form of intelligence include speed and power of abstraction and the ability to handle skilfully long chains of reasoning. The young child gains his/her initial and

most fundamental knowledge in this area through confronting objects, in ordering and re-ordering them, and in assessing their quantity. At this preliminary stage, logical-mathematical intelligence quickly becomes remote from the world of material objects. Through the course of development, one moves from objects to statements, from actions to the relations between actions, from the realm of the sensori-motor to the realm of pure abstraction and, ultimately, to the highest regions of logical, mathematical and scientific thought (Gardner *et al.*, 1996, 207).

Linguistic intelligence
This intelligence involves skills in, and sensitivity to, the semantics of language, sensitivity to phonology, a mastery of syntax and a sensitivity to the pragmatics of speech. It seems to be the most widely and democratically shared gift across the human species. All normal children develop extraordinary language skills during the first four or five years of life. The most skilled linguists in the world have not been able to write rules that account for the forms of utterances of childhood. Some scholars think that children are born with considerable 'innate knowledge' about the rules and forms of language. The poet is the exemplar *par excellence* of linguistic ability: s/he is superbly sensitive to the shades of meaning of words (Gardner *et al.*, 1996, 205).

Spatial intelligence
Central to this intelligence is the capacity to perceive the visual world accurately, to modify one's initial perceptions and to be able to recreate aspects of visual experiences, even without relevant physical stimuli. The most basic operation, upon which other aspects of spatial intelligence rest, is the ability to perceive a form or an object. This can be tested by multiple-choice questions or by asking an individual to copy a form. Spatial intelligence is an invaluable asset in our society, used to great effect by artists, sculptors, architects and scientists. Einstein was an example of someone with extremely well-developed spatial intelligence and it would appear that his most fundamental insights were derived from spatial models rather than from pure mathematical reasoning (Gardner *et al.*, 1996, 207).

Musical intelligence

This intelligence involves sensitivity to and expertise in pitch, rhythm and timbre. This gift is shared by a great number of people across many cultures. The composer illustrates the gift in a highly developed state. Areas of the right hemisphere of the brain are involved in the perception and production of music. If these areas are damaged, musical ability is impaired. Some autistic children, who cannot speak, can be very gifted in music and can be accomplished instrumentalists, thereby underscoring the independence of musical intelligence (Gardner *et al.*, 1996, 207).

Bodily-kinesthetic intelligence

A central characteristic of this intelligence is the ability to use one's body in highly differentiated and skilled ways for expressive and instrumental purposes. Skill in the manipulation of objects goes hand in hand with skill in the use of the body for functional or expressive purposes. Control of bodily movement is localised in the motor cortex of the brain, with each hemisphere dominant or controlling bodily movements on the contra-lateral side. The highly skilled performer has evolved a series of procedures for translating intention into action over the years. The hallmark of expertise is the knowledge of what is coming next, which allows for the overall smoothness of performance. There are many forms of bodily expression, including dance, acting, athletics, gymnastics, and various sports. Another aspect of this intelligence is the development of the capacity to manufacture and to transform objects directly with one's body and through the use of tools (Gardner *et al.*, 1996, 209).

Intrapersonal intelligence

Central to this intelligence is the ability to examine and be aware of one's own feelings, motivation and behaviour. Gardner sees this intelligence as developing from an ability to distinguish pleasure from pain and to act on that discrimination. This intelligence is highly developed in the novelist, who can write introspectively about feelings, in the patient who comes to a deep knowledge of his/her own feelings, or in the wise elder who draws upon the wealth of inner experience to help and advise others. Gardner has emphasised the role played by this intelligence in enabling individuals to build an accurate mental model of themselves and to draw on such a model to make good decisions about their lives. Thus, this intelligence may act as a 'central intelligences agency' enabling individuals to know their own abilities and perceive how best to use them (Gardner *et al.*, 1996, 209-211).

Interpersonal intelligence
This intelligence involves an ability to read and understand the intentions and desires of others. It is highly developed in political and religious leaders, in skilled parents, teachers and individuals in the caring professions, such as therapists. Early in life, this intelligence is seen in the ability of young children to discriminate among the individuals in their environment and to discern others' moods. In its most developed forms, interpersonal intelligence manifests itself in the ability to understand, act on, and shape others' feelings and attitudes for good or otherwise (Gardner *et al.*, 1996, 211).

Naturalist intelligence
Central characteristics of this intelligence include an ability to recognise flora and fauna, to make other consequential distinctions in the natural world and to use these productively. This is the latest intelligence to be recognised and, to date, little has been written about it (Shores, 1995).

Consequences
As every intelligence is part of our genetic heritage as humans, everyone has certain core abilities in each of these intelligences. The earliest stage of an intelligence is described by Gardner as a raw patterning ability and this predominates during the first year of life. The subsequent stage involves use of a symbol system. As development progresses, each intelligence is represented in a notational system. This is the second-order symbol system, where the marks on paper represent symbols. In our culture, this system is usually tackled in a formal educational setting. The final stage

is where the intelligences are expressed through a wide range of vocational and avocational roles. This usually begins during the adolescent years and continues throughout adulthood, where intelligences achieve mature expression in a variety of pursuits (Gardner, 1993, 28).

Though we all possess each intelligence to some degree, there are some who are believed to be 'at promise'. This implies that they are highly endowed with the core abilities and skills of that intelligence. Conversely, there are those who are said to be 'at risk' in an intelligence. These people are likely to fail tasks involving that intelligence in the absence of special aids. The natural growth rate varies from person to person and the difference in growth rate is even more pronounced when we include people in the 'at promise' and/or 'at risk' categories in our discussion.

Gardner suggests that it may be possible to bring a larger number of children to an 'at promise' level if intensive intervention happens at an early stage. He believes that in pre-school and elementary school years, instruction should emphasise opportunity. In the case of very gifted children, discovery of powerful talent often seems difficult to prevent. However, for those whose talents do not emerge naturally, Gardner says that 'specifically designed encounters with materials, equipment, or other people can help a youngster discover his or her own metier' (Gardner, 1993, 29).

Lazear (1991, xvii) says that all human beings are retarded in certain problem-solving skills, while simultaneously being gifted in others. He believes that this knowledge should help us to believe that we can continue to develop our intelligent behaviour throughout our lifetime. Teachers should, therefore, ensure that they encourage students to pursue their own interests and help them to become independent and life-long learners. The eight intelligences listed above might be regarded as eight 'gateways' to knowledge: any concept can be approached through any one or more of these gateways, depending on the gifts of the individual person. To concentrate on two of them, as has been done by focusing almost exclusively on logical and linguistic intelligences, would obviously be a serious disadvantage for those students generously gifted with other intelligences, as well as depriving all students of opportunities of using other 'gateways' to knowledge. Moreover, even if students make great use of their giftedness in other intelligences, our present system of assessment does not provide opportunities to display these abilities, nor, indeed, are all of them recognised as useful, or even valid, in society at large.

Problems with traditional tests

From what we have said above, it is evident that, from the perspective of the theory of multiple intelligences, traditional intelligence tests were geared, largely, if not exclusively, to measure abilities in the areas of logical-mathematical and linguistic intelligences. Children who were weak in these areas, even though highly gifted in the other six intelligences, would inevitably score poorly. The multiple intelligences theory suggests that assessment should be context-appropriate. Therefore, assessment should use familiar tasks in a typical setting and it 'should highlight problems that can be solved in the materials of that intelligence' (Gardner, 1993, 31).

Rather than being imposed at times during the year, Gardner believes that assessment should be part of the natural learning environment. He defines assessment as 'the obtaining of information about the skills and potentials of individuals with the dual goals of providing useful feedback to the individuals and useful data to the surrounding community' (Gardner, 1993, 90). Initially, assessment would have to be introduced explicitly, but he believes that, after some time, it would occur naturally on the part of both student and teacher, with little need for explicit recognition on anyone's part. It would, of course, be incumbent on the assessor to provide helpful feedback to the student. This could involve identifying areas of strength and weakness, giving suggestions on what to study, pointing out which habits are productive, and indicating what could be expected in the way of future assessments. Gardner stresses that it is important that some of the feedback takes the form of concrete suggestions and indicates individual relative strengths, regardless of the ranking of that student in the group. Assessment, then, becomes a central feature of the education system (ibid, 93).

Gardner and his colleagues are engaged in a number of

teaching projects in the US involving the use of the theory of multiple intelligences. He believes that the main points of the approach could be taught to teachers and made available to interested schools. It is estimated, however, that a move to a more qualitative form of education, involving a multiple intelligences approach in schools, would likely increase costs significantly. The question as to whether the benefits to be gained would justify the additional cost is one that relates to values as much as to, if not more than, research.

Re-organisation of schools

A consequence of the multiple intelligences perspective is the realisation that, instead of one dimension, we all have several relatively independent intelligences, generally acting in combination. From an education viewpoint, it is important that each child's strengths and weaknesses be identified at an early stage. Striking differences between individuals raise serious questions about the wisdom of having all children involved in exactly the same curriculum and, even more important, of presenting that curriculum in the same way.

Hitherto, the accepted view of schooling might be termed a 'uniform view', in the course of which progress was assessed by regular formal testing. The aim was to administer these tests under uniform conditions and to inform the relevant partners in education of the scores achieved. In the case of the two state examinations, Junior and Leaving Certificate, tests were nationally normed to facilitate maximum comparability. Almost inevitably, those subjects that lend themselves more easily to such assessment tended to be valued most. While one can see some advantages of this procedure in complex society, empirical research in recent years shows that, among former students, there is significant dissatisfaction in this country with schooling as it stands (Hannan & Shorthall, 1991).

What type of education do we want in the future? It is evident that no individual can learn even a small percentage of existing knowledge. Therefore, choices must be made and they may as well be informed choices. As we learn more about the differences between individuals, it becomes increasingly difficult to treat all children in the same way. It is 'inappropriate on scientific grounds and distasteful on ethical grounds' (Gardner, 1993, 114).

At present, students at second level in Ireland are assessed in most subject areas by written tests, culminating, at the end of five or six years, in the Leaving Certificate examination. Some subjects have oral, aural and/or practical assessment, but the primary emphasis is still on the written paper. Elsewhere (Drudy & Lynch, 1993, 240), it has been observed that scope for the development of the personal intelligences is notably, even conspicuously, lacking in our schools. Moreover, the absence of a systematic forum for the development of interpersonal competence is particularly lamentable: apart from being directly connected with employment opportunities, especially in public relations and service occupations, it is now understood to be central to human happiness and fulfilment, as well as being urgently needed in an increasingly divided world.

Changing the system

Many people at the Department of Education are well aware of the need to adapt the present system of education, especially at second level, to meet the needs of children with a wide range of abilities. As late as 1991, the OECD examiners referred to the second-level curriculum as a 'derivation from the Classical Humanist tradition with an overlay of technological/ technical/vocational subjects and a leavening provided by development projects'. Many members of the teaching profession are also not only similarly aware but actively engaged in attempts to bring about change. A report of the Curriculum Action Awareness Group in 1990, based on the responses of Principals from voluntary secondary schools, called for 'a radical overhaul of the Senior Cycle Programme and its associated system of assessment ... [which] exposes students to a very narrow range of academic skills... resulting in a mismatch between candidate's abilities and interests and aptitudes on the one hand and the syllabus and examination on the other' (NCCA, Dec 1993).

Though awareness of the need for change in curriculum and teaching methodologies at second level is growing, it is extremely difficult to make even a small change in a well-established nation-wide system of education. Nevertheless, there are many with hope who believe that change will eventually come when sufficient people become sufficiently concerned. All change begins with awareness of the need to change.

Experiments at change
The following brief summary records some of the significant attempts that have been made to change the second-level school programme, and methods of teaching and assessment. Some of these attempts have now concluded, others are in progress and yet others are just beginning.

1   Transition projects
These projects, established in 1978, ran until 1987 and were among the most important initiatives in curriculum development in this country. They were instrumental in the development of several school programmes suitable for use at second level (Gleeson & Granville, 1996, 120). Many schools now have incorporated a transition year into their six-year second-level programme to run after the completion of the Junior Certificate and before the senior cycle. The purpose of this year has been described by the Department of Education as 'to promote the personal, social, educational and vocational development of pupils and to prepare them for their role as autonomous, participative and responsible members of society' (Department of Education, 1994, 4).

2   The Senior Certificate
This pilot project, begun in the early 1980s, was supported by European Union funds and grew out of pre-employment courses which had been running since 1977. The course was developed in two centres, in Dublin by the Vocational Education Committee (VEC) and at the Curriculum Development Unit in Shannon. Different, but complementary, aspects of the course were developed in each of these two centres. In Dublin, a Vocational Preparation and Training Programme (VPTP) was

evolved. This was initially a one-year programme (VPT-1) with emphasis on participation and evaluation of progress, in which the National Curriculum Values in Education (NCVA) co-operated, rather than formal assessment through examination. The essentials of this course were subsequently incorporated into the Leaving Certificate Applied, which will be described below.

The Senior Certificate was developed at the Shannon Curriculum Development Unit in the 1980s. This was a two-year alternative programme, intended for students who regarded the normal Leaving Certificate as too academic, leading to a special certificate, which a number of employers recognised as providing a good preparation for employment. It proved to be one of the most innovative experiments in teaching and assessment in Irish education in decades. The essentials of the approach, methodology and curriculum content were later incorporated into the Applied Leaving Certificate.

3 New Leaving Certificate alternatives
In 1993, the Minister for Education, following the work of several planning committees, issued guidelines about the restructuring of the Senior Cycle (M31/93, M47/93). Henceforth the Leaving Certificate would be available in three forms: the traditional Leaving Certificate course, the Leaving Certificate Vocational Programme and the Leaving Certificate Applied Programme, popularly, though not officially, abbreviated to LC, LCVP and LCAP, respectively.

Leaving Certificate Vocational Programme
The Leaving Certificate Vocational Programme is a full two-year alternative Leaving Certificate course. The main difference between it and the traditional Leaving Certificate syllabus is that it gives students an opportunity to do a greater number of practical subjects (up to four), and a smaller number of 'theoretical' subjects. The programme is available in many second- level schools but does not significantly differ from the traditional Leaving Certificate either in teaching methods or assessment. From the point of view of curriculum development, its innovative component has to do more with the grouping of

subjects than with educational approach or methodology. It does, however, suit students who prefer practical subjects and/or plan to pursue a career in one of the crafts or some aspect of technology or applied science.

Applied Leaving Certificate

The Applied Leaving Certificate is the successor of the Senior Certificate and, like its predecessor, qualitatively, if not quantitatively, is a very significant innovation in Irish second-level education. It was emphasised that the Applied Leaving Certificate would not be a 'sawn-off' version of the traditional Leaving Certificate. It is a two-year course with an innovative modular form of course structure and a specific emphasis on active teaching and learning experiences. A feature of the programme is the strong community dimension, embracing work experience and out-of-school learning. The programme incorporates a common curriculum for all students, with a particular weighting on vocational specialisms. It has three basic elements:

a) Vocational Preparation: including guidance, work experience, English and communication, enterprise education and preparation for work.

b) Vocational Education: including two specialist areas of vocational occupation, together with mathematical applications and information technology.

c) General Education: including modules in arts education, social education, languages and leisure and recreation.

Unlike the traditional national certificate programmes, there is a conscious integrative, cross-curricular dimension to this new programme. This is manifested in a variety of ways, notably in the Student Tasks, nine of which are carried out by students in the course of their two-year programme. Assessment is through credit accumulation in three distinct but complementary modes: completion of modules (40 credits), nine student tasks (27 credits), external examination (33 credits). The award of Applied Leaving Certificate will be on the basis of overall performance in the programme, with grades of Pass (60 credits), Merit (70 credits) and Distinction (85 credits) out of a total maximum of 100 credits (Gleeson & Granville, 1996, 120).

A notable feature of the implementation of the new Applied Leaving Certificate has been the hesitancy of some schools, especially voluntary secondary schools, to take part. The basic reason for the lack of acceptance (on the part of parents, students and public, as much as, if not more than, principals and teachers) of this course is its low academic status. It does not give direct access to third-level education via the CAO/CAS routes. Another serious threat to the wider acceptance of the programme is scepticism on the part of parents, students and public. The enthusiastic adoption of the programme by some of the long-established voluntary secondary schools would probably go a long way towards allaying the fears of some parents and students about the usefulness of this programme *vis-à-vis* the traditional Leaving Certificate. The availability of this course in a school would also enable the school to provide for a much wider range of talents and abilities, as well as offering additional opportunities for the personal fulfilment of a greater number of students.

Another way to counter scepticism about the Leaving Certificate Applied would be through planned positive discrimination in favour of those students who take the course. While it does not qualify for direct access to third-level education via the CAO/CAS routes, special arrangements could be made for students who take this course to gain entry to selected third-level courses and training opportunities. This could be done through post-Leaving Certificate courses. The Circular Letter of the Department of Education (M47/93) is unequivocal about this in principle; 'It is intended that the Applied Leaving Certificate will be fully integrated into the envisaged system for certification of educational and training qualifications ... (and that) it will provide an access to third level educational qualifications'.

There are, of course, inherent dangers and difficulties in any positive discrimination and I do not wish to minimise the difficulties of attempting to treat all young people equally, though differently. Neither do I wish to ignore the argument that if the Leaving Certificate Applied is suitable for the 'alternatively' talented children, it should be just as suitable for all children, including those who do particularly well in the present system.

In summary, we might say that the Leaving Certificate Applied has a welcome emphasis on breadth and balance of knowledge, as well as on the application of knowledge and skills to the solution of practical problems. It seeks to recognise and reward a very broad range of intelligences, abilities, competencies, achievements and practical skills. It emphasises experiential learning rather than book learning; it provides short-term goals and intrinsic motivation, has significant community involvement, has work experience at its core, and focuses on process as distinct from product. Altogether, it would seem to meet the requirements of the type of programme outlined by Gardner to develop a broad range of intelligences, and promises to give those students, not particularly gifted with the two traditionally recognised intelligences (linguistic and logical-mathematical), an opportunity to use and develop their talents which neither the traditional nor vocational preparation forms of the Leaving Certificate provides.

4   The Nagle-Rice Project
The idea of the Nagle-Rice educational project grew out of a suggestion from the Presentation Brothers in 1993 that one of the ways in which the 150th anniversary of the death of Edmund Rice, founder of the Christian and Presentation Brothers, should be marked was by means of a project aimed at students who appeared not to be benefiting from the traditional second-level curriculum and methods of teaching. The suggestion was elaborated in a memorandum submitted to and welcomed by the Irish leadership team of the Presentation Brothers. After discussion, it was decided to invite other congregations in the 'Presentation family' (Presentation Sisters and Christian Brothers) to participate in the project. They agreed, and Anne Fleischmann, a teacher in St Brigid's Secondary School, Killarney, who was already well known for her creative teaching methods and her promotion of the Senior Certificate programme, was

appointed to lead the project (Feheney, 1993). There was a small management committee, comprising representatives of the leadership teams of each of the three congregations (Presentation Sisters, Christian Brothers and Presentation Brothers), with myself as administrator. The Minister for Education approved the secondment of Anne Fleischmann as director of the project, while the three congregations pledged to meet all other expenses, including the salary of a substitute teacher.

Aims of the project
The aims of the Nagle-Rice project were listed as follows:

a) To make an effective educational response to students whose gifts, inclinations and interests are insufficiently acknowledged and developed in the content and pedagogy of the present post-primary curriculum and in the pattern of assumptions, expectations and evaluations which endorses and is endorsed by that curriculum.
b) To broaden the understanding of intelligence of students, parents and teachers by using the multiple intelligences framework, and by developing a multidimensional approach to teaching and learning which would enable students to work from their areas of strength and improve their less developed intelligences.
c) To develop new learning partnerships between students, parents, teachers and the school community.
d) To insert the work of the project into the mainstream of post-primary schooling so that it will continue after the project terminates. (Fleischmann, 1995)

Stages in the project
Starting in 1993, the project has gone through several distinct stages. The first one involved working with individual teachers, later with groups of teachers, from about a dozen selected schools, in the course of which problems with academically-weak students and classes were explored and examples of effective intervention shared. The Action Research approach, as outlined by McNiff (1992), was used (Fleischmann, 1994).

The next stage involved working with clusters of students who, themselves, became action researchers, exploring the ways in which they learned best. Later, links with parents were initiated, in the course of which they were introduced to the theory of multiple intelligences and invited to give examples of ways in which their children displayed, at home, signs of intelligence that were not able to find expression in school. This was followed by workshops on multiple intelligences for groups of students (Fleischmann, 1995).

At the same time, workshops on multiple intelligences for teachers in the schools participating in the project were begun, both at primary and second level. Efforts were also made to build links between the sixth-class teachers in the primary schools and teachers in the second-level schools, again using multiple intelligences as a framework. More recently, links were established between staff involved in this project and the Department of Education at University College Cork, with the focus on ways of developing new forms of assessment to suit a multiple intelligences approach (Fleischmann, 1996).

Reflections

To date, the Nagle-Rice project has been in operation for four years and is expected to run for a further year. Some tentative conclusions might be expressed as follows:

a) The present approach to teaching, assessment and examinations, in the second-level system especially, is so well established that any significant change would be equivalent to a paradigmatic shift – a change of vast proportions.

b) Limited success has been achieved in helping and supporting individual teachers in selected schools but, even here, the boundaries have proved to be very non-porous. Because of the way second-level schools are organised, each teacher tends to operate in his/her own classroom independently of his/her colleague, with very little actual sharing of methodology or practice. The assumption that all, or even a majority, of teachers can soon be converted to the approach and methods of a small minority, even when these latter are obviously strikingly successful, has not proved true in practice. Moreover, many of our teachers are themselves products of a didactic style of teaching and they will need considerable help to widen their teaching skills and be at ease in the role of facilitators of learning rather than skilled imparters of information. This does not mean, however, that basic knowledge of the theory of multiple intelligences has not been spread to a wider teacher audience, but there is, for many, a great chasm between knowing about something and practising it in the classroom.

c) Principals and staff need great encouragement and support if they are to work up sufficient confidence to back educational experiments like this. This is illustrated in a story, which, though sounding apocryphal, is true enough. It concerned a senior member of staff of one school, who counselled caution in respect of projects of this nature. His case was as follows: if word got out to the public that their school was particularly successful in making provision for academically weak students, one consequence might be that prospective parents of 'bright' students would be scared away, thinking that the school was specialising in academically weak students. This could lead to some parents of 'bright' students bypassing that school when choosing a second-level school for their child!

d) The Nagle-Rice, like other similar projects, was a means of bringing trustees and other members of the school community into contact with one another and involving them in work aimed at the direct welfare of a minority group not appearing to benefit from the educational opportunities on offer. As such, it was a reminder to all concerned that our educational system does permit pilot projects and that these can have an effect on the system as a whole. The project also has some symbolic effect, even if this is limited to the people directly or indirectly involved. And symbolic gestures can have a powerful inspirational effect too, as the story of the 'Widow's Mite' shows, and as Mary Robinson has reminded us, through her hospitality towards and visits to under-privileged groups during her presidency.

The matter of Christian ethos

The fact that a significant number of young people who fail to benefit adequately from second-level education are in voluntary secondary schools should be of particular concern to the Trustees of these schools. The reason for this is that the congregations who own these schools have a 'preferential option for the poor', and children not gifted with what might be termed the two popular forms of intelligence, and who are consequently educationally disadvantaged, would be expected to benefit from this special concern. The ethos of these congregations is *a priori*, in theory if not in practice, preferentially on the side of these 'alternatively talented' children, who are at a severe disadvantage in the traditional second-level system. We have seen that these children, consequently, under perform, are considered failures and have low self-esteem. This is not consonant with treating each child as a unique human being. Moreover, the subjection of all children to a single system which, of itself, begets failures, is surely inimical to the community of learning that Catholic schools purport to create. The Catholic school would, therefore, appear to have a duty to work towards a change from the present uniform approach in teaching and assessment towards one that offers the option of an approach informed by the spirit, if not the theory of multiple intelligences. We are, of course, speaking here of an option, an alternative choice available to students and parents, not something imposed on them.

Multiple intelligences is, so far, only a theory, and not the only theory about human intelligence. It has its critics, though these are far outnumbered by its supporters, among whom teachers and professional educationalists are increasingly found (Gardner *et al*, 1996, 213). Multiple intelligences is also, however, an optimistic theory, one that affirms and holds out promise to all children, but particularly to those who consider themselves failures because of poor performance in traditional intelligence tests and examinations. It would seem in keeping with the ideology and ethos of Catholic schools to work towards a wider acceptance and recognition of as many of the human intelligences as possible. This, however, will not happen of itself: awareness will have to be raised among members of the entire school community, staff training initiated and appropriate policies put in place. The time will then, hopefully, come when the matter will even receive explicit mention in school mission statements. Perhaps this is an appropriate task for the next millennium? Who among us does not look forward to a time when all our children will be happy in school and treated equally, if differently? Then, there will be no children of a lesser God.

9

Feminism in the Catholic School

Bernadette Flanagan PBVM

Feminism is a word that usually produces a visceral reaction. It is also a word surrounded by great confusion. Sometimes I have heard comments like, 'I believe men and women should work in partnership but I'm not a feminist'. What exactly does the word 'feminist' mean to somebody who makes that type of remark? I have also noticed that even amongst those who are happy to describe themselves as feminists, there is an absence of agreement on what they mean by this term. So is there any place for feminism in the Catholic school, if the term itself is so nebulous as to convey no concrete and consistent meaning?

Choosing to surrender to intellectual defeatism can hardly be an acceptable approach to educationalists. For, whatever else feminism may be, it is a powerful world-wide phenomenon which is deeply affecting all social reality and, as such, is of concern to those who form young people to live in a global community. As far back as 1963, Pope John XXIII in his encyclical *Pacem in terris* identified the changing place of women in society as one of the 'distinctive characteristics' of our age, a 'sign of the times' (Par. 41), to which the Christian community must attend if it is to effectively live and preach the Gospel. Therefore, it would seem necessary to try to understand the nature and the goals of feminism, since any educational responses to this movement will need to be rooted in a clear definition of its precise nature in a Christian context.

What is feminism?
Feminists are unhappy with sexism. Historically, sexism has maintained that persons of the male sex are inherently superior to persons of the female sex. In a pattern analogous to racism, this prejudice denies women access to certain roles and opportunities

on the basis of physical and/or psychological characteristics alone. Sexism expresses itself in a patriarchal social structure which operates by assigning the significant leadership positions in society preferentially to men. Religious patriarchy is one of the strongest forms of this structure, for it understands itself to be divinely established. Sexism also expresses itself in androcentric thinking. This is reflected in one set of skills and one way of relating, those more commonly found amongst men being better valued in society.

Feminists respond to the reality of sexism in different ways. Liberal feminists are predominantly concerned with the political and legal situation of women in society and their major goal is the achieving of equal rights for women within the prevailing socio-political order. Cultural feminists, on the other hand, focus on the special contribution women could make to a better world. They contend that women are peace-makers, more nurturing, less competitive and so could, in appropriate spheres, if given the opportunity, uniquely transform contemporary culture. Both of these types of feminism emphasise the different contribution women could make side by side with present structures. A third type of feminism tries to avoid speaking of sexual oppression in isolation from economic and racial factors. These socialist feminists view patriarchy as an alliance among oppressors across racial and class lines and believe it will ultimately be undone by the abolition of the economic system which grounds the classic social order. By contrast, however, radical feminists view patriarchy as the basic dominant system in which other hierarchical relationships, such as colonialism and racism, are rooted. The creating of a new society will be anticipated in this view by an era of positive discrimination in favour of women. Their belief is that deliberate steps have to be taken to dismantle patriarchy in its own right.

While initially, then, it can seem that feminism is concerned about equality, what is really at issue is different perceptions of the realities of likeness and difference. 'Likeness' feminism, which is evident in the liberal and radical forms, wants a situation where men and women will enjoy circumstances in life that are alike in opportunity, though not necessarily identical. So, they ask for equal entitlement to consideration for jobs. To the suggestion of the existence of sex differences which might rule them out, they would respond that these differences were small in number and trivial in type. 'Difference' feminism, which is evident in the cultural and socialist forms, emphasises differences between women both within and across groups. It is focused on the fact that while all women are women, no woman is only a woman. This type is particularly sensitive to the enormous gaps between economically advantaged and disadvantaged women. Because this view searches more widely for the roots of disadvantage, it may, in the long term, provide a more comprehensive analysis of the place of gender *vis-à-vis* access to the conditions in which a person's life may flourish.

Feminism and gender development

As feminism, particularly in its post-modern form, strives to be more attentive to the reality of difference, the real nature of the question of distinctions between men and women gets thrown into relief. At the heart of such a debate is the question of gender formation. It is interesting to note, however, that, despite the ubiquity of debates about gender issues in the Christian Churches, gender as an issue in itself has received very little attention. This is despite the fact that we cannot deny the impact of gender on the structuring of our subjectivity, relationships, life chances and practices. But, while being gendered pervades life experience, contemporary critical studies of gender seem also to indicate that the gendering process is incomplete, contradictory and contingent (Butler, 1990; Fuss, 1990; Flax, 1990; Morgan, 1992).

An enquiry into the nature of gender roles, the development of gender identity and the scope of gender relations, therefore, goes far beyond the differences between men and women. Gender is a complex, dynamic and self-reflexive phenomenon. As such, it challenges educational agencies to interact with it in a way that goes beyond operating out of categorical assumptions about empirical differences. Instead, education must engage with the complexity of interdisciplinary theories of gender at a profound level. These theories portray a human nature that is not essential but existential (Graham, 1995, 187-90). However, while gender is a complex and constructed phenomenon, it cannot be regarded as simply an incidental aspect of the human being. The decisive impact of gender as a form of social relations is suggestive of a model of human nature that is profoundly relational. In a Christian context this model draws its deepest inspiration from the life of the Trinity. While talking about God as 'one' in theology has always been intended to avoid suggestions of divisions in the deity, to say that God is three has affirmed community as a distinctive aspect of God, an aspect that human beings are invited to mirror (Johnson, 1993, 204). Authentic human being is thus only fully realised within communities that respect the dynamic, evolutionary nature of personhood, including its gendered dimensions.

The primary challenge, therefore, that feminism poses to educational agencies is the necessity for them to create communities of learning where the reality of being men and women together in the world can be explored. This stands in contrast to systems which organised themselves by assuming that the self was best defined in relation to others. Feminists have highlighted how studies of personality formation now point out that this latter perspective was primarily formed from male experience and had its roots in the nature of the relationship of the young boy with his mother. Needing to become himself, the boy becomes a self by separation, opposition, conquering the need for the significant other, his mother. When carried unnuanced into adulthood, this stance can soon lead to the ideal of the solitary self, which defines its power in adversarial relationships with others (Keller, 1986). If the experience of the young girl with her mother were integrated into personal development theory, quite a different vision of a full humanity would emerge. A girl becomes a true self, not by total separation, but by a dialectic of identification and differentiation. Rather than 'me' meaning 'not the other', the self understands its identity as intertwined with the other. Within the paradigm, neither heteronomy, exclusive other-directedness, nor autonomy, in a closed egocentric sense, would be the model informing educational practice. Thus, school communities are challenged by feminism to place their energies behind a moral revolution which displaces the ideal of an ego-driven, autonomous self with one that values mutual relationship.

Feminism and God-language

This educational challenge will, in a Christian context, be intrinsically linked to the type of language used to describe God. Gordon Kaufman has pointed out that speech referring to God 'sums up, unifies, and represents in a personification what are taken as the highest and most indispensable human ideals and values in a community' (Kaufman, 1981, 32). An audit of God-language would, therefore, seem imperative for every Christian school community which wishes to nourish in its members an experience of God that is neither oppressive nor idolatrous. Feminism's critique of God-language has not only been concerned with the inadequacies of former ways of speaking about God, but has also been attempting to generate a new language.

Traditional God-language has often oppressed the imagination by drawing imagery and concepts for God, like King and Lord, almost exclusively from the world of ruling men. In this way, men who ruled acquired a God-like status, while women, children and other men were marginalised. Relationships of dominance and subordination were thus canonised and a static definition of the nature of maleness and femaleness was made normative. Drawing solely on male metaphors to refer to God was also idolatrous in that it contributed to obscuring the divine image made visible in male and female (Gen 1:27).

This traditional patriarchal notion of God grew out of a dualist rather than a mutual notion of personhood. Many of the attributes of God, such as omniscience and omnipotence, laid an implicit stress on solitariness. It emphasised in a one-sided fashion the absolute transcendence of God over the world, God's untouchability by human suffering and the all-pervasiveness of God's dominating power. Today, speech about God is being reshaped to include intrinsic relatedness to the world, alliance with human flourishing and liberating care for the oppressed. Speech about God today is recognised to lie at 'the intersection of mighty concerns' (Johnson, 1993, 19).

Amongst these great concerns is the way God-language impacts on women's experience of themselves as persons and on their perception of their place in the social order. The International Commission for English in the Liturgy, which was set up to implement Vatican Two's move to the vernacular in liturgical worship, has urged that this issue 'must not be thought of as a theoretical problem, or a minor one; it is an immediate, real and pressing problem for many Christians and, therefore, for the whole Church' (ICEL, 1978). The Commission also pointed out that 'the range of symbols used determines the scope of religious understanding', and that, through them, 'one comes to perceive one's self and others' (ibid.).

The search for emancipatory speech about God will, in the Christian community, be guided by the Bible. Three biblical images for God could be particularly powerful in addressing the reality of sexism; namely spirit, wisdom and mother. In the Hebrew Scriptures (Old Testament) the word for spirit, *ruah,* is of grammatically feminine gender. Images that accrued around the spirit often gave expression to this linguistic fact. In particular, the symbol of the bird was a symbol of female deity in ancient Near-Eastern religions. Therefore, when hovering like a nesting bird over the egg of primordial chaos in the beginning (Gen 1:2), or sheltering those in difficulty under protective wings (Ps 17:8), there are inevitable echoes of femaleness. Informed by this tradition, the early centuries of Christianity made explicit use of female imagery to characterise God's spirit. Reclaiming invocations of the Spirit in prayer, like the following prayer from the tradition of Syrian Christianity, may, therefore, be one effective means of countering sexism:

> The world considers you a merciful mother.
> Bring with you calm and peace,
> And spread your wings over our sinful times.
> (Pataq-Siman, 1971, 155)

For sixth-class students, moving into secondary school, the activity of the Spirit has been brought to the foreground of consciousness for them through the experience of Confirmation.

Efforts to develop a less sexist God-language could well build on this foundation.

Another, even more explicit way of speaking about the mystery of God with a female symbol is by employing the biblical figure of Wisdom. In an educational setting this tradition has a certain natural appeal. In the Bible, the Book of Wisdom describes most elaborately the work of Wisdom. She is the fashioner of all that exists (7:12) and has delivered Israel from oppression (Chapter 10). Given the fact that Judaism is a monotheistic religion, Wisdom was not a second divine being but rather was Israel's God in female imagery. Biblical scholars generally agree that personified Wisdom was the answer of Orthodox Judaism to the threat of loss of membership to the cult of the goddess Isis (Kloppenborg, 1982). As such, it was an effort to present the God of Judaism in what was then a popular image. Consequently, it challenges contemporary communicators of the religious tradition to present it in a way that speaks to present-day sensibilities. Amongst the Gospel writers, John is distinguished from the others by the extent to which he identifies Jesus with the figure of Wisdom. In this way John is highlighting divine relatedness to the world. Wisdom in Jesus is not distant, dominating transcendence, but draws near, bringing new life. Any attempt to retain tasks of ordering and directing the social or religious realms in relation to men, would be in opposition to the personification of God's wise, directive presence in female imagery.

A third type of female image for God in the Bible draws on women's experience of bearing, birthing and nursing new life. In an illuminating study, Phyllis Trible has shown how the Hebrew term for God's merciful love is derived from the word 'womb' (Trible, 1978, 33). Thus, when God is spoken of as merciful, the word used conveys a sense of a womb trembling, yearning for its former inhabitant, grieving at the pain of intimate loss. This psychic mode of being compassionate is attributed to men, as well as to women and God, in the Bible, as is the case for Joseph of the multi-coloured coat, who 'yearns' for his brother Benjamin (Gen 43:30). By employing the metaphor of mother to describe the nature of God's love, men and women are challenged to live life with tenderness and kindness.

Conclusion

Feminists are deeply aware of the historical and cultural restriction of women and their experiences to a narrowly defined place within the world order. Those who have investigated the historical origins of this patriarchal arrangement have drawn attention to the fact that the development of strong kingships led to the decline of female religious imagery (Lerner, 1986, 145). Thus, religious belief and practice assumed some importance in providing a public, systematic set of symbols which expressed the appropriate place and way of being for man and woman in the world. Man belonged to the public space, woman to the private. Attitudes of dominance, separateness and distance became canonised. A social valuing of capacities for relatedness, intuitive wisdom and partnership was not upheld in the symbolic order.

We are at a turning point in history. For the past three thousand years Western civilisation and its precursors, as well as most other cultures, have been based on philosophical, social and political systems in which men – by force, direct pressure or through ritual, tradition, law and language, etiquette, education and the division of labour – determined what part women should or should not play, and in which the female was everywhere subsumed under the male. Educational agencies have the choice of being midwife to the birth of a new consciousness, inspired by feminism, or of being curriculum technicians, straining to include a greater range of products on already overcrowded shelves. If communities of learning are concerned with nourishing a particular sensibility, as well as teaching subjects, then the symbolic order within which the school operates must be addressed. Feminism is not simply concerned with access to scientific subjects for girls, home economics for boys and gender-stereotyping in textbooks. It recognises instead that the possibility of such developments is helped or hindered by the images of the ideal world-order which have become established in Christianity. Real change then will require that a school community reviews how its religious symbols speak of the role of women and that it develops, in images, rituals and religious education, models which reflect the image of God in both man and woman together.

PART V

ADMINISTRATION

10

THE CHANGING ROLES OF TRUSTEES AND BOARDS OF MANAGEMENT

Teresa McCormack PBVM

The purpose of this paper is to explore the evolving nature of the role of school trustees and to discuss how that role relates to the role of Boards of Management. It is hoped that the paper will have some relevance for the trusteeship of all types of school. However, it focuses specifically on the situation of approximately 360 Catholic voluntary secondary schools in Ireland, where the trusteeship is held by religious congregations and which are attended by about half of the country's post-primary students.

Interest in issues about trusteeship is of relatively recent origin. Indeed, the term 'trustee' itself seems to have only begun to achieve currency in the 1970s, although most of the involvement of religious in schools was, in fact, grounded in the concept of trusteeship from the outset.

History and context

Involvement by religious congregations in the provision of education in Ireland dates back to the eighteenth century. For most congregations, their entry to education was a response to extreme poverty among Catholic families at the time and to their exclusion from almost all social institutions. The founders of the indigenous congregations, in particular, realised that the absence of educational opportunities predestined the children in these families to continued marginalisation. Religious set up schools for poor Catholics with the clear aim of empowerment so that the marginalised of one generation could, in the next generation, participate fully and meaningfully in developing Irish society. These schools had a particular founding intention or mission, which specified that the school would provide Catholic education for the children of an area where parents wished to avail of it. Within the framework of Catholic education, the school's mission set out some basic principles and core values, derived from the congregation's philosophy or charism. As the Vatican Congregation for Catholic Education put it, in 1988, 'each congregation brings the richness of its own tradition to the school, found in its original charism' (35).

Thus, the mission of a Catholic school might specify:
- the priority goals and objectives of the school (often expressed in terms of the development of the whole person);
- how, in a very general way, the goals and objectives are to be pursued (e.g. a balanced curriculum or a special emphasis on a particular subject, such as music);
- whom the school is meant to serve (e.g. poor children or people with special learning needs).

The early schools established and run by religious were so successful that they quickly became part of a new establishment. After independence in 1922, the role of religious congregations as providers of education, especially at second level, became more and more central. In his study of Irish educational expenditure, Tussing (1978) showed that the contribution of religious congregations was one of the main reasons why the Ireland of the 1970s 'by a long chalk the poorest country in the EEC, [could] afford such a highly developed [education] system' (54).

In the 1970s, the influence of the Second Vatican Council brought about very significant changes in the self-understanding of those involved in Catholic schools and gave rise to a new vision of Catholic education. Religious enthusiastically embraced the new vision of Catholic education, recognising in it many of the radical features that prompted their founders to establish schools. In particular, they tried to embrace the challenge of the Council to promote Catholic schools that were open to the modern culture,

> ... affirming what is positive about modernity in terms of democratic principles, human rights and the struggle for social justice, while at the same time negating the destructive dimensions of modernity such as excessive individualism, a market-led capitalism and the

exploitation of nature. Above all the Catholic school must be able to talk meaningfully and imaginatively about the mystery of God in the face of modernity and the emerging strands of post-modernity. (Lane, 1997, 131)

Trustees also responded to the challenge of the Council to give meaningful roles to parents and lay teachers by delegating the conduct of the school to a representative Board of Management, based on Articles of Management. These articles, agreed between trustees and the other school partners, specify that the school must function in accordance with the religious and educational philosophy of the congregation concerned. Lay people also began to be appointed as principals of voluntary Catholic schools.

Voluntary schools in their early days were run almost totally at the discretion of their owners/trustees. The state had little or no control over what happened in these schools. The discretion enjoyed by trustees has been progressively constrained because schools are dependent on funds from the state and because the state began to exercise considerable control over curriculum and assessment. It is important to note, however, that state support for denominational education is protected by the Irish Constitution.

Despite the ongoing changes, religious continue to believe that, by exercising the role of school trustee, they can exercise a positive and distinctive influence on the educational experiences of young Irish people and on society as a whole. The next section of this paper will attempt to define trusteeship. This will be followed by a discussion of how trusteeship affords opportunities to influence what happens in schools. A final section of the paper will examine some of the challenges that arise in attempting to provide for trusteeship in the future. The legal and other aspects of trusteeship are outlined more fully in CORI (1996).

Defining trusteeship
As noted already, when religious congregations established schools, they did so with a particular intention or mission (the provision of Catholic education, in line with the congregation's

religious and educational philosophy). Their responsibilities, therefore, are distinctive and have a legal as well as a moral basis. The legal basis derives from the fact that the congregation is the owner of the school in two senses. First, the title of the 'real' property (land and buildings) is usually registered in the name of members of the congregation. Secondly, the congregation owns the enterprise of the school itself, i.e. that enterprise (or mission) for which the school was established. As legal owner, therefore, the congregation holds the school in 'trust' for the purposes (mission) to which the congregation is committed – hence the use of the term 'trustee'. Trustees have a fiduciary relationship towards other persons (beneficiaries) and are obliged to honour the trust. On this basis, trustees have two distinctive and important types of responsibility in relation to the schools with which they are associated:

a) those that relate to ensuring that the school, in its ethos and otherwise, is consistent with the founding intention (i.e. the trust), and

b) those that relate to the legal and financial responsibilities associated with ownership of the land and buildings in which the school is situated.

It is the responsibility of the religious congregation to interpret the founding intention (trust) in the light of prevailing circumstances and to try to ensure that the school remains true to its mission. To an increasing extent trustees work in partnership, through their Boards of Management, with parents, staff and the wider community. This approach has the advantage of bringing into dialogue the visionary dimension of the congregation's philosophy and the day-to-day practicalities of running a school.

It follows from what has been outlined so far, that a definition of the trusteeship of Catholic voluntary schools would need to have four elements.

a) It should indicate that the trust relates to a responsibility for Catholic education.

b) It should state that, within the overall responsibility for

Catholic education, each congregation has a religious and educational philosophy which it must ensure is reflected in the ethos of the school.

c) It should make clear the legal basis for the trustee role.

d) It should establish that decisions about the future of the school rest ultimately with the trustee, albeit following extensive consultation.

The relationship between trustees and school management

When the Conference of Religious of Ireland (CORI, formerly CMRS), on behalf of religious congregations, began, in the 1970s, to promote Boards of Management for voluntary secondary schools, it sought to put in place a framework which would enable decision-making to be shared with teachers and parents, while taking account of the distinctive responsibilities of trustees. For example, the Articles of Management recognise that decisions about certain matters deriving from the ownership of the school, can ultimately be made only by trustees. These include decisions about the future of the school (closure, amalgamation, etc.) and decisions relating to capital expenditure.

However, the articles also recognise that the school is most likely to be effective when its day-to-day management is carried out in partnership between trustees, parents, teachers and the wider community, and when its future is planned through dialogue among all the partners. It is, therefore, not always helpful to think in terms of a delineation of reserved and delegated functions. In fact, trustees need to retain an interest and an involvement in all aspects of school life because every aspect of school life has the potential to impact on the school in a way which might shift it away from its founding intention. For example, a decision about something as seemingly innocuous as school uniforms could have the effect of making it difficult for some students to attend. There are, of course, some matters in which trustees will take a particular interest because they are critical to the overall direction of the school. Enrolment policy and provision for religious education are two clear examples. Trustees have an obligation to ensure that decisions in these and other areas do not result in a serious departure from the school's basic principles and core values. In general, trustees need to establish ways of working with their school partners to ensure that the principles and values of the congregation's religious and educational philosophy are reflected in the school's ethos and in its policy and practice. Some of these ways of working are discussed in the next section.

Changing roles and strategies of influence

Until relatively recently, religious congregations regarded the exercising of their trusts in relation to influencing school ethos as a fairly straightforward matter. The managers, principals and a large proportion of staff were members of the congregation. This meant that everybody in key positions in the school subscribed to a shared value system (the congregation's religious and educational philosophy) on which the founding intention of the school was based. If questions arose about whether the prevailing ethos was in line with that philosophy, these questions could usually be resolved informally within the congregation.

As discussed already, from the mid 1970s, new ways of exercising trusteeship began to emerge in response to the call of Vatican II for greater lay involvement and to the fall in vocations to religious life, which made it difficult for congregations to supply personnel to occupy positions as principals and managers. These new ways of exercising trusteeship were based on the Articles of Management, in conjunction with strategic documents setting out the congregation's religious and educational philosophy.

A proactive role in schools

In general, religious congregations are happy with the existing model of management and recognise that it affords them some important opportunities to influence school ethos while working with the other partners and through the Board of Management. Thus, religious congregations are in a position, through the trusteeship of their schools, to advance the Catholic vision of education and, at the same time, make a valuable and distinctive contribution to the type of experience which children will have in these schools. However, there is a growing realisation that, in attempting to influence what goes on in schools, religious congregations have to compete, very often, with a number of factors at national and local level which may have the effect of influencing the school in a direction different from that favoured by the congregation. Arising out of this realisation, many congregations are attempting to develop a more proactive role in relation to the schools with which they are involved.

Effectively, trustees need to be in a position to:
a) articulate clearly the principles and values of a distinctive educational philosophy consistent with the congregation's charism and with the founding intention of the school,
b) engage proactively with the school to promote that philosophy and monitor the extent to which it is being implemented, and
c) intervene in situations where there is a serious departure from that philosophy.

A variety of methods is used by trustees to monitor and influence what is happening in their schools (e.g. through trustee nominees to the board, by school visits, through their involvement in staffing decisions, school development planning and annual reporting, and the provision of education and training). In the vast majority of cases, when problems arise, they are dealt with through dialogue and negotiation. The ultimate sanction of dismissing a board exists to deal with a very small minority of cases where discussion and negotiation fail to resolve the issue. In exercising their trusteeship in a proactive way, trustees are taking steps actively to promote the desired ethos rather than simply checking for its existence periodically (see CORI, 1996 for a fuller discussion of the proactive role of trustees).

Influencing national policy
As noted earlier the influence exercised by trustees is only one of a number of factors that act as a determinant of a school's ethos. It is, therefore, not sufficient for trustees to operate only at the level of the individual school. They also need to seek out ways of engaging with the other determinants of ethos. One of the most

significant of these determinants is the educational policy framework in which individual schools operate. It is on this basis that, for a number of years, religious congregations have been devoting a good deal of energy and resources **to seeking collectively to influence decisions that are taken at national level.** One of the ways in which this is being done is through the efforts of CORI to become more influential in terms of national policy. It is on the basis of this kind of rationale that CORI, through its Education Commission and Office, has devoted a major part of its time and effort to research and analysis in order to develop its own policy positions. It then tries to disseminate these policies in discussion documents and through participation in conferences, submissions, advocacy, and by forming alliances and working with media. Since 1992 a significant part of this work has related to the debate on education that followed publication of the Green Paper. It has also involved trying to reach agreement with others on what **values should be institutionalised in any new structures** that become necessary either because of the decline in the direct involvement of religious or for any other reason.

Through their involvement in the process of public debate about policy, religious have tried to highlight deficiencies in Government policy from the perspective of a Gospel-based vision of education. There is evidence that the contributions of religious to public debate have had some positive outcomes. The targeting of resources to those who are disadvantaged and recent proposals to make the system more participative, although they fall short of what religious would consider ideal, are examples of where the collective voice of religious appears to have been heard. The increased recognition of the importance of the trustee which, as will be shown in the next section, has occurred in recent years can also be attributed to the arguments of CORI and others in the public debate.

The challenges ahead

Those involved in the trusteeship of schools will face many challenges in the early years of the twenty-first century. It seems certain that the role of trustees will become increasingly important, while, at the same time, the resources available to those who traditionally acted as trustees (particularly religious congregations) will continue to decline.

There is now a very strong consensus in Irish education that the most appropriate way of accommodating the growing pluralism in society is through the availability of a diversity of school types. There is a commitment on the part of Government, arising from a corresponding concern in contemporary society, to try to ensure that, as far as possible, parents will be able to choose schools that reflect their religious, ethical or cultural values. Trustees are crucial in ensuring that there is clarity about the philosophy and ethos which each school is trying to promote and between which parents can exercise their choice.

The role of trustees was the subject of much interest during the education debate over the last five years. The 1992 Green Paper, which initiated that debate, is now recognised as having undervalued the importance of trusteeship. However, this weakness in the Green Paper was rectified by the White Paper in 1995 which acknowledged the particular functions of trustees in relation to 'the continuity of the ethos of the school... including a distinctive religious ethos' (146). The White Paper did, however, recognise, that ethos is an 'organic element' which arises from the actual practices of a school and, as such, is a concern of all of the school partners.

When the first draft of the Education Bill, 1997, was published there was a lot of concern that the Government seemed to be reverting to the thinking of the Green Paper on trusteeship (see CORI, 1997 for an outline of these concerns). However, following extensive lobbying by CORI, the Minister for Education issued amendments on 22 April 1997, which more accurately reflect the policy positions of the White Paper.

As awareness of the importance of trusteeship continues to grow, so also does the realisation that existing arrangements for the trusteeship of Catholic voluntary schools need to be changed. One of the factors giving rise to the need for change is the fact that we are fast approaching the time when it will not be possible for religious congregations to exercise trusteeship themselves. In particular, the combined effects of the age profile of religious, the declining number of vocations and the movement by religious into new ministries will make it increasingly difficult, over the next twenty to thirty years, for congregations to discharge their functions as trustees. Therefore, congregations need to identify existing structures or establish new ones that will be capable of carrying on the work previously done by the congregations themselves.

Even if congregations were not experiencing a decline in membership, there would be a number of arguments for considering new structures for the trusteeship of schools. There is no solid basis for believing that the continuation of Catholic education depends on the direct involvement of religious. The provision of Catholic schools is, in fact, a responsibility of the whole Catholic community. According to this kind of thinking, religious, having made a valuable contribution to establishing a network of Catholic schools, can move on to identifying and meeting urgent educational needs that cannot be met by others. Therefore, many religious believe that, even if the decline in membership of congregations was not taking place, it would be appropriate to begin to devise forms of trusteeship based on partnerships between congregations and others.

Another factor that gives rise to the need for change in relation to trusteeship is an increased emphasis on the role of Boards of Management. There is now a widespread commitment to ensuring that all schools have Boards of Management that are representative of parents, teachers, the wider community and trustees. There is also acceptance of the belief that the role of boards needs to be enhanced by assigning to them the responsibility for the 'effective educational management and provision in a school' (White Paper, 1995, 146) and by ensuring that they are accountable for the way they exercise their responsibilities. To an increasing extent, it is likely that boards will be accountable to the state in relation to meeting the needs of students through appropriate curriculum and assessment, as well as being accountable to their trustees in relation to protecting and promoting the ethos of the school. In other words, boards will increasingly have 'a dual mandate' – from the State as well as from their trustees.

The changes that are envisaged for Boards of Management obviously have serious implications for trustees. In particular, **all** trustees will have to begin to develop the mechanisms and processes for relating to their boards, which, to date, only some have put in place. Thus all of those involved in trusteeship will need to establish ways of relating systematically with their boards. They will need to negotiate with their school partners on how to engage proactively with their schools in areas such as school development planning. Trustees will also need to agree with the state on the provision of education, training and ongoing support of Boards of Management.

Another implication of the changing role of Boards of Management arises from the new relationship that boards will have with the state. In the context of this new relationship, it will be increasingly important for trustees to be proactive, not just at the level of the individual school, but also at the level of the whole system. Trustees will need to work individually and collectively (e.g. through CORI) to bring their particular perspective to bear on the process of developing the policy framework in which their individual schools operate and which has a major influence on the living ethos of all schools.

11

STAFF DEVELOPMENT AS EMPOWERING AND ENABLING

Eileen Doyle

Context

An appreciation of the background to the present concern with staff development in schools is important. Without it, one runs the risk of thinking that such professional development only began in Ireland with the windfall of EU funding and the establishment of the In-Career Development Unit (ICDU) of the Department of Education in 1994. In addition, a sense of the history of what teachers and managers were doing before that year may result in greater empowerment for all concerned (Treston, 1995, 5).

Primary teachers in Ireland have a long tradition of attendance at professional courses, particularly during the school holiday period.[1] Attendance by secondary and vocational teachers received an impetus in the mid-eighties when the work of the Interim Curriculum and Examinations Board began to influence curriculum change, and, to date, these numbers have continued to increase.[2] That is not to say that secondary teachers prior to 1984 did not attend courses. A flashback thirty years to 1967 and the beginning of free education shows that thirty-six summer courses were organised by the Department of Education for secondary teachers. All the courses took place in July and August and were generally of five days duration. Some eight courses were provided in Gaeilge and French, seven in Biology, one in Physics, twelve in Mathematics, one in History, one in Geography, one in Domestic Science, two in Physical Education, one in Civics and two in Music. An interesting feature was that a number of these courses were continuation ones from 1966. A complaint and an insightful suggestion came from the editor of the newly published journal of the Association of Secondary Teachers of Ireland (ASTI) when he wrote:

> Almost every month ... there are notices of refresher

courses for teachers in a variety of places ... (to which)
teachers from all parts (come) at inconvenient times ....
Has it not occurred to the powers that be that if students
can be taught by television so can teachers?
(*The Secondary Teacher,* October 1966, 5)

Until the late 1960s professional development courses were
directed to the individual teacher in the classroom. The
emphasis, therefore, was on developing teacher competence in
subjects taught, whether by primary or secondary teachers.
Methodology did not stress collaborative learning and teaching.
In a sense, a teaching staff was a number of individual teachers
working as lone professionals with children or adolescents.[3] The
catechetical movement from the early 1970s, with its innovative
approach to teacher education, contributed in no small way to
thinking about teachers as staff and their professional
development as including staff development.[4]

Changes in the state examination syllabuses or the
introduction of a new subject such as Civics tended to be
accompanied by courses for teachers[5]; while these could not be
labelled 'staff development', it is probable that they empowered
and enabled subject teachers to deal with course changes. In a
sense the model was a dependency one on provision which was
external to the school. Throughout the 1970s the Department of
Education's 'revised courses' and ensuing courses were a topic of
concern for the ASTI.[6] The timing of courses was dictated by the
fact that secondary teachers superintended and marked the
Intermediate and Leaving Certificate examinations. That
professional development courses for teachers seemed to be the
prerogative of the Department of Education was unquestioned.
But by the 1980s 'who controls the curriculum' in schools was an
issue for the Churches:

Education is too important a matter to be left to teachers
or educational administrators.
(Irish Council of Churches, 1982, 22, 4.6)

A strategic concern about *staff* development was a logical focus.

A number of subject associations had been organising courses with financial assistance from the Department. Some associations became more active than others, and bodies such as the Irish Association for Curriculum and Development (IACD) made important contributions to professional development. A remarkable aspect of teachers' professional development since the establishment of the ICDU is the Department's allocation of funding to the teacher unions and the managerial bodies to organise professional development programmes.[7] It is perhaps a recognition of the historic involvement of teachers and school managers in promoting the realities of teaching and learning.

The nuns

The Conference of Convent Secondary Schools (CCSS) represented the largest managerial body of voluntary secondary schools and, from its foundation in 1929, actively promoted professional development among its members, the religious congregations of women.[8] The historical records show small but increasing support for lay teachers to attend courses in the 1940s, 1950s and early 1960s.[9] From 1966 the numbers of nuns and brothers at summer courses increased: one lay commentator rejoiced that 'the nuns had found a voice'.[10] Moreover, it was the nuns who led the way in what is now 'staff development'.

From 1969, in the wake of the Second Vatican Council, the CCSS encouraged school principals to begin what the organisation actually called 'staff development'. In retrospect it might be said (not unkindly) that such development was done to school staffs rather than with them. Usually the format was a lecture by an invited guest, often a priest, sometimes a layperson, more often than not male, and always chosen by the principal or/and manager. The talk was followed by questions rather than discussion. Topics tended to be related to theology and scripture, Catholic education, dealing with adolescents, involving parents, coping with leisure time. Perhaps unknowingly, it paved the way for later work on the ethos and philosophy of schools. Initially, between one and two hours were given to this 'staff development': some form of timetable intervention was arranged either by shortening the school lunch-break or afternoon classes so as to enable pupils to finish early. At times, the lecture session would be arranged to continue after the official end of the school day. Staff needs analysis, pre-planning, involving teachers in the design and evaluation of the in-service, were not part of this early staff development.

The first formal professional development courses for school principals were organised in 1973 by the CCSS and took place during school holidays. Many school managers also attended. Efficiency in the administration and management of schools was the main focus. Educationists, including a number of prominent trade union officials, as well as lecturers and educationists from the United Kingdom and Northern Ireland, and, from 1977 onwards, from the Irish Management Institute (IMI), were involved.

By the end of the 1970s, the methodology in use had moved considerably beyond the lecture mode. Three factors contributed to a more process-led training for school principals. One was a publication by the Conference of Major Religious Superiors (now the Conference of Religious of Ireland, CORI).[11] Another was the human resource management emphasis by personnel in the IMI and their skilful work with teams, groups and use of video training. The third resulted from the establishment in the early 1980s of the much-maligned Health Education Bureau (HEB), which provided professional development and training over a five-year period for tutors, including a number of principals. From 1977 onwards, 'the staff day' became a feature in the majority of CCSS schools and in a growing number of other schools. However, many schools had no framework within which to situate staff development days (Duffy, 1995, 278).

From the mid-1970s, numbers of primary and second-level teachers from Ireland, including CCSS principals, were regularly attending summer schools in the UK. In addition an increasing number of nuns, brothers and priest teachers were participating in summer schools in the US and Canada, and some religious were studying abroad for longer periods. Catechetics, counselling and aspects of adult education were the most popular courses sought because they were seen as fundamental to developing Catholic education. A feature of many of those courses was the opportunity for those interested to attend continuation programmes over a number of summers and to build a portfolio of professional development. To evaluate the effect on staff development in Irish schools of contact with educational thinking in other countries is not, however, quantifiable. Neither is it possible at this stage to quantify the contribution made by Trinity College, Dublin, through its approach in the new Masters in Education programme from the mid-1970s. What is true, however, is that innovative ways of thinking about schools and programmes of staff development were being studied by principals and managers.[12] There was a visible shift from the once-off 'injection model' of professional in-service to a recognition of the complexity of change and development in schools. An uncertain future for religious in schools was also part of the context, as focused in the FIRE Report (1973).[13] Comprehensive and community schools were by then a reality in Ireland and the challenge of the larger school was increasingly a concern of those who attended courses in places like Loughborough College and Swansea University.

Undoubtedly, a significant occurrence in staff development in many secondary schools was the CCSS invitation to Dr. Douglas Hamblin to be the main speaker at a week-long conference in pastoral care in July 1978. Even then, his vision of professional development focused on promoting the capacity of teachers to analyse their work at different levels so that pupils would experience the integration of the pastoral curriculum. (Hamblin, 1989). The conference, which was attended by 511 teachers from Irish secondary schools, consisted of interactive workshops, task groups, lectures and planning sessions on developing appropriate professional skills to structure pastoral care in a school organisation. Schools were encouraged to send groups of staff rather than a lone teacher in the hope that a collaborative approach to working with pupils would be the focus. While it is true that a large number of schools began to develop more systemic ways of ensuring appropriate student care, ways that, in turn, necessitated staff development, there is, as yet, no adequate research nor, indeed, available records to give an accurate picture.[14]

In November 1978 school trustees and managers were reminded that the Catholic school should be 'a community' where pupils are taught 'within an educational framework or structure professing the truth of the Christian message and its relevance for life' and that the attainment of its aims depended 'above all on ... the teachers' (Religious as Managers Report, 1978, 2-5). One of the functions of the 'manager as employer' was 'ensuring the on-going formation of the staff through in-service training' (Report, 8, 4.3). By 1980 annual staff days or half-days were taking place in almost all CCSS schools, as well as in many other second-level schools. Moreover, some school principals enabled groups of staff to visit other schools, mainly in the Republic and Northern Ireland, as part of the staff development programme. The 'staff day' was custom and practice by the time the Department of Education agreed to repeated requests from the managerial bodies and the ASTI for a 'recognised staff day' in each school year.[15]

Towards a definition

If staff are 'those in authority within an organisation especially teachers in a school' (Oxford, 1996), and development is 'the act or an instance of developing, the process of being developed, a stage of growth or advancement, a full-grown state', then staff development is not something one may do to teachers, though it may be done with them. Development will necessarily include meeting the individual teacher's legitimate personal and professional needs (Hyland and Hanafin, 1997, 144-8). In the context of staff development these will need to be contextualised within 'the four levels of organisational behaviour' (Tuohy and Coghlan, 1994 and 1997). A staff that is working on its own development, or/and a staff with whom an outsider to the school is working, will need certain requisites for their task. On the one hand, the staff will need to be 'authorised or licensed or given power or be made able to' pursue their task or, in a word, they will need to be empowered; on the other hand, the staff will need to have 'the means or authority' to make the task of development possible: they need to be 'enabled' (Diggins, Doyle, Herron, 1996, 41-2). A consultant or facilitator does not *manage* staff development though s/he will hopefully assist teachers in managing the process (Gregorc, 1995). Some staff members, as a result of the empowering and enabling process, may decide to begin or add to their professional[16] development portfolios (Inset Service, 1997, 1-4).[17] But reflection and analysis need to be the 'platform' (Diggins, 1997; Starratt, 1996) from where 'empowering' and 'enabling' are realised:

> Empowerment is a notion with a spring in its step; unhappily to step is more often than not constrained in ways which are not immediately apparent.
> (Fielding, 1994, 31).

The continual quest for truth that comes from reflection will not lose sight of the purpose of inservice: it is about improving the educational experience of pupils; and 'the only way education is going to change is if the classroom teacher makes it happen' (Kohn, 1993, 9; Glasser, 1993). Discerning teachers have always recognised the significance of purposeful work in classrooms.[18]

Who owns?
The activity of empowering and enabling in the context of staff development cannot be divorced from the Board of Management as employer (Cavaleri and Fearon, 1996; Main, 1985, 112) or, indeed, in the Irish context, from the chief executive officer (CEO) in the vocational school system.[19] Neither can staff development be disconnected from the professional development of school principals in their increasingly complex role (Lyons, 1997, 5; Leader and Boldt, 1994, 93-101) or from the ultimate purpose of education.[20] The fact that any one teacher employee may spend more than forty years in the same school, the age gap with their pupils increasing annually, demands a response from a school board in terms of staff development. (Farrelly, 1987; Doyle, 1985, 9). [21] Yet it is vital that the teaching profession promotes 'its own reconstruction... (although) being reconstructed by others... requires less courage but probably involves more hardship and demoralisation' (Barber, 1996, 207). One aspect of whole school development planning is enabling

teams of teachers to organise for themselves 'professional explorations' in other schools. The process of these explorations (Diggins, Doyle, Herron, 1996) has proved to be significant in staff culture change: this has been particularly powerful in schools where the majority of staff did not have experience of school systems other than their own or did not have post-graduate career breaks or opportunities.[22] Providing for substitution is an essential support.

Developing skills in dealing with the interpersonal politics of schools is often neglected in staff development planning. At second level, in particular, teachers have come from a tradition and culture of isolated professionals. Some issues that staffs may need to deal with include 'the self-science curriculum' (Goleman, 1996, 303-4), organising purposeful meetings, time management, effective teamwork, evaluation, dealing with staff bullies who may have made some colleagues 'voiceless', particularly at meetings (Spaulding, 1997, 39-55). Empowering teachers to analyse the current reality through a process of reflection and professional articulation is often the starting point in staff development. That is not to claim that each member of staff will choose to participate. Many members of staff will readily verbalise their ideal of a sixth-year graduate from their school: someone with independence, confidence, a positive self-image, spiritual awareness, and ability to make decisions. But identifying educational experiences within the normal school day, when pupils are enabled to develop such qualities and abilities, often proves to be difficult. Situating aspirations and aims within what pupils actually experience is often a high step towards more conscious realisation of what adults in a school may honestly believe is happening (Sotto, 1994, 88-99; Gardner, 1991, 254).

Employers have a role in empowering teachers to develop 'career anchors' (Mayo, 1991; Schein, 1978) and thus encourage a culture within which to 'classify their potential... not label' it (Mayo, 1991). The 'multiplicity and diversity' of teachers' roles, along with 'their increasing complexity and unpredictability' (CDCC, 1996, 3-6), highlights a lacuna in the Irish system: the absence of a formal professional code.[23] Part of the process of staff development is moving towards a shared understanding of a school philosophy, vital to empowerment (Starratt, 1993). Otherwise, 'the philosophy of the "centre" may become unduly powerful in deciding educational vision and direction' (Hargreaves, 1997, 9-21).[24] The benefit of a professional code could help to clarify and enrich the concept and status of what it means to be teachers of children and young people. It might also help in avoiding the 'quest for a "suit proof"' system (Mahon, 1995, 79). A significant degree of autonomy, self-criticism, openness and willingness to learn is demanded. And the Catholic school system has been challenged to promote the reality of 'the school as open community':

> Partnership between a Catholic school and the families of the students must continue and be strengthened: not simply to be able to deal with academic problems that may arise, but rather so that the educational goals of the school can be achieved.
> (Vatican, 1988, 27-8).

Approaches to staff development are often influenced by a particular concept of teacher role. The future restructuring of 'middle management' roles in Irish second-level schools may increase the number of professional development co-ordinators on staffs but 'managing staff development is not the responsibility of one person alone' (Baccharach & Mundell, 1995). How many primary and second-level boards have a strategic policy of staff development which young teachers are made aware of when being employed?[25] For the cultures and structures of a school to develop, the board will need to go beyond simply sanctioning resources of time and money (Spark and Hirsh, 1997). If the board remains at a distance from the work of development, there is the danger of what Goleman calls 'the illusion of unanimity' (1997, 186-7) with regard to the education philosophy that should energise a school community.[26]

A variety of ways

Leonard and Dundon (1996, 15-17) have reiterated the close links between professional development, professional culture in schools and teacher action research in its several forms. Callan (1994) provided opportunities for teachers in fifteen second-level schools to reflect on their school culture through a form of appraisal. Stoll and Fink (1996) have explored issues related to changing school culture - often the key task in staff development. The role of a Board of Management merits appropriate research so as to develop models of staff-management collaboration for whole school development. In a representative sense, the board is the wider community. Many boards in the UK seem to concentrate on staff development without examining the role and function of boards or the wider school community (Earley, 1994). One study examined the relationship between school principals and chairpersons of boards (Esp, 1995).[27] Most recently, Crease and Bradley (1997, 105- 15) have signalled the importance of joint work groups between school board members and staffs in promoting development. A number of secondary schools in Ireland are beginning to use this approach. If 'faith in the individual and collective capacity of people to create possibilities for resolving problems' and the 'use of critical reflection and analysis to evaluate ideas, problems and policies' is to be alive in democratic schools, there needs to be an understanding that 'democracy is not so much an ideal to be pursued as an idealised set of values' to be lived (Apple & Beare, 1995, 10). Such development is unlikely to happen of itself: well planned and evaluated programmes can help[28] a school community to balance the see-saw of that 'paradoxical place between our daily experiences and our dreams of the future' (Aronowitz and Giroux, 1993, 205; McGuiness, 1993, 15).

For school boards or individual principals to make arbitrary decisions about programmes of staff development would be to ignore the fact that adult learning needs to be purposeful, focused and self-directed (Stoll & Fink, 1996, 154-55). Work at primary and second level supports a whole school approach (Drumcondra and West Dublin Reports, 1993-6): in-service with individual teachers or groups has been found to be less effective in changing schools. Evaluation by the Association of Secondary Teachers of Ireland (ASTI) recommends full staff development (ASTI, 1996-7).

Effective management will sometimes be inspirational[29] in promoting staff development, as is evidenced by the work of some CEOs and secondary managers since the early eighties. Management involvement needs to recognise that the four domains of teacher responsibility (planning and preparation, developing an appropriate classroom environment, teaching for learning, and professional responsibilities) have a certain cultural sensitivity, whether in Australia, the United States, Canada or Ireland (Danielson, 1996, 29). An understanding of the cultural sensitivity in a denominational or a multi-denominational or non-denominational school could be enriched by combining the perspective, insight and energy of management and staff. Without such a clear understanding, nobody in a denominational school may remember to ask, for example, 'What is the cost, to Christian values, of seeking state support for religious endeavour?' (Whyte, 1997, 283). Or nobody in a primary, secondary or vocational school may ask, 'what is the cost to the values that this school promotes of releasing teachers for courses during the school day?' Other questions may be significant: how would one recognise a school where staff development was effective? What have been the experiences of recently retired teachers? What might a parent experience in such a school? Or a pupil, a teacher, a substitute teacher, a trainee teacher? What is the school atmosphere like for the maintenance personnel, the school secretary, the school principal? Or visiting local politicians or clergy or sales representatives? What is break- time or lunch-time like in a school where staff and management (which includes parents) are creatively working on development?[30] How educational are its school rules? (Martin, 1997; McGuiness, 1993 and 1989). How do teachers choose - or decline -to describe staff development to the board? Is the ideal of 're-creating ourselves' through learning so that, as a staff, we 'reperceive the world' (Senge, 1990, 14) and the school? This reperception can be crucial in how we see ourselves as professionals, how we cope with the complexities of life in the classrooms and how we anticipate and deal with stress.

Conclusion

Over the past thirty years, in-career development has become established practice among primary and second-level teachers, principals and managers. While individual professional needs continue to merit attention, the current focus in schools is on staff development. The Department of Education with the NCCA continues to provide training programmes for subject or course change. A number of organisational, methodological and professional elements may be similar in all schools. Boards of Management could adopt similar policies of in-service. The assistance of the same range of consultants, education centres, university and college education departments might be sought. But no two schools are the same. Staff awareness and perception of their professional in-service needs will vary. Staff response to in-service will differ from school to school. Variables that contribute to that different response will include: the ability of the principal to hold and to communicate an educational vision; individuals' awareness of their own stage of personal and professional growth; internal structures for managing and evaluating learning and teaching; how teachers and principal deal with human conflict; the degree of openness to development; the willingness to acknowledge that staff development is hard work.

Appropriate planning by staff *and* school boards may result in the best of two worlds: the continual development of the school community and a daily experience in classrooms which the professionals and their pupils are proud to share. The classroom, rather than the staffroom, is the heart of the school. But, unlike the classroom with the isolated teacher, in the school where staff development is effective, there is a network of classrooms, rather than a series of separate and independent ones. Here, teachers are enabled to work with pupils in a coordinated way and their school system empowers and nourishes their professionalism.

12

CHALLENGES OF EDUCATIONAL LEADERSHIP: MEANING, COMMUNITY AND EXCELLENCE

David Tuohy SJ and David Coghlan SJ

Traditionally in Ireland the work of the school principal has been seen as embracing all aspects of schooling. Little distinction has been made between leadership and administration, and less attention has been given to the development of a Christian ethos. In general, the main focus of the principal's role has been internal, with priority given to the efficient running of the school and the maintenance of good relationships among the staff. This was understandable in an environment in which there was little external change or challenge to schools, where societal values about education were constant, and the roles of different stakeholders in the school were well-defined and accepted by everyone. However, there has been a notable shift in the status of education over the past twenty years. Increased Government involvement in policy setting, a massive increase in participation by students, parental and business representation in governance structures, as well as demands for specific social and economic products from schools are all signs of the times for education. This rapidly changing external environment has brought new demands on school management. Nowadays, the role of the principal not only embraces the administration of internal factors, but must also embrace leadership roles with regard to the external forces that impact on the school.

Increasingly, a distinction is made between administration and leadership. Administration is typically described in terms of working within a system to keep it in operating order. Leadership, by contrast, is typically described in terms of the capacity to articulate vision, to generate commitment and enthusiasm around values, to form culture and to lead change. This distinction between administration and leadership is useful as it helps focus attention on what is happening in a system and may point to what needs to happen. We all know of people in official positions who are good administrators; the operational and physical system runs efficiently and smoothly. However, there is a general unease that they are efficient about the wrong things, that their priorities are wrong or, perhaps, the future is not being considered. By contrast, we may have had experience of a principal who is very inspirational, who can generate great enthusiasm about projects and has a great sense of purpose and vision. However, the same person is a poor organiser, and the day-to-day details get neglected, resulting in chaos and frustration.

It is unfair to cast leadership and administration in any sort of good or bad relationship with each other. Both are essential. Starratt (1995) illustrates that as leaders work to create vision, administrators are required to enshrine the vision in the operational structures and policies of the school. Both need to work together in transforming vision into the working structures and programmes. Administrators need the leaders to talk them through the vision so that they can build congruent institutional forms. Principals who play both roles can reflect on how they can move from one role to another – creating vision and then institutionalising that vision in the operating structures of the school. In this chapter we examine the forces that affect leadership in schools today, and characterise the focus of leadership as meaning, community and excellence. We then look at the way leadership and administration complement one another in developing these areas at individual, team, inter-team and school levels.

Forces in school leadership

Duignan and Macpherson (1992) outline the work of school leadership as embracing three main areas – ideas, people and things. The realm of ideas reflects on what is right and what is significant for the school. In this area, the school leader is involved in clarifying value and in strategic planning and appraisal of abstract ideas and proposals for school development. The realm of people involves the way in which ideas are adopted as significant meaning for members of the school community. They give rise to new paradigms of teaching and learning, resulting in developmental professional practice. The realm of things gives attention to the practical issues of performance and resources. Practice is constantly evaluated in terms of the desired vision, and resources are aligned for the more efficient achievement of these goals.

Sergiovanni (1984) presents five forces of leadership and excellence in schools: 'technical' human, educational, symbolic and cultural. Under technical he includes the administrative tasks of the school leader – planning, organising, co-ordinating, time-tabling as so on – which are important to maintain efficiency and keep the school in running order. 'Human' comprises the school leader's human-relations role in encouraging, building and maintaining morale, using participation, managing conflict and in general enabling people to attain satisfaction. The 'educational' dimension is the leader's professional knowledge and expertise in the theory and practice of education and schooling, which is exercised through design and delivery of curriculum, supervision, in-service training and so on. 'Symbolic' expresses the role the school leader has as principal – presiding over ceremonies, representing the school to the outside world. 'Cultural' embodies articulating values and purposes, socialising new members, reinforcing the values of the school in a working culture. Sergiovanni concludes that technical, human and educational activities are the hallmarks of competent schools. By themselves they are not sufficient to attain excellence. Excellence requires that adequate attention be paid to symbolic and cultural forces.

Following the focus on the moral purposes of schooling in Starratt, Sergiovanni and Duignan and Macherson, we will develop the proposal that Christian leadership in schools embraces three main areas of vision – meaning, community and excellence (Starratt, 1996). The development of these areas requires leadership and administrative skills that include clear ideas about the meaning of each term, how the Christian ideal integrates with a secular humanist education, as well as developing structures and programmes which facilitate others to share this vision (Fig. 12.1).

MEANING   **COMMUNITY**

Leadership
Developing Vision

Leadership
Developing culture
of teamwork

Administration
Structures that
embody the vision

**SCHOOL
LEADERSHIP**

Administration
Delegating and
personnel
management

Leadership
Setting standards
of quality

Administration
Measuring efficiency
and effectiveness

EXCELLENCE

Fig. 12.1: *Three challenges for educational leaders and administrators.*

In the area of 'meaning', there needs to be some common vision on what the school is trying to achieve, on the balance to be achieved between the personal, spiritual, career and economic goals that the school curriculum can achieve. The Christian school will typically embrace values that are in tune with popular culture, but will also promote certain counter-cultural values which challenge the self-interest of students and parents. This is institutionalised in the choice of curriculum, the subject choices available to the students, the way teachers develop a critical approach to their own subject area, the influence of the hidden curriculum arising from structural balances between subjects, the importance given to success at curricular and extra-curricular activities, and myriads of other rituals within the school which communicate and institute value. In Christian schools, the role of religious education, liturgical and paraliturgical activities, prayers in the classroom can contribute to the meaning aspect of school vision. So also will the way in which other subjects are seen as containing a religious dimension, or whether there is a rigid separation between the secular and the religious. Leadership in this area of schooling looks to developing symbols and rituals that promote a rich and deep religious culture.

'Community' requires a vision on how people within the school should work together and relate to one another. As the school curriculum prepares students to take their place in the adult world, they are given an appreciation of the way that world works, of the interdependence between groups in society, and between countries on the international stage. Students also experience community in the school itself. This is institutionalised in the discipline code, in the way teachers deal with students and in the way students deal with one another. Also involved is the way in which different groups are integrated into the school. The school will have an admissions policy which regulates which students are admitted. It will also have a policy on class placement, which regulates how students are organised and integrated into the school. Practices of ability-streaming and mainstreaming of special-needs students have major implications for the type of community which the school portrays and values. Similarly, school policy on assessment can affect the spirit of co-operation and competition that is generated among pupils, and is seen as the proper way of interacting with peers. Other areas of community development promote the involvement of teachers and parents in school governance through the establishment of democratic structures and disseminating quality information through newsletters and parents' associations to enhance the quality of participation. In Christian schools, building a community based on Gospel values is a constant challenge embracing many areas of school life.

The vision of 'excellence' reflects on the standards that the school promotes. This embraces academic, behavioural and extra-curricular areas. It includes both the performance of students and the professionalism of the teaching staff. Involved in this vision is a realistic assessment of the potential and capacity of the individuals involved. The goals thus set are both challenging and achievable. In Christian schools, there will always be a concern with excellence, that individuals develop their talents and that these talents bear fruit 'one hundred fold'. The development of these talents can be seen from a criterion perspective, where all individuals try to reach a prescribed standard. A second approach is norm-referenced, where success is judged in comparison to others. The Christian approach tends to be criterion-referenced, where the competitive culture is highly norm-referenced. Therefore, the concerns of the Christian school will not just be with the excellence of acquisition, but also with the excellence of distribution. The measurement of excellence in Christian terms is influenced by a Christian understanding of meaning and value, and a concern for neighbour and community.

The work of leadership
The process of leadership in schools involves viewing the school as a social system in which sequences of interaction link and integrate in a systemic pattern as actions enforce and reinforce each other (Tuohy, 1995). One particular application of a systems approach views the school as comprising four levels of participation and behaviour – the individual, the face-to-face team, the inter-departmental group and the organisational (Rashford & Coghlan 1994, Tuohy & Coghlan 1994, 1997). These reflect four levels in which the work of school leadership and administration is exercised.

At Level I, the principal is involved with individuals. This level describes the relationship between the individual and the school, and the way in which the school is integrated into the wider framework of personal life and career goals. From a leadership perspective, this involves having the individual committed to the goals, values and culture of the school. The outcome of this relationship is an appropriate bonding relationship. Students participate in the post-primary school against a general background of family support and values, developing personal identity and peer identification through adolescence, and future career aspirations. A major concern of schools is to develop structures that help the individual student to integrate these areas of development with the values and culture that the school promotes. In Christian schools, particular attention will be paid to helping the student understand the spiritual dimension of their own development, and developing bonds which extend beyond the school, to their parish, to the Church and to the person of Jesus. Promoting a sense of teacher-bonding with the school involves understanding the psychological contract and career motivation of the individual teacher and how this is integrated with family interests and external attractions. Helping teachers, especially those involved in secular subjects, develop a Christian vision of teaching, may be a particular challenge.

The challenge may focus on how the content matter of their subject helps students understand and promote God's creation. Alternatively, it may focus on process and whether teachers identify Christian teaching more in terms of Jesus' Sermon on the Mount, teaching the disciples on the road to Emmaus, or confronting the Pharisees and Sadducees. The principal must then find means of responding to these factors in a way that enhances the teachers' participation in the school. The principal may also be involved in finding ways to promote the bonding of parents to the school, by helping them appreciate the values and culture of the school and how these contribute to the development of their child. This enlists the parents' help in promoting and enhancing the school value system.

A more complex approach to participation exists in establishing effective working relationships in a face-to-face team (Level II). At this level, the principal is involved in promoting effective teamwork. This gives an increased sense of community and shared ownership with the task of the school. Ensuring that students are offered opportunities to learn through co-operative projects within the curriculum, through service projects involving people less fortunate than themselves, and that they begin to understand the use of power and process by running student societies and committees is all part of the symbolic and cultural perspective on school leadership. Teachers may also be involved in teams relating to a particular subject department, curriculum-development or team-teaching project or some devolved management team. Parents also like to be involved in the school, and providing some experience of focused teamwork can promote the quality of that involvement. The experience of effective teams can lead to greater motivation among participants and higher quality decision-making within the school, especially when the team is built around a core element of meaning in the mission of the school.

An even more complex involvement exists in terms of the inter-departmental group, where the work of multiple teams and groups must be co-ordinated in order to achieve inter-disciplinary and inter-departmental tasks and maintain a balance of power among competing interest groups (Level III). For the principal, this means the development of a middle-management structure which is used to extend the knowledge and co-ordinate the functions of complex aspects of school management. Ensuring that middle-management is aware of, and working out of the key vision of the school, is the essential task at Level III. As well as the technical, human and educational expertise involved, this level requires symbolic and cultural management which celebrates the congruence between performance and vision, and addresses areas that are not congruent. Perhaps the most powerful symbol at this level is the distribution of resources – physical and human. This makes a powerful statement as to the values and priorities within the system. Resources are a key element in the empowerment of vision in the school. In developing the Christian dimension of the school, co-ordinating the informative and formative dimension of students' development is a key issue. Integrating the formation element of retreats, class or year Masses, celebration of other sacraments, and extra-curricular activities, such as Vincent de Paul societies, with the information-level academic programmes is a Level III activity.

Finally, the most complex level of participation is the relationship of the school to a changing external environment. The key task for any organisation is its ability to adapt to environmental forces that drive change (Level IV). The principal's work is to the unified effort of all participants in the school towards the end of making the school effective, responsive, service-oriented and functional in its external environment. Communicating the school vision to external bodies such as government, community interests, parish clergy, trustees and boards of management, as well as reporting back to the staff on the concerns of these bodies, are vital roles played by the principal in the management of cultural forces. It may be that the principal is the agent in implementing the strategic concerns and plans of the trustees (Coghlan, 1997). It is equally important to find means of dealing with these concerns in a way that facilitates mutually satisfactory relationships between the school and the parties involved. This dialogue is particularly important if the vision of education for the school embraces how students may be integrated into the Church community as adults.

It can be seen clearly that the four levels are integrally inter-related and inter-dependent. Not only must the issues of each level be consciously managed, but the effects of one level on another must also be afforded equal attention. Within the school, some individuals may have specialist commitments to particular aspects of the process. Nevertheless, the main role of effective leadership and administration is to ensure a holistic view of the process of school management, with particular attention to creating, maintaining and developing links between the four levels. School leaders in their symbolic and cultural roles create vision and articulate values of meaning, community and excellence. In their technical, human and educational roles they institutionalise these values in the operation of the school. This involves both individuals (Level I) and teams and committees (Level II) internalising the values and philosophy of the school, the values operationalised in the structure and balance of programmes and resources in the school (Level III), and in its mission and service to the community (Level IV). School leaders, therefore, act as leaders and custodians of how meaning, community and excellence are actualised across the four levels (Table 1).

LEVEL	MEANING	COMMUNITY	EXCELLENCE
I Individual	Helping individual teachers, students and parents have a personal vision which includes a Christian perspective.	Encouraging participation by individual teachers, students and parents in school activities.	Leading the professionalism of the school and linking teaching with student learning.
II Team	Providing opportunities for teachers to have dialogue on meaning, through discussing the syllabus. Providing students with opportunities to discuss and debate issues of personal, local, national and international importance.	Providing opportunities for teamwork and experiences of community. Understanding the process of group dynamics and how to build teams, and help others build teams.	Providing teams with realistic and challenging goals. Setting norms of high standards and excellence. Delegating responsibility for standards of implementation, and giving feedback which celebrates success.
III Inter-Departmental Group	Leading discussion on how individual activities (curricular and extra-curricular) contribute to the overall curriculum and vision of the school, e.g. co-ordinating the work of the chaplain, pastoral care and career guidance with the academic timetable.	Overseeing how different groups are integrated in the school. Chairing and leading articulation of the discipline code with the help of year heads, form tutors and classroom teachers.	Selecting teachers of high quality and providing staff development which maintains a good balance of skills in the staff. Obtaining and distributing resources that promote the goals of the school vision.
IV Organisational	Promoting the school's vision by developing links with key groups in the wider community; Keeping up to date on developments that will affect the school and keeping members of the school community informed about such issues.	Liaising with the wider community by giving external groups opportunities to bring their point of view to the school. Promoting the participation of the school in activities initiated by external groups.	Promoting the strengths of the school among other groups, particularly in relation to the achievement of strategic aspects of the school vision.
Inter-Level	Ensuring that there is a congruence between the way an academic programme or staff-development initiative is aligned with the development of personal visions and meanings and with the school vision.	Ensuring that there is a congruence between the way an academic programme or staff development initiative is aligned with the development of personal visions and meanings and with the school vision. Ensuring that individuals and groups have an opportunity to be involved in a way that is fair and equitable. Developing a sense of celebration which promotes individual and group success and which promotes reflection on the inter-dependence of individuals and groups	Promoting high standards for all activities in the school. Giving feedback on the importance of each contribution to the excellence of the school culture, and celebrating successes.

Table 1: Focus of attention for School Leaders in Each of Three Areas at the Four Levels of Action

Conclusion

Leadership and administration are frequently characterised in terms of the caption – 'Leaders do the right thing; administrators do things right.' These roles are interdependent in the person of the school principal. Leadership is required to create vision, and administration is required to make it work. We have focused on the leadership and administrative work of the principal in three areas – meaning, community and excellence. We have shown how both roles in these three areas involve attention to individuals, teams, inter-team co-ordination, and the school in its wider community context. In Christian schools, this activity is informed by a faithful reading of Gospel values and the invitation to develop a personal relationship with Christ. Christian vision becomes a powerful force in responding to the leadership challenge of creating meaning, community and excellence.

PART VI

THE FUTURE OF CATHOLIC SCHOOLS

13

CATHOLIC SCHOOLS AT THE CROSSROADS: AN AMERICAN PERSPECTIVE

Andrew M. Greeley

Introduction

In this paper I propose to treat two subjects:
1.) A survey of major research on Catholic education.
2.) A suggestion that future research might focus on 'social capital' in Catholic schools.

Research on Catholic schools

In 1958 Peter and Alice Rossi began a tradition of research on Catholic schools that has continued for forty years in their study of schools in Fitchburg, Massachusetts. To their surprise they found that the Catholic schools they observed simply did not fit the stereotypes common in the academic establishment at that time. Rossi would later enunciate the principle, not always attended to in some inadequate research, that it was the residual behaviour in later life of those who attended Catholic schools that was the most appropriate measure of their success.

The first published evidence of what Catholic schools were like was in James Coleman's *The Adolescent Society*. The Polish working-class high school for young men in Chicago didn't fit the stereotype either. It was in ways a splendid place, for reasons that Anthony Bryk would explain thirty years later in *Catholic Schools and the Common Good* (1993). Between *The Adolescent Society* and *Catholic Schools* a trajectory of research findings answered most of the questions about Catholic schools thirty to forty years ago. I cannot think of a single one which was not good news for Catholic schools. I will outline them briefly, usually without reference to details of the findings of particular studies, by proposing a series of questions and the answers to them:

1. Are Catholic schools academically inferior? Are they strongholds of anti-intellectualism, as Professor Donovan of Boston College once argued?

The answer to this question is a flat 'no'. By every imaginable measure, Catholic schools are superior to their public counterparts, even when all appropriate background variables have been taken into account, even, in the case of the 'High School and Beyond' study, previous academic scores.

2. Is the academic success of Catholic schools the result of selective recruiting or successful retention of better students?
Again the answer is the opposite of what those who ask the question usually suspect: in fact, the success of the Catholic schools is strongest among the disadvantaged students (those with academic, emotional, disciplinary and familial problems and who lack a home environment conducive to success). Moreover, the success of the Catholic schools increases as these problems pile up on students. Finally, the contribution of Catholic schools to disadvantaged students does not vary with race – it is present in white and brown and black, perhaps because the Catholic schools were designed, like Coleman's working-class Polish school, to serve poor immigrants.

3. Is the success of the Catholic schools, especially with disadvantaged young people, the result of tight disciplinary control?
Again no. Rather, the Catholic schools, as Anthony Bryk has shown, are successful because they make greater academic demands, provide stronger community support, and give more personal attention to students – just what the promotional literature of Catholic schools promised, perhaps often with their fingers crossed in hope. Coleman argued that the Catholic schools are indeed the 'Common Schools' in that they did for the disadvantaged what the public schools claim to do but, in fact, fail to do.[1] He also argued that much of the success of these schools results from the 'social capital' they have at their disposal, another way of saying the same thing that Bryk said, a subject to which I will return when discussing a new direction for research on Catholic schools.

4. Are Catholic schools divisive? Do they produce men and women who are more likely to be prejudiced than those who go to public schools?

The answer is a flat no. Quite the contrary, those who attend Catholic schools are less prejudiced than Catholics who attend public schools, and less prejudiced than all public school graduates. Moreover, they are also more likely to be pro-feminist. All of these statements are true even when social class and educational achievement are held constant.

5. Is not the religious impact of Catholic schools less important in a time of turbulence and change, such as these decades in the wake of the Second Vatican Council?
The answer, monotonous by now, again is no. Quite the contrary, the effects of Catholic education on adult religious behaviour has been stronger in the post-counciliar years than before, perhaps because they have the 'social capital' of being plugged into the Catholic information network.

6. Are not the apparent effects of Catholic education on adult behaviour the result of the parental religious background of those who attend Catholic schools?
The answer again is in the negative. In fact, Catholic schools have an impact independent of parental background even in a comparison between those who attended Catholic schools and those who did not, but would have if Catholic schools had been available. The evidence on how the Catholics schools have accomplished this religious impact is consonant with the findings about the schools' academic impact – the real effect is less in the classroom than in the social network the schools create.

7. Is not 'religious education' (formerly called CCD) an adequate substitute for the Catholic school?
I know of no evidence that 'religious education' has any independent impact at all on the subsequent adult behaviour of those who participated in it. It may be necessary to support such programmes, if only to assure the parents of those children who do not attend Catholic schools (often because the Church refuses to build such schools) that the Church has not lost interest in them. The case for such programmes has not been made, at least not with any data to back it up. I am not sure, given the

argument that Catholic schools create powerful social networks which account for their impact, that it will ever be possible to make the case.

8. *Can the Church afford the money to maintain a subsidy for Catholic schools?*

'Subsidy' is an inaccurate word. In fact, the proper word is investment, for, as the late Bishop Bill McManus, God be good to him, used to say, the funding of Catholic schools is an investment.

The extra contribution to Sunday collections of parents with children in Catholic schools on a national average picks up the cost of such schools, and those who attended such schools are likely to be generous in adult life. Catholic schools are indeed a capital investment, bingo with a purpose, as my colleague Michael Hout remarks. The reason that there has been a three-decade moratorium on the construction of Catholic schools is that Catholic contributions (in terms of proportion of income and hence free of inflation) have fallen to half of what they were three decades ago, with the resultant loss of perhaps eight billion dollars in income per year. Spread this out over ten years and the Church has lost the eighty billion dollars that it would have if Catholics contributed as much today as they did in the early 1960s and as Protestants do today.[2] Moreover, with this kind of money available, Catholic schools would not have to price themselves out of the market and could pay their teachers a living wage. The financial problems of the Church, as acutely as they affect Catholic schools, are not in fact something caused by Catholic schools or even by a decline in their appeal.

Incidentally, Catholic school-Catholics are more likely, both when they are in high school and in college, to volunteer for community service – strikingly more likely. This is true even when one excludes the 'compulsory' volunteering that is required at many Catholic high schools – a phenomenon that perhaps only Catholicism could produce (and not unlike the forced confessions on the Thursday before First Friday of not so many years ago, a sacrilege which, for all I know, still continues).

9. Are Catholic schools 'worth it?' Is the pay-off commensurate with the costs?

This is a value question, not a research question. It implies that the Church might well spend the money on other and more worthy projects – projects which the clerical elite will choose, of course. Such a question assumes that there exists a body of wisdom and a group of wise men who can determine where Catholic money goes, and that the money expended by parents on Catholic schools will be available for projects the wise men propose to support. Such an assumption is, of course, false. Close the Catholic school and the Sunday collections go down. Don't open one and the Sunday collections are not comparable with parishes that have a Catholic school. The pertinent response to this question comes not from research findings but from consumer behaviour – the willingness of many parents to pay for Catholic education whenever they can get it. They think the schools are 'worth it'.

No social research is perfect, there is always a possibility that more sophisticated, more insightful, more sensitive approaches may later impose greater clarity, nuance and refinement on a given project or a whole tradition of investigation – and it is the latter that is at issue here. But it is most unlikely that the basic trajectory of the scholarship I have described will be altered very much. There are answers to the crucial questions about Catholic schools which have existed since, let us say, 1950. In every instance the answers are favourable to Catholic schools, so favourable indeed that one wonders how the questions could have arisen in the first place. Their persistence and, perhaps, even their origins, can be accounted for by the continuation of anti-Catholic bigotry in the educational establishment and Catholic self-hatred. It is worth noting, however, that the reviews of *Catholic Schools and The Common Good* showed a decline in hostility to Catholic schools.

It is perhaps worth while to comment here that I have no institutional reason to be on the side of Catholic schools. I have never taught in one (save for Catechism classes in my early years in the priesthood); I have never been affiliated with Catholic colleges or universities or diocesan school offices; none of my research has been funded by the Church. If I provide this favourable report on them, it is because the evidence compels me to do so.

One expects in the research business to offend those whose institutions have been found wanting in the research enterprise. One is surprised, however, when those who should be delighted by favourable findings want to reject them. 'I disagree with your writing on Catholic schools', someone will say. Or, 'what you describe is not true in my parish'. The only answer to such comments is to respond, 'I will not take your disagreement seriously until you produce high-quality national sample data to prove me wrong and, moreover, while your parish may be interesting, an anecdotal report about it is irrelevant to the research findings being reported'. Only in a group that does not understand social research – and perhaps does not want to – would such comments even be raised. On the other hand, when someone says that what I have described is true in their parish, I am pleased, but not because events in a single parish add any certainty to research findings.

After time, it seems to me, the fate of the research tradition I have described is not so much that the relevant consumers challenge it, but rather they simply ignore it. Catholic educators, perhaps for reasons of mass masochism, no longer deny the good news about their work. Rather, they pretend it doesn't exist. At one point, I thought that this was personal: they did not mind good news about Catholic schools so long as it was not from me. I now perceive that they do not want good news from anyone. They ignore not only my work, but the work of Coleman and his colleagues, and Bryk and his colleagues too. As I search for an explanation of this odd behaviour, I tend to conclude that it results from both self-hatred and the intense identity crisis caused by the Second Vatican Council and the end of the theories of immigrant Catholicism (protect the faith of the immigrant).

In any case, serious, quality research on Catholic schools has produced no evidence to confirm the null hypotheses of failure and inferiority that have for so long been the conventional wisdom about Catholic schools. Beyond that, this researcher sayeth not. If for extraneous reasons some wish to deny or ignore the findings, that is their business and their problem.

Further research: social capital
The notion of 'social capital', introduced into contemporary social science in great part because of the efforts of the late James Coleman, has become very popular lately, not without good reason. Not only does it bridge the gap between economics and sociology (Coleman 1988, Greeley 1997)[3], it also provides a very useful tool for analysing social structure. Social capital, in brief, is the extra resource for achieving certain goals available to members of a relational network (social structure), precisely because of the existence of the network. The resources, according to Coleman, exist not only in the individuals but in the network itself. These are resources that the actors would not have if they were not in the network. In his seminal 1988 article on the subject, he cited Catholic schools as a classic example of the extra pay-off in educational outcome which social capital makes possible (social capital generated in part by the overlapping networks of membership in a Church community and in a community of the parents of schoolchildren).

Coleman sees the social capital resources in the networks that are external to the school institution. Bryk sees parallel resources as internal to the school institution – greater personal interest in students and enhanced social support.

Since the basic questions about the right of Catholic schools to exist have been answered by the research tradition I have described above, I propose that, should anyone be interested in further research on Catholic schools (a supposition I do not consider to be self-evidently true), the origins and operation of social capital in those schools might profitably be explored, both to further human understanding of social capital and, perhaps, to facilitate the expansion of its resources in Catholic schools and in the rest of the Church. The results of such research might shift the weight of opinion in the Catholic community in the direction of the notion that Catholic schools are an enormously valuable resource.

Other research evidence has confirmed the evidence of

Weber and Durkheim that there are stronger community ties (all over the world) among Catholics than there are among Protestants. The work of Bryk and Coleman specifies spectacularly one operation of those community ties. If one is to believe David Tracy, this community ethos is but an aspect of the larger phenomenon of the 'sacramental' or 'liturgical' imagination (or, if one wishes, the 'analogical' imagination). I am not altogether sure how one might conceptualise sacramentality and liturgy as social capital. Perhaps the relationships of communal worship intensify yet more the resources available for joint action in a network.

The slow and painful process of research on the Catholic phenomenon has demonstrated that Catholicism has two enormously rich and fruitful assets uniquely available to it – stronger community ties (and orientations towards community) and more imaginative metaphorical resources, particularly as they are expressed in communal liturgy. My point is not that these resources (I might almost call them graces) are there and not being used, but that they are there and are operating, however imperfectly, to the benefit, however limited, of the Catholic heritage and people and, also, to the benefit of those who, though not Catholic, attend Catholic schools. It would be folly, I think, not to learn more about how they work. However, in a Church institution, concerned mostly about what the Catholic right-wingers will say and what the papal nuncio will think, one does not expect much interest in such apparently complex and perhaps unintelligible phenomena. Moreover, one can not anticipate that the Catholic liberal élite, preoccupied as it is with the deficiencies of the Church institution, will come to believe that there is any grace or, if one wishes, Grace) left in the heritage, especially since this grace, like the spirit (or, if one wishes Spirit) operates softly, gently and imperceptibly like the wind.

There are scholars who are exploring the impact of social capital on secondary education. One could hardly expect them to be interested in the special social capital that is provided by Catholicism's communal/liturgical imagination in Catholic schools. If Catholics don't study this phenomenon, then who will? Can the impact of religious imagination be studied? Surely it can. Yet, in all candour, I see no evidence that anyone inside the Catholic school establishment is willing or able or even interested in studying it. I assume that, before the research starts, there has to come into existence an awareness that religion is story before it is anything else and after everything else, and that Catholicism has, far and away, the best stories.

Conclusion

By way of summary, research on Catholic schools has produced more positive and supporting findings than anyone might have expected thirty-five years ago and, indeed, more than many Catholics and many Catholic educators are willing to admit today. Further research might well explore the communal and liturgical imaginations that currently function, however imperfectly, in the Church and in the schools, and which, apparently, generate substantial social capital. Such research might facilitate the search for solutions to the difficult policy issues that Catholic schools face, not as a result of their failure, but of their success (complicated by the sharp decline in Catholic contributions).

I often regret that I ever became engaged in this area of scholarly investigation. It has been a waste of time. Doctrinaire slogans, conventional wisdom, shallow ideology, pessimism and nonsense have dominated the discussion of Catholic education for so long that I have little hope that mere findings, no matter how solid, will be taken seriously. Certainly my own work, and that of the research heritage I have described, has had no impact at all.

14

THE FUTURE OF THE CATHOLIC SCHOOL: AN ENGLISH PERSPECTIVE

Gerald Grace

Introduction

The future of the Catholic school (in this case, of Catholic voluntary-aided and grant-maintained schools in England)[1] is, from one perspective, an occasion for hope and optimism. Catholic schools, both primary and secondary, have been well placed in the public league tables of academic and test results which are, in contemporary England, an important source for the making or breaking of a school's reputation and public image. In addition to support from local Catholic communities, the schools are much sought after by parents of other Christian faith communities and by members of other faiths. In many areas, therefore, Catholic schools are filled to capacity and are, in fact, oversubscribed by parents who are attracted by the Catholic school's reputation for academic success and for taking spiritual and moral formation seriously. As Cardinal Hume (1997, 25-6) has put it:

> The Church's aim has always been to provide a place at a Catholic school for every Catholic child. Great strides have been taken towards achieving that goal. Today, Catholic schools are increasingly popular, not only because of the good academic results they often achieve, but also because many parents sense that a Catholic school might help their children to develop the self-discipline, moral resilience and spiritual maturity so necessary in surviving exposure as young adults to the winds of secularism and materialism in our society.

The decision by the British Prime Minister (an Anglican) and his wife (a Catholic) to send their son to a Catholic grant-maintained school in London appeared to confer public and political legitimacy upon a schooling system that has, even as late as the 1970s, been subject to political calls, especially from the Left, for its abolition on the grounds of social divisiveness, covert selection and the general undermining of the effectiveness of the state system of schooling.[2]

If we distinguish in educational analysis between *surface level analysis* and *deep structure analysis*[3] it is possible to conclude that, at a surface level, the future for Catholic schools in England looks bright. The schools have most of the surface and visible indicators of success and effectiveness, i.e. good academic and test scores, a reputation for spiritual and moral excellence, and for the 'good discipline' which exemplifies this, a strong position in the competitive internal market for schooling which developed in the 1980s, the support of parents ('customers'/'consumers') extending well beyond the Catholic community, and official and political legitimacy and approval at a high level in the British state. There is much here to give confidence for the future.

However, analysis at the deep structure level prevents the development of triumphalism about Catholic schooling and encourages, instead, thoughtful reflection about its visible success and more systematic research into the changing culture of Catholic schooling. This paper is written as a contribution to deep structure analysis by looking carefully at some of the contemporary challenges for the future of Catholic schooling in England and with reference to the available research.

Challenges for the future of Catholic schooling
1. *Common good v individual self-interest*
The Sacred Congregation for Catholic Education, in publications such as *The Catholic School* (1988), asked all Catholics to consider 'the Catholic school's fundamental reasons for existing' (8). The Sacred Congregation provided a basic framework to guide such thinking, as follows:

to provide a service which is truly civic and apostolic. (9)

This is the basis of a Catholic school's educational work. Education is not given for the purpose of gaining power but as an aid towards a fuller understanding of, and communion with, man (sic), events and things. Knowledge is not to be considered as a means of material prosperity and success but as a call to serve and to be responsible for others. (43)

first and foremost the Church offers its educational service to 'the poor or those who are deprived of family help and affection or those who are far from the faith' (44-5)

For the Catholic school mutual respect means service to the Person of Christ. Cooperation is between brothers and sisters in Christ. A policy of working for the common good is undertaken seriously as working for the building up of the kingdom of God (46).

This fundamental call to be of service to the poor (in economic, family and spiritual terms) has been a powerful constituent of the culture of Catholic schooling since the Second Vatican Council in many countries, including the USA, England, Ireland and Australia. Bryk *et al.* (1993), in a major research study, *Catholic Schools and the Common Good*, have argued that many Catholic schools in the US serving inner-city communities have been informed by 'an inspirational ideology' (301) which has made them qualitatively different from public (state) schools. This inspirational ideology has celebrated the primacy of the spiritual and moral life, the dignity of the person, the importance of community and the moral commitments to caring, social justice and the common good as the visible fruits of the faith. Catholic school principalship in these contexts has been strongly influenced by the spiritual, economic and moral capital of the various religious orders, which have provided most of the leadership positions until recently. Working with such a culture of 'the preferential option for the poor', Bryk *et al.* have demonstrated that Catholic schools have made considerable contributions to the common good of American society by their effective academic, spiritual, moral and social service to the most deprived and disadvantaged communities.

The detailed research reported in *Catholic Schools and the Common Good*, while celebrating these achievements in the past, concludes in sombre terms. Contemporary conditions in the USA are beginning to demonstrate that market forces and market values in education and the inexorable circumstances shaping institutional survival and financial solvency are threatening the historical mission and values of Catholic schooling. As the strategic subsidy[4] which the religious orders provided in personnel and in cultural and economic capital for the educational mission to the poor weakens over time, Catholic schools in areas of the greatest need are closing while those in the affluent suburbs are prospering. These trends are confirmed by the research of O'Keefe (1996) in a paper evocatively entitled, 'No Margin, No Mission'. Surveying the pattern of Catholic school closures in poor inner-city areas of the USA, O'Keefe calls for renewed efforts in the Catholic community as a whole to sustain the educational mission to 'some of the most underprivileged children in the United States' (193).What is being described here is the growing triumph of profit margin (market culture in education) over educational and spiritual mission (the option for the poor). As market forces in education grow stronger, and as the ability of the Catholic Church and of the religious orders to countervail these economic forces becomes weaker, the future of Catholic schooling may look bright in the suburbs but grim in the inner city, where its priority mission should be.

For English Catholic schools in the maintained sector of education there are similar challenges for the future, but realised within different socio-political and cultural contexts, the most significant of which is the existence of substantial state funding for denominational education. However, developments in the 1980s and 1990s arising from the educational reforms of governments influenced by the ideologies of the New Right have led to major changes in the culture of education and in the general working environment of schools. The introduction of local management of schools (with individual devolved budgetary responsibility), empowered school governors (to strengthen the parental voice in education), grant-maintained status (to encourage autonomous independence from local education authorities), open pupil enrolments (to encourage 'customer'/'consumer' choice among schools) and a political and ideological climate celebrating a competitive market in education, the survival of the fittest as demonstrated by public academic league tables and the need for the closure of 'failing' schools; all of these radical changes have attempted to transform the culture of English schooling so that all schools are subject to the discipline of individual competitive success, measured, visible and cost-effective.

Catholic schools in England face challenges in the future from a new culture of education which, at its worst, involves the commodification of education,[5] the marketisation of school cultures and processes and the celebration of an ethic of individual and autonomous school 'success', regardless of the fate of other schools. These developments do not articulate easily with Catholic values in education, where spiritual and moral culture is given precedence over material success, where education is seen as a service and not a product, and where notions of the common good and of the well-being of community institutions take precedence over individual self-interest. In other words, the space, identity and voice of contemporary Catholic schooling in England is now more directly challenged by individualistic and market values than ever before in its history. In these circumstances, the critical question for Catholic school leaders (the hierarchy, the head teachers and the school governors) is: Can a legitimate balance be found between Catholic values and market values or will market forces in education begin to compromise the integrity of the special mission of Catholic schooling? Can Gospel values survive in the face of a more direct relationship with the market-place and education?

Richard Pring (1996) has argued that the philosophy of the market-place is incompatible with the distinctive idea of the nature and purpose of schools. In particular, in placing the market and individual self-interest at the centre of educational arrangements, the reforms of the 1980s, he argues, undermine Catholic educational values, which emphasise the importance of community and concern for the common good. My own research (Grace 1995, 1996) demonstrates that the struggles between concern for the common good and the advancement of school self-interest constitute major ethical and professional dilemmas for Catholic head teachers in England. Stated in its starkest form, it is beginning to be realised by head teachers that there is little market yield or measurable return for schools which continue to operate a preferential option for the poor or even a fully open-door policy for all the children and youth of the local community. In a market economy for schooling, the imperatives of visible and measurable success, financial balance and high league table positions, all combine against commitment to 'customers' who are lacking in both cultural and economic capital and the 'right attitudes' to schooling. The temptation is, therefore, to 'play the market' or to 'go upmarket' by adopting a more calculating policy on who is admitted to the school, who is excluded from the school, who is entered for external examinations at secondary level, etc. At present, Catholic head teachers are struggling with these market temptations and dilemmas:

> Catholic schools really must keep the explicit link between Christ and person-centred education.... How do we square our vocational vision of pupils as persons with the market vision of economic units? How does this affect our treatment of special educational needs? How does this affect our admissions policy? (Female secondary head teacher, quoted in Grace 1995, 176).

The moral and professional dilemma that is currently facing Catholic head teachers (primary and secondary) in England is the recognition that a competitive market culture in schooling is making it much more difficult to be in the service of the poor, the troublesome, the alienated and the powerless. Success can be achieved with such children and young people (as the Catholic Bishops' report, *The Struggle for Excellence*, 1997, demonstrates), but at a greater cost in terms of time, resources, staff commitment and educational support, and it can only be fairly judged in relative rather than in absolute terms. As questions of cost and cost-effectiveness become more dominant in English schooling culture, and as public and visible 'success' continues to be judged in absolute terms, the integrity of Catholic schooling in the future is, at a deep structure level, under threat. Catholic schools may continue to score successes in the new culture of schooling in England but this may be at the price of fidelity to 'the poor or those who are deprived of family help and affection or those who are far from the faith'.

It is clearly in recognition of this threat to the spiritual, moral and educational integrity of Catholic schooling in the future that the Bishops' Conference of England and Wales has issued an authoritative commentary on *The Common Good in Education* (1997). In calling for more solidarity, partnership and co-operation among Catholic schools, the bishops say:

> it remains the Christian duty of individual schools themselves to promote the common good and support 'the poor, vulnerable, powerless and defenceless' by:
>
> • reviewing and, where necessary, amending their selection procedures
> • sharing specialist resources wherever possible with those that have few or none
> • helping unpopular schools to improve their public image
> • working at local, diocesan and national levels to ensure an equitable distribution of the resources available to education. (*The Common Good in Education*, 17)

Future research will have to investigate the extent to which Catholic schools remain faithful to their own mission statements, the exhortations of the Sacred Congregation for Catholic Education, and the call from the bishops for solidarity and commitment to the common good. In the struggle between moral purpose and material success, an important **values audit** will have to be undertaken of the integrity and distinctiveness, at a deep structural level, of Catholic schooling culture in England.

2: The nature of future Catholicity

In considering 'the Catholic school's fundamental reasons for existing' (8), the Sacred Congregation for Catholic Education laid emphasis upon the contribution of the Catholic school to the salvific mission of the Church. Thus it asserted 'the Catholic school forms part of the saving mission of the Church, especially for education in the faith' (1988, 13). What 'education in the faith' entails, what the evidence of its relative success or failure can be said to be, and what forms of Catholicity are actually realised in the living cultures of different types of Catholic school are currently topics for debate and for research in England.

Thomas Groome (1996) has claimed that what makes a school Catholic is, among other things, the presence of five theological characteristics:

- a positive anthropology of the person is a realistic but optimistic understanding of people as capable of sin but essentially good;[6]

- a sacramental life and a sacramental consciousness i.e. an awareness of the presence of God as mediated by the liturgical sacraments;

- a communal emphasis i.e. that we find our identity, our true selves and our salvation in a relationship with others;

- a sense of tradition i.e. the importance of tradition and history in the development of the Christian story;

- an appreciation of rationality and learning i.e. the illumination of faith by reason wherever possible.

To what extent in the past Catholic schools in England actually realised a culture of Catholicity of this type is difficult to assess, given the paucity of systematic research with such a focus. However, there are influential writers who believe that the Catholicity of the schools was much stronger in the past than it is in the present or will be in the future. James Arthur (1995), in *The Ebbing Tide: Policy and Principles of Catholic Education*, argues that Catholic schools in England, which were originally founded on a 'holistic' model ('concerned with the transmission ... of Catholic faith – its beliefs, values, character and norms of conduct' (233)), are being transformed over time into educational cultures based upon 'dualistic' and 'pluralistic' models. For Arthur, the 'dualistic' Catholic school separates the secular and religious elements of education, regarding the Catholic ethos of the school as something additional to its secular academic programme, and 'it does not assume that a majority of children come from believing families' (227). The 'pluralistic' school is based on the assumption that all single-faith schools offer an educational setting which is narrow and divisive ... and this school model would involve accepting other faiths into Catholic schools' (229). The analysis contained in *The Ebbing Tide* suggests that English Catholic schooling of the holistic type is giving ground, especially at secondary-school level, to dualistic and pluralistic models of schooling, and that this constitutes part of the ebbing tide of Catholicity. In support of this thesis, Dr Arthur constructs an illuminative (although fictional) case study of St Michael's secondary school in which the Blessed Sacrament is reserved in the school chapel at the opening of the school in 1960 and removed from a very different St Michael's in 1996. The symbolism is powerful and intentional: a central feature of Catholicity in the schools, the sacramental life and the consciousness that goes with it, is disappearing, and Catholic schools in England in the future will 'become institutions practically indistinguishable from those under LEA control' (253).

This analysis has provoked much controversy within the Catholic educational community in England. For some, it has given expression to their deepest fears that Catholic schools are undergoing a process of incorporation into a multi-faith pluralism which will extinguish the rich distinctiveness of the Catholic faith. Worse than this, the dualistic school appears to relegate religion to being a footnote to the serious academic text of achieving measurable successes. However, for others, Arthur's analysis is based upon a golden-age construct of Catholicity in the past and a too pessimistic reading of the different forms that Catholicity can take in contemporary schooling. Peter Hastings (1996), for instance, believes that much of the Catholicity of English schooling in the past was oppressive in its culture and immature in its outcomes. For Hastings, the future for a mature Catholicity must be found in schools that – value openness and intellectual challenge.

From a research standpoint, there is much to be done in this contested area. This is why I have worked to establish a Centre for Research and Development in Catholic Education at London University, Institute of Education.[7] James Arthur's thesis of ebbing Catholicity is not actually based on extensive fieldwork research in Catholic schools.[8] While intuitively appealing, it remains at the level of a hypothesis to be tested. Similarly, the notion that a vital and authentic Catholicity is tied to a particular form of the sacramental life must be investigated in detail. As part of a pilot study for a more extensive inquiry into the contemporary role of Catholic secondary schools in inner-city areas in England, I have been involved in research consultations with a sample of head teachers. This has revealed that, while the celebration of the Mass may be relatively infrequent in such schools, many of the head teachers assert that Catholicity is being 'realised in other ways'. Future research will need to probe the validity of such claims and to explore what head teachers, teachers and pupils understand by other forms of Catholicity. The question of what constitutes the Catholic ethos of a school is another contested area which needs investigation. For some the issue is necessarily tied to the proportion of Catholic pupils (practising or nominal) who are present on the school roll. For others, this is a narrow and mechanistic view which fails to take into account the contemporary faith pluralism of inner-city communities and the need for Catholic schools to be of service to 'those who are far from the faith'[9] (Sacred Congregation, 45).

Just as Catholic school leaders have to consider what legitimate balance can be made in the future between the imperative demands of market survival and those of spiritual and moral mission, so too they have to consider what is the proper balance that should be made between the generation of a distinctive Catholic ethos on the one hand and a pluralistic and ecumenical openness to all faiths or even to non-faith on the other.

Those who support the analysis given in *The Ebbing Tide* argue that a great strength of Catholic religious and educational culture is the richness of its symbolic life and its ritual practices. This richness, in their view, should not be lost to Catholic school culture in the future in the mistaken pursuit of modernity, pluralism or ecumenism. Thus, McClelland (1992, 6-7) argues:

> The crucifix should not be discarded from classrooms as a gesture to religious pluralism. Neither should representation of saints be relegated ... in the interests of a false ecumenism. Nor should pious religious practices be abandoned on the altar of individual freedom. All these things are daily reminders of that communion of saints which lies at the heart of the theology of the Catholic school. Such schools will not overcome the materialism of the age ... (in this way).

Peter McLaren (1993) has suggested that ritual and symbolism have a powerful effect on the formation of young people and on the process of 'making Catholics'. The power of ritual and symbolism is to be found precisely in their appeal to the imagination, the emotions and the sense of the dramatic, which are particularly salient during adolescence. In his ethnographic study of a conservative Catholic school, 'St Ryan's', McLaren concluded that:

> Overall, a broad range of Catholic symbols were translated by classroom rituals into graphic and readily comprehensible messages which constituted a compelling way of viewing reality and the student's location within that reality. (184)

While such observations seem to support the case for renewing a strong form of Catholic ethos in the future, there are also counter-arguments which suggest that a 'strong' form of Catholic ethos may, in practice, be oppressive and alienating in religious formation and inhibiting to open and critical intellectual inquiry. As well as this, it may seem to signal Catholic exclusiveness and closure to other faith communities rather than inclusiveness and openness to the challenges of contemporary pluralism.

For Bernadette O'Keeffe (1992), the future for Catholic schools in England must be in the direction of greater openness. Such openness is already a *de facto* feature of many Catholic schools in inner-city areas where substantial 'other faith' school populations exist. For O'Keeffe, it should now become a principled development for the future, where faith rather than denomination 'would seek to achieve the integration of differences into a collaborative and fruitful whole' (45).

There is a wariness in the English Catholic community about greater openness and the possibility of inter-faith schools. The historical legacy of the citadel school (as a bulwark against enemies of the Faith) and of triumphalist truth claims (against the truth claims of other faiths) is far from exhausted. At this present juncture, there appears to be a sincere commitment to dialogue with other faiths (which is an advance over no dialogue) but little evidence of such dialogue being realised in many concrete educational projects which advance the inter-faith educational mission.[10] It is significant, in this connection, that Bishop Vincent Nichols, addressing Catholic educators on 'The Church's mission in education in a multi-faith society', observed:

> Catholicism is not a breakaway movement or a protest. It is not a denomination. Rather it is a response to the revealed truth – a truth which possesses it, and not a truth which a Catholic can ever pretend to possess. (1997, 58)

Much more debate and much more research will be required in the future to assist the Catholic educational community in England in its deliberations about what sort of Catholicity should be looked for in the schools.

Conclusion

There is not space here to do justice to the full range of issues that will impinge upon the future of Catholic schooling in England. Among these are questions to do with the tensions between Catholic grant-maintained schools and Catholic voluntary-aided schools; tensions between hierarchical counsel and guidance on the future of schools and the voice of a more confident and assertive group of parents; issues to do with the future of Catholic independent schools and matters relating to the future role of religious orders and their changing mission in education. While all of these are important, it is the argument of this paper that the two most profound questions are the nature of the educational mission being realised in the schools in an age of market culture, and the nature of Catholicity being realised in the schools in a more secular and pluralistic age.

Catholic schools in England are currently enjoying great surface structure success, popularity and acclaim from official sources. What their status is at the deep structure level of educational, spiritual, moral and ethical integrity, is a more complex issue, in need of much more debate, dialogue and research inquiry.[11] Catholic schools, by reason of their special mission, have to pay particular attention to the verse in St Matthew's Gospel which asks: 'What shall it profit a man to gain the whole world and to lose his own soul?' It is not being suggested here that Catholic schooling in England has lost its soul, but it is being suggested that, for the future, more investigation should be undertaken on the state of its educational soul.[12]

Acknowledgements

I would like to thank Professor Richard Pring and Dr James Arthur for comments received on the first draft of this paper.

15

THE FUTURE OF THE CATHOLIC SCHOOL: AN IRISH PERSPECTIVE

J. Matthew Feheney FPM

Introduction

There could scarcely be a more appropriate time to consider the future of Catholic schools in Ireland than the eve of the first comprehensive educational legislation in the history of the state. The Education Act now pending, which is likely to be based largely on the last Government's White Paper on Education, should be a milestone in Irish education, comparable to those great educational events of the past: the Stanley Letter of 1831, which led to the setting up of the Irish National Schools, the Colleges (Ireland) Act of 1845, the Intermediate Education Act of 1878, the Ministers and Secretaries Act of 1924, which led to the setting up of the Department of Education, the Vocational Education Act of 1930 and the introduction of free second-level education in 1967. It is doubtful if there will be any legislation in the area of education of comparable importance for many years to come.

Though the broad future of denominational schools seems assured in the promised legislation, few would deny that these schools are facing a testing time in the future. It could even be argued that they are at a crossroads and that their future will be affected not only by the decisions that will shortly be taken, but also by failure to take decisions. And as far as decisions are concerned, is it not likely that, in the future, as so often in the past, we will blamed more for our sins of omission than for those of commission?

Any examination of the future of Catholic schools must also consider their past and present. At second level we have four types of school in Ireland: voluntary secondary, of which there were 445 in 1995; comprehensive schools, of which there were 16 in 1995; community schools, of which there were 61 in 1995; and, fourthly, 246 (1995) second-level schools under the local

Vocational Education Committees. While the first three, constituting nearly 70 per cent of the total, have much in common in the way they relate to and operate under the Department of Education, the fourth category, known variously as vocational schools or community colleges, operate under the supervision of the local Vocational Education Committees, hereinafter abbreviated to VECs (Department of Education, 1995).

While the comprehensive and community schools, together with those under the VECs, are non-denominational, the vast majority of the 445 voluntary secondary schools, constituting more than 50 per cent of all registered post-primary schools, are Catholic. There are also a small number of voluntary secondary schools under Protestant and other management. The vast majority of Catholic voluntary secondary schools (64 per cent) are single-sex day schools, while a decreasing number, also single-sex, are boarding schools. Many of the Catholic schools, especially those with boarding facilities, have a long history, extending back, in some cases, to the last century.

While the sixty-one community and sixteen comprehensive schools are intended to cater for children of all or no religious denomination, the adjective 'inter-denominational' would be an inadequate, and possibly a misleading description of them. The majority of the community schools came into being as a result of the amalgamation of smaller voluntary secondary schools, sometimes including a local VEC school, and either the local bishop or a religious congregation is a co-trustee of the school plant and property. Moreover, the local bishop, and religious congregations where they are involved, have a generous representation on the Boards of Management of both comprehensive and community schools. It is obvious, therefore, that though not expressly Catholic, these two types of school have strong Catholic connections. The connection between the Catholic Church and VEC second-level schools is also strong, if complex, with minor variations from area to area. In all areas, however, the local Catholic bishop has generous representation on Boards of Management, in addition to having the right to nominate a salaried Catholic chaplain to each VEC school.

Though lack of space will not permit me to go into the details of the Articles of Management of either community or VEC schools in this paper, I would like the reader to bear in mind that, though not *de jure* Catholic schools, they have, nevertheless, strong links with the Catholic Church, and what I have to say about Catholic schools in this paper will be applicable in varying degrees to many of the schools in these three categories (Drudy & Lynch, 1993, 6-16).

The past

All but a few of the older second-level schools in Ireland date from the passing of the Intermediate Education Act of 1878, when provision was made to give partial financial aid to schools preparing students for state examinations. The students originally patronising these schools were from the better-off classes, since the main source of finance for the operation of the schools and the payment of teachers' salaries came from student fees. Though at first most of these schools were under the direction of religious orders or congregations, they were gradually joined by diocesan 'junior seminaries', which aimed at providing would-be diocesan priests with a good preparation for entry to the national seminary in Maynooth or one of its diocesan counterparts.

There was no significant change in this state of affairs until after the Second World War, when some primary schools, especially those under Congregations of Brothers and Sisters, began to add post-primary departments. These departments became known as 'Secondary Tops' and prepared students for the Intermediate and Leaving Certificate examination, normally taken only in second-level schools. The Department of Education was content to approve the arrangement provided the staffing level was the same as that which obtained at primary level. Though this initiative involved considerable additional work for the teachers, especially since no free periods were available for the preparation of lessons and marking student assignments, it was extremely successful, and this was the route through which several of our fine Catholic schools of today evolved to voluntary secondary status. The 'Secondary Tops' also provided a much-needed and significant service in certain provincial towns and suburban areas where there were no second-level schools. In particular, they played a crucial role in the future careers of many students from lower-income families, who, being unable to afford attendance at a boarding school, would, otherwise, have had no access to second-level education.

The sequence of the development of the present system of state aid to Catholic voluntary secondary schools, therefore, has progressed through several stages. Starting with the Intermediate Education Act of 1878, a system of payment by results was initiated. This was followed by the payment of incremental salaries to teachers in 1924. Then, with the introduction of free second-level education in 1967, the Department of Education initiated a system of capital grants for the provision of the necessary school buildings. All this state aid affected neither the private ownership of school buildings nor the denominational character of the education offered. Today, therefore, though the Department of Education has considerable prescriptive and regulatory powers in regard to these schools, having control over curriculum and assessment, it, nevertheless, provides state aid for capital as well as operational expenditure, including teachers' salaries, for what, in legal terms, are privately owned schools.

The present

In the early years, the teachers in second-level schools were drawn almost exclusively from the religious orders or congregations managing these schools, or from diocesan priests in the case of the 'junior seminaries', but, gradually, lay men and women were employed in small numbers. Following the Second Vatican Council and the start of the decline in religious vocations, the number of religious personnel in these schools decreased. At the same time, the enrolment in almost all of these schools increased rapidly, leading to many new teaching appointments, which went mainly to lay men and women. Student numbers in voluntary secondary schools jumped from 76,843 in 1961 to 157,234 in 1971 (Department of Education), while the number of teachers increased by 40% between 1968 and 1974 (Barry, 1984, 147). As the number of vocations to teaching congregations continued to fall, the religious personnel in second-level schools continued to decrease sharply. In voluntary secondary schools it was down to 50 per cent in 1966, fell to 34 per cent in 1971 (FIRE, 51) and to 10 per cent in 1993 (CORI, 1996). At present (1997), the vast majority of teachers in voluntary secondary schools, and increasingly the principals, are lay people. Some Catholic second-level schools now have no religious or clerics on the staff and, with fewer and fewer young people entering the religious life, and even fewer opting for a teaching career in second-level schools, all indications are that this change will not be reversed for a generation or two, if ever.

The future

Catholic schools of the future will, as far as we can see, be staffed almost exclusively by lay people, be administered by lay principals and will be managed by Boards of Management that will be almost totally lay. The trustees, for the foreseeable future, however, will be the local Bishops or members of the religious congregation involved. It is obvious, therefore, that Catholic lay men and women will, in practice, be the chief custodians of the ethos of Catholic schools in the future. A very important question, therefore, is: How are we helping these lay men and women prepare for this great task? I would suggest that there are two aspects to this preparation, one concerned with structures and the other with staff training and development. I would, moreover, contend that while we have made significant progress in developing appropriate structures for the future, we have been slow, if not negligent, in promoting staff training and development.

Planning new structures

Any historical survey of Catholic second-level education in recent years will point to the FIRE report (1973) as the source and inspiration of many of the policies of trustees in regard to the administration of these schools over the last quarter of a century. The FIRE (an abbreviation for The Future Involvement of Religious in Education) report was commissioned in 1972 by a joint body comprising the Irish Episcopal Commission on Post-primary Education and the Education Commission of the

Conference of Major Religious Superiors (now CORI). Its compilation was an act of foresight and wisdom.

The FIRE commission examined the state of Catholic post-primary education in Ireland at the time, envisaged the possible developments over the following quarter of a century and made appropriate recommendations. The implementation of the recommendations of the FIRE report was greatly facilitated by the fact that the trustees of the majority of the Catholic second-level schools were members of CORI – the main inspiration of the report and the body which, through its education commission, articulates and co-ordinates policy for Catholic second-level schools in Ireland. Among the policy changes recommended by the FIRE report and implemented by Catholic schools under religious trustees – though not to the same extent, perhaps, by the local bishops – were the sharing of management with parents and teachers through the introduction of Boards of Management, collaboration of small single-sex schools in provincial towns and suburban areas and the amalgamation of smaller single-sex schools to form either co-educational voluntary secondary or community schools. After long negotiations, Boards of Management were constituted in accordance with Articles of Management, jointly agreed by CORI, the Department of Education and ASTI, the teachers union to which the majority of teachers in voluntary secondary schools are affiliated.

The enlightened leadership in the CMRS, which led to the FIRE report and its implementation, has been continued by CORI through its education commission and education office. One of the more recent fruits of the pro-active work of this body is a trustee handbook, *The Trusteeship of Catholic Secondary Schools* (CORI, 1996), which takes a radical look at the future of trusteeship. This document states that it is 'guided by a recognition of the fact that many congregations are seeking ways of transferring their existing obligations, such as school trusteeship, to others'. Some of the ideas informing this thinking are explored in an article by Teresa McCormack elsewhere in this volume. The important point to remember, however, is that trustees are not considering abandoning their Catholic schools, or transferring them to the state or one of the VECs, but are actively involved in devising ways in which, despite the absence of a physical presence, they will be able to exercise the role of trustees 'pro-actively in schools so that their Congregation's religious and educational philosophy is a significant source of influence in the schools' (CORI, 1996, xi).

An important development in recent times has been the setting up of congregational education offices, especially by those congregations with significant involvement in education. In addition to developing expertise in educational administration and acquiring experience in problem solving, especially in the areas of trusteeship, Boards of Management and finances, it is hoped that these offices will promote staff development. In the counties Cork, Kerry and Limerick, the Christian Formation Resource Centre, set up in 1992 by trustees of voluntary secondary schools, was the model for and precursor of some of these congregational education offices, especially in the matter of staff development.

Effectiveness of Catholic schools

Before dealing with the training and development of personnel who are going to be responsible for Catholic education in Ireland in the future, I would like to look briefly at some of the recent studies of Catholic schools abroad. Though few studies have been done on the effectiveness of Catholic schools in Ireland, the same is not true of the USA, Australia and Britain. In 1993 Anthony S. Bryk, University of Chicago, and associates, published an important study, *Catholic Schools and the Common Good*. This and the work of other US researchers is reviewed by Andrew Greeley in chapter 13 of this volume. In brief, this research has shown that Catholic schools are making a unique contribution to the education of Americans, especially those from deprived backgrounds, and are doing this in a strikingly successful way. Bryk's research confirmed a conclusion of an earlier researcher, James Coleman, that Catholic schools are now doing what it was originally envisaged public schools would do but had not actually done (Bryk *et al.*, 1993, 57). Catholic schools in the USA are also succeeding in transforming themselves from educational institutions into communities of learning and are utilising the internal dynamics of community groups to achieve their educational aims (Greeley, 1997, 79).

In Australia, Marcellin Flynn has carried out some very significant research into the work of Catholic schools. This research has especially drawn attention to the influence of the 'hidden curriculum' in Catholic schools and has shown that this has a more powerful influence on students than even the formal curriculum, including religious education. Flynn's findings have highlighted the importance of school ethos as one of the most potent ways of influencing students, particularly at second level (Flynn, 1985, 296; 1993, 421). The ethos might be regarded as part of what US researchers have called the 'social capital' of Catholic schools (Greeley, 1997, 80).

In Britain also, in recent years, there have been some important studies of Catholic Schools, among which James Arthur's *The Ebbing Tide* (1995) has attracted not only interest but debate. Another important recent study is *The Contemporary Catholic School: Context, Identity and Diversity,* edited by Terence McLaughlin, Joseph O'Keefe SJ and Bernadette O'Keeffe (Falmer Press, 1996). One consequence of the great interest in Catholic schools in Britain, and one that is also an indication of the fact that this topic has attracted the attention of the academic world, is the setting up of a Centre for Research and Development in Catholic Education at the Institute of Education, University of London, one of the great centres for educational research and teaching in the English-speaking world. Professor Gerald Grace is director of this centre and is also one of the contributors to this volume.

If, therefore, there has been a new awakening of interest in and appreciation of Catholic schools in the three largest and most influential English-speaking countries in the world, it is more than likely that, in due course, something similar will occur in this country. Moreover, this interest in Catholic schools on the part of professional educationists is not due to any inherent interest in the Catholic religion, but is due to the remarkable success, as proved by empirical research, of these schools in meeting new educational challenges, especially those resulting from the unhelpful social and economic changes taking place in the world. There seems to be no good reason why Catholic schools in Ireland should not be able to render a service comparable to that rendered by their counterparts in the inner cities of the USA. To do this, however, Irish Catholic schools will not only have to organise themselves to meet the challenges ahead, but they will also have to achieve congruence between their words and their deeds. They will really have to do what they say (and have long said) they purport to do. And this brings us to the training and development of personnel.

Staff training and development

It is very clear from studies, such as those of Bryk and team in Chicago, that the success of Catholic schools in the USA is due not only to helpful and supportive structures but also to principals and teachers who know what they are doing and how to do it. Not, indeed, that the standard of tuition in secular subjects in these schools is significantly better than that in public schools, but, rather, that Catholic schools are characterised by an atmosphere of pastoral care and a deliberate attempt to create community (Bryk, 1996, 28-34). It is the skills and expertise that promote and foster these characteristics that are missing from much of our current staff development, but which must be included in future. Because of the high academic standards for entry to the teaching profession in Ireland, teachers are, in the main, well equipped to teach, as far as secular knowledge and information is concerned. The same is not true, however, in respect of Christian theology and interpersonal skills, especially those needed to relate to and influence young people.

There are no theology faculties in any of the Colleges of the National University of Ireland and the theological formation of many excellent teachers, including principals, came to an abrupt stop at the end of their second-level schooling. There is, consequently, a great imbalance between the level of their religious literacy and their general education and professional expertise as teachers. This poses serious problems when, as is now happening, and as will happen regularly in the future, a school staff is invited to examine the philosophy of the school, to formulate vision and mission statements and to work out aims and objectives in keeping with the Catholic ethos of the school. I am not here referring to an exercise in composition by a few articulate people. Rather, I have in mind putting in place a process, involving not only all members of staff, but also, members of the entire school community, in the course of which the vision of the founder will be re-examined, discussed and re-stated in contemporary language. Following this, the same process must be used to formulate a mission statement, after which, aims and objectives can be agreed. To ensure that all this work does not remain at the conceptual level, concrete steps must be listed as a means of embodying the aims and objectives.

When new teachers are being engaged, they have a right to see the vision and mission statements, as well as the aims and objectives, so that they can make a conscious decision to associate themselves with the mission of that particular school. While, in the past, acceptance of the philosophy and mission of the school could be assumed, either because the applicant was personally known to the principal of the school, or acceptance was conveyed by means of some cryptic or non-verbal signal, understood by both principal and teacher, it is nowadays necessary to spell this matter out.

The majority of our Catholic schools were founded during a period of virtually universal religious practice, when religious values were taken for granted. In this period, it was also taken for granted that evangelisation was the primary *raison d'être* of a Catholic school. The founders of these schools were motivated by considerations of charity and service. They were continuing a tradition begun by eighteenth- and nineteenth-century founders such as Nano Nagle, Edmund Rice, Catherine McAuley, Mary Aikenhead and others. These schools grew and flourished, and their administration is now in the hands of a new generation of teachers, not all of whom have, as yet, fully internalised the values of these founders. We are now faced with a new challenge: to enable these schools to articulate a vision, forge a rationale and put supporting structures in place which will see them through the next century. The ideals of the original founders need to be restated in contemporary language, using contemporary metaphors, if they are to be spiritually nourishing.

Evidence from overseas has underlined the contribution relevant research can make in supporting those people involved in managing, leading and teaching in Catholic schools. This, unfortunately, is a point that needs constant repetition, if not labouring. Though much effort has been invested in building and staffing Catholic schools in this country, very little effort has been devoted to articulating a Catholic philosophy of education. Kavanagh attributes the comparatively little attention given to research and policy development, not only in the Catholic Church but even in the Department of Education, to the fact that the second-level school population has been expanding steadily for almost forty years and most of the resources were devoted to the actual provision of schooling, with little left for more long term research, review and planning (Kavanagh, 1993, 2). In the future, however, not only the 'how' but also the 'why' of Catholic education will have to be the subject of ongoing high quality research.

Critique of Catholic schools
James Arthur, whose important critical study (*The Ebbing Tide*) of Catholic schools in England was mentioned above, proposes a schema for the classification of Catholic schools in England. Though I readily recognise that conditions are very different in our two countries, Catholic schools being only a tiny minority in England but an overwhelming majority here, nevertheless, Arthur's schema and terminology can help us not only to see our schools in a wider perspective, but may also provide an instrument with which to critique them.

Arthur divides Catholic schools in England into three categories: dualistic, holistic and pluralistic. At present we have few, if any, Catholic schools that would meet the criteria advanced for classification as pluralistic, so, in the interests of saving space, I will omit this category from my brief consideration. Arthur's next category is dualistic schools. The underlying reality of the dualistic Catholic school is that, although it is a single institution, it conducts two separate activities within itself. Arthur says:

> The 'dualistic' model separates the secular and religious aims of the school – not only in its teaching, structures and practices, but also in the minds of its pupils. On this model there are two realities set together – one specifically Christian and the other secular…. The Catholic ethos of the school is seen as something additional. (Arthur, 1995, 227)

Arthur's holistic Catholic school stands out in sharp contrast to the dualistic one. The holistic school attempts to form policies that follow post-Conciliar principles, viewing the school as an educational setting within which a critical synthesis should occur between culture and the Catholic religious vision. In claiming to be Catholic, the school commits itself to pursuing the meaning, values and truths specific to the Catholic faith. On this model, the Catholic school does not merely provide that which other schools fail to provide, nor is its purpose to be a shelter from the world. Rather, it seeks to establish a partnership with parents in being the seed-ground for the apostolic mission of the Church. In the words of Arthur:

> This model views the Catholic school as being inspired by the unifying vision of Christ, and as being integrally bound up with the work of the Church, which gives it its special character, a character which resides in the possibility of teachers, pupils and parents uniting as a community around a Catholic conception of school life inspired by the Gospel and the Church. The Catholicity of the school depends on there being a body of people whose lives are imbued by the Catholic faith, and who are therefore able to bring the light of Christ into every aspect of school life. (Arthur, 1995, 231)

The Irish situation

While not wishing to delay unduly in this section of the paper, I think it would be very helpful for the principal and staff to examine their school with a view to ascertaining where they see themselves in the continuum between the holistic and dualistic categories. There is some potential in Arthur's schema for the evaluation of schools from the point of view of how well they fulfil their primary purpose, which all official statements agree is evangelisation – in practice as well as in theory. Any such evaluation must, of course, not only be based on the analysis of external criteria, but must also take the spirit of the school and the personal influence of the principal and staff into account. The 1977 Roman document, *The Catholic School* (CS), emphasises this point: 'The extent to which the Christian message is transmitted through education depends to a very great extent on the teachers. The integration of culture and faith is mediated by the other integration of faith and life in the person of the teacher' (CS, 1977, 16-17, No. 43). Moreover, Arthur's holistic school is, to some extent, another name for the ideal Catholic school, and, in an imperfect world, one cannot hope to encounter the ideal very often, if ever.

In the absence of empirical studies, and of necessity relying on personal experience only, I would hazard a guess that the majority of Catholic schools in Ireland fall somewhere between the holistic and the dualistic categories. It is difficult to think of a school that meets all the requirements of the holistic category, while I can think of many that, though striving to be holistic, fall some way short of it, yet are not fully dualistic either. This does not mean, however, that many of the features of the dualistic school are not to be found in the average Irish Catholic second-level school. One of these features is the apparent over-concern with examination results. The founders of many of these schools, especially those originally catering for students from more deprived backgrounds, were very anxious to present tangible proofs of their schools' effectiveness, especially in the areas of examination results and sporting achievements. This was necessary for the self-esteem of both students and teachers, who were concerned to show that they were as good as students and teachers in the more exclusive boarding, 'private' and diocesan colleges. The cumulative effect of this over-concern with results has been to place a high value on material success, thereby providing a fertile ground for the 'points race', which is of more recent origin. There is no denying, however, that long before the advent of the 'points race', there was extremely keen competition among Catholic voluntary secondary schools for outward symbols of academic success, such as university scholarships. Perhaps this was one of the sins of commission?

McClelland has also noted this weakness in respect of Catholic schools in England:

> The weakness of the Catholic school, however, has often been its inability to establish a confident internal polity that eschews that element of divisiveness inherent in the attempt to develop practices operating in secular schools: aggressive competition, the premium placed upon worldly success, the use of selfish rewards ... the need for outward conformity in social attitudes. (McClelland, 1991, 173)

Conclusion

In conclusion, therefore, we might say that while, at second level, many comprehensive and community schools are virtually Catholic, the only *de jure* Catholic schools in Ireland are those classified as voluntary secondary. There would appear to be a promising future for these schools for several reasons. Though not without weaknesses in the past and the present, they have a good record of service. They are esteemed not only for the religious and character formation they provide, but also for the high academic standards they have established and the success they enjoy in motivating their students. The trustees of these schools have shown that they are pro-active, are anticipating the social changes likely to come about in the future and are actively planning to adapt the management of the schools to meet these changes. The education commission of CORI, including its secretariat education office, has been the cutting edge of this pro-active work.

In addition to the Catholic voluntary secondary schools, which are *de jure* Catholic, there are many comprehensive, community and VEC schools that are virtually or *de facto* Catholic. By this I mean that the vast majority of the students and teachers are Catholic, that the school has a Catholic chaplain, that religious education is an integral part of the school curriculum and that the ethos of the school is virtually, if not expressly Catholic. It is, nevertheless, true that these schools are designed to cater for students of all denominations and that their Catholic ethos is dependent on the teachers and parents of the students for the time being. If, therefore, at some future time, the religious affiliation of the people in the catchment area were to change significantly, so, surely and inevitably, would the ethos of the school. It is in the event of this happening in the future that we must envisage the possibility of some, or even many, of the present community, comprehensive and VEC schools becoming, in the future, what Arthur calls 'pluralistic' schools. If we accept that what can happen will probably happen, it is important to ensure that voluntary secondary schools survive, since, at some future date, they may be the only Catholic schools available.

We have also noted a new appreciation of Catholic schools abroad, especially in the USA, Australia and Britain, arising from the results of empirical research which found Catholic schools to be remarkably successful. They were found to be especially successful in creating school communities out of educational institutions. This success is even more striking with children in deprived communities.

There are, however, many challenges facing Catholic schools. These challenges include supporting management and teachers with relevant and quality research, creating an effective middle management, and promoting widespread, relevant and effective staff training and development. There must be ongoing evaluation of and in all Catholic schools with a view to helping them discover how effective they are in realising their aims and objectives. They have always been good at conceptualising. Now they must put appropriate performance indicators in place so that they can see in what ways they are successful in living out their mission statements – and in what ways they fail to do so. In the final analysis, young people are evangelised in school only by teachers who are, themselves, convinced believers. It was Paul IV who said, 'Modern man listens more willingly to witnesses than to teachers, and if he does listen to teachers, it is because they are also witnesses' (Paul VI, 1975, 52, par. 14).

Greeley reports that some bishops and clergy in the US have

neglected Catholic schools for the simple reason that they find it too much trouble to raise funds to support them, even though the money would be forthcoming if sought (Greeley, 1997, 78). In Ireland, this situation is unlikely to arise in view of the fact that Catholic schools are generously endowed by the state. However, even if this were not so, there are many parents who would be willing to make sacrifices to support these schools for the sake of a Catholic education for their children. Catholic schools in the English-speaking world were conceived and born, not with the help of state aid, but in the absence of it. And it was the English bishops, in a period of great poverty and hardship for the Catholic community after the restoration of the hierarchy in 1850, who penned one of the most moving and unequivocal appeals on record on behalf of Catholic schools:

> Do not rest until you see this want supplied; prefer the establishment of good schools to every other work. Indeed, whenever there may seem to be an opening for a new mission, we should prefer the erection of a school, so arranged as to serve temporarily as a chapel, to that of a church without one. (Bishops, 1997, 117)

This is a statement that all trustees, principals and Boards of Management of Catholic schools could, with benefit, reread and ponder.

BIBLIOGRAPHY

Introduction

Arthur, J., *The Ebbing Tide* (Leominster: Gracewing, 1995).

Bryk, A.S., Lee, V.E. and Holland, P.B., *Catholic Schools and the Common Good* (Harvard: Harvard University Press, 1993).

Congregation for Catholic Education, *The Catholic School* (London: Catholic Truth Society, 1977). *Lay Catholics in Schools: Witnesses to Faith* (London: Catholic Truth Society, 1882) *The Religious Dimension of Education in a Catholic School.* Dublin: (Veritas, 1988).

CORI. *The Trusteeship of Catholic Voluntary Secondary Schools.* (Dublin: CORI, 1996).

Department of Education, *List of Second-Level Schools* (Dublin: Department of Education, 1995/96).

Flynn, M., *The Effectiveness of Catholic Schools* (Homebush, NSW: St Paul, 1985).

Flynn, M., *The Culture of Catholic Schools* (Homebush, NSW: St Paul, 1993).

Gardner, H., *Frames of Mind. The Theory of Multiple Intelligences* (New York: Fontana, 1993).

John Paul II, *Catechesis in our Time (Catechesi tradendae)* (Slough: St Paul, 1982).

McLaughlin, T.H., 'The Distinctiveness of Catholic Education', in McLaughlin, T.H. (1996), O'Keefe, J. and O'Keeffe, B. *The Contemporary Catholic School* (London: Falmer, 1966).

Vatican II, *Declaration on Christian Education (Gravissimum educationis)* (Washington, DC: National Welfare Conference, 1965).

Chapter 1: The Crucifix in the Classroom

Arthur, J., *The Ebbing Tide: Policy and Principles of Catholic Education* (Leominster: Gracewing, 1995).

Bosch, D. J., *Transforming Mission: Paradigm Shifts in Theology of Mission* (Maryknoll, NY: Orbis Books, 1992).

Bryk, A. S., Lee, V. E., and Holland, P. B., *Catholic Schools and the Common Good* (Cambridge: Harvard University Press, 1993).

Bryk, A. S., 'Lessons from Catholic High Schools', in

McLaughlin, T., O'Keefe, J. and O'Keeffe, B. (eds.), *The Contemporary Catholic School: Context, Identity and Diversity* (London: Falmer Press, 1996).

Coleman, J. S., 'Schools and Communities', in *Chicago Studies* 28.3. November 1989.

Cooper, B., 'National Crisis, Catholic Schools, and the Common Good', in McLaughlin, T., O Keefe, J. and O Keeffe, B. (eds.), *The Contemporary Catholic School: Context, Identity, and Diversity* (London: Falmer, 1996).

Cross, F. L. and Livingstone, E. A., *The Oxford Dictionary of the Catholic Church* (London: Oxford University Press, 1974).

Gallagher, M. P., *Questions of Faith* (Dublin: Veritas, 1997).

Gilkey, L., *Catholicism Confronts Modernity: a Protestant View* (New York: Seabury, 1975).

Groome, T. H., 'What makes a school Catholic?' in McLaughlin, T., O'Keefe, J. and O'Keeffe, B. (eds.), *The Contemporary Catholic School: Context, Identity and Diversity* (London: Falmer, 1996).

Haldane, J., 'Catholic Education and Catholic Identity', in McLaughlin, T. O'Keefe, J. and O'Keeffe, B. (eds.), *The Contemporary Catholic School: Context, Identity, and Diversity* (London: Falmer, 1996).

Lane, D., 'Afterword: The Expanding Horizons of Catholic Education' in Hogan, P. and Williams, K. (eds.), *The Future of Religion in Irish Education* (Dublin: Veritas, 1996).

Lesko, N., *Symbolizing Society: Stories, Rites and Structure in a Catholic High School* (London: Falmer, 1988).

McDonagh, J., 'Catholic Education and Evaluation', in *Papers Presented at a Conference on The Catholic School in Contemporary Society* (Dublin: CMRS, 1991).

Murray, D., *A Special Concern: the Philosophy of Education: A Christian Perspective* (Dublin: Veritas, 1991).

Murray, V., 'Other Faiths in Catholic Schools: General Implications of a Case Study', in McLaughlin, T., O'Keefe, J. and O'Keeffe, B. (eds.), *The Contemporary Catholic School: Context, Identity and Diversity* (London: Falmer, 1996).

O'Donnell, C. *Ecclesia: A Theological Encyclopedia of the Church* (Collegeville: Liturgical Press, 1996).

O'Keeffe, B., 'Catholic Schools in an Open Society: The English Challenge', in McClelland, V. A. (ed.), *The Catholic School and the European Context, Aspects of Education,* Journal of the Institute of Education (Hull: University of Hull, 1992).

O'Keeffe, B., 'Beacons of Hope' in *The Tablet,* 24 May 1997.

Report to the Bishops of England and Wales, *Signposts and Homecomings: the Educative Task of the Catholic Community* (Slough: St Paul, 1981).

Sacred Congregation for Catholic Education, *The Catholic School* (1977).

Sacred Congregation for Catholic Education, *Lay Catholics in Schools: Witnesses to Faith* (1982).

Sacred Congregation for Catholic Education, *The Religious Dimension of Education in a Catholic School: Guidelines for Reflection and Renewal* (1988).

Seymour, J. L., O'Gorman, R. L. and Foster, C. R., *The Church in the Education of the Public: Refocusing the Task of Religious Education* (Nashville, Abingdon Press, 1984).

Chapter 2: The Operative Goals of a Catholic School – A Case Study

Andrews, P. (1994), 'Pluralism Revisited', *Studies,* Vol. 83, No. 330, summer 1994.

Buetow, H. A.: *The Catholic School: Its Roots, Identity and Future* (New York: Crossroad, 1988). Cited in Ramsay, W. and Clark, E. E., *New Ideas for Effective School Improvement* (London: Falmer, 1990).

Clare, J., 'Catholic Schools Do Well', *The Tablet,* 10 February 1996.

Coleman, J. S., Hoffer, T. and Kilgore, S., *High School Achievement: Public, Catholic and Private Schools Compared* (Chicago: University of Chicago Press, 1981).

Coleman, J. S. and Hoffer, T., *Public and Private High Schools: The Impact of Communities* (New York: Basic Books, 1987).

Ester, P., Halman, L. and deMoor, R., *The Individualizing Society: Value Change in Europe and North America* (Tilburg: Tilburg University Press, 1994).

Flynn, M., *The Effectiveness of Catholic Schools* (Homebush, NSW: St Pauls, 1985).

Flynn, M., *The Culture of Catholic Schools* (Homebush, NSW: St Pauls, 1993).

Fogarty, M., Ryan, L. and Lee, J., *Irish Values and Attitudes: The Irish Report of the European Value Systems Study* (Dublin: Dominican Publications, 1984).

Greeley, A. M., *The Catholic Myth, the Behaviour and Beliefs of American Catholics* (New York: Collier Books, Macmillan, 1990).

Greeley, A. M., 'Are the Irish Really Losing the Faith?', *Doctrine and Life*, March 1994, pp. 132-42.

Hogan, P., 'Schooling, Religious Tradition and the Default of God', *The Furrow*, July 1985.

Lane, D., *Catholic Education and the School – Some Theological Reflections* (Dublin: Veritas, 1991).

Lambert, R., Millham, S. and Bullock, R., *Manual to the Sociology of the School* (London: Weidenfeld & Nicholson, 1970).

MacMahon, B., *Listening to Youth: The Views of Irish Youth on Their Religion* (Dublin: Dominican Publications, 1987).

McGreil, M., S J, 'The Social Tasks of Education', *Studies*, Vol. 83, No. 330, summer 1994.

OECD, *Report: Review of National Policies for Education – Ireland* (Paris: OECD Publications, 1991).

Sachs, J., *The Persistence of Faith* (London: Weidenfeld & Nicholson, 1991).

Sacred Congregation for Catholic Education, Rome, *The Catholic School* (London: Catholic Truth Society, 1977).

Whelan, C. (ed.), *Values and Social Change in Ireland* (Dublin: Gill & Macmillan, 1994).

Chapter 3: Religion, Culture and Schooling

Bhreathnach, N., 'Towards a Coherent Philosophy of Education', *Irish Education Decision Maker* (8: 4-10, 1994).

Congregation for Catholic Education, *Religious Dimension of Education in a Catholic School: Guidelines for Reflection and Renewal* (London: Catholic Truth Society, 1988).

Coutty, M. 'Laïcité, Passion Francaise', *Le Monde de l'Education, de la Culture et de la Formation*, 246, March 1977.

Department of Education/An Roinn Oideachais, *Memorandum V. 40; Organisation of Whole-time Continuation Courses in*

Borough, Urban and County Areas (Dublin: Department of Education, 1942).

Department of Education/An Roinn Oideachais, 'Notes on the Teaching of Civics' (Dublin: Department of Education, 1966).

Department of Education/An Roinn Oideachais, *Curraclam na Bunscoile: Lámhleabhar an Oide/Primary School Curriculum*: Teacher's Handbook (Dublin: The Stationery Office, 1977).

Department of Education/An Roinn Oideachais, *Rules and Programme for Secondary Schools* (Dublin: The Stationery Office, 1986/87).

Government of Ireland, *Education for A Changing World: Green Paper on Education* (Dublin: The Stationery Office, 1992).

Government of Ireland, *Charting Our Education Future: White Paper on Education* (Dublin: The Stationery Office, 1995).

Hyland Á. and Milne, K., *Irish Educational Documents*, vol. 1 (Dublin: The Church of Ireland College of Education, 1987).

Hyland Á. and Milne, K., *Irish Educational Documents*, vol. 11 (Dublin: The Church of Ireland College of Education, 1992).

Johnson, R., 'The Schooling of the English Working Class, 1780-1850', in Roger Dale, Geoff Esland and Madeleine MacDonald (eds.), *Schooling and Capitalism* (London and Henley: Routledge and Kegan Paul/Open University Press, 1976).

McLaughlin, T. H., 'Education for All' and Religious Schools in G. Haydon (ed.), *Education for a Pluralist Society: Philosophical Perspectives on the Swann Report*, Bedford Way Paper No. 30 (London: University of London, Institute of Education, 1987).

Oakeshott, M., *On Human Conduct* (Oxford: Clarendon Press, 1975).

Whitehead, A. N., *Religion in The Making* (Cambridge: Cambridge University Press, 1926).

Williams, K., 'Religious Ethos and State Schools', *Doctrine and Life*, 42, 9: 561-70, 1992.

Williams, K., 'Practical Learning: a Neglected Aspect of a Christian Education?', *Doctrine and Life*, 44, 2: 100-5, 1994.

Williams, K., 'State Support for Church Schools; Is It Justifiable?' *Studies in Education*, 11, 1: 37-47, 1995.

Williams, K., 'Parents' Rights and the Integrated Curriculum, *Doctrine and Life*, 47, 3: 142-50, 1997a.

Williams, K., 'Religion in Irish Education: Recent Trends in Government Policy', in Pádraig Hogan and Kevin Williams (eds.), *The Future of Religion in Irish Education* (Dublin: Veritas, 1997).

Chapter 4: The School as an Agent of Evangelisation
Arbuckle, G. A., *Earthing the Gospel: An Inculturation Handbook for Pastoral Workers* (Homebush, NSW: St Paul, 1990).
Archdiocese of Brisbane, *Becoming a More Evangelising Parish: A Resource for Leaders* (Brisbane, 1994).
Buetow, H. A., *The Catholic School: Its Roots, Identity and Future* (New York: Crossroad, 1988).
Crawford, M. and Rossiter, G., *Missionaries to a Teenage Culture: Religious Education in a Time of Rapid Change* (Sydney: Christian Brothers Province Resource Group, 1988).
Dulles, A., 'Seven Essentials of Evangelisation', *Origins* 25: 23, 1995.
Dwyer, B., *Catholic Schools: Creating a New Culture* (Newtown, NSW: E. J. Dwyer, 1993).
Flynn, M., *The Culture of Catholic Schools: A Study of Catholic Schools: 1972-1993* (Homebush, NSW: St Pauls, 1993).
Groome, T. H., 'What Makes a School Catholic?' in McLaughlin, T., O'Keefe, J. & O'Keeffe, B., *The Contemporary Catholic School: Context, Identity and Diversity* (London: Falmer, 1996).
Habermas, J., *The Theory of Communicative Action: The Critique of Functional Reason*, Vol. 2 (Boston: Beacon Press, 1987).
Haldane, J., 'Catholic Education and Catholic Identity' in McLaughlin, T., O'Keefe, J. & O'Keeffe, B., *The Contemporary Catholic School: Context, Identity and Diversity* (London: Falmer, 1996).
Johnston, K., & Chesterton, P., *The Poor and Catholic Schools* (Sydney: Conference of Leaders of Religious Institutes, NSW, 1994).
Knight, J., 'The Political Economy of Industrial Relations in the Australian Education Industry 1987-1991', *Unicorn*, November 1992, Vol. 18, No. 4, 1992.
Lane, D. A., *Catholic Education and the School: Some Theological Reflections* (Dublin: Veritas, 1991).

Ó Murchú, D., *Our World in Transition: Making Sense of a Changing World* (Sussex: Temple House Books, 1995).

Ó Murchú, D., *Quantum Theology: Spiritual Implications of the New Physics* (New York: Crossroad, 1997).

Sobrino, J., *The True Church and the Poor* (London: SCM, 1985).

Tarnas, R., *The Passion of the Western Mind: Understanding the Ideas That Have Shaped Our World View* (New York: Ballantine Books, 1991).

Treston, K., *Transforming Catholic Schools: Visions and Practices for Renewal* (Brisbane: Creation Enterprises, 1992).

Chapter 5: Teaching Religion to Young People Today

CCEA., *Religious Studies 1997, Draft Syllabus and Coursework Memorandum, Proposals for Consultation.* (Belfast, 1994).

Gallagher, M. P., 'New Forms of Cultural Unbelief' in Hogan P. and K. Williams (eds.), *The Future of Religion in Irish Education* (Dublin: Veritas, 1997, pp. 19-31).

Lane, D. A., 'The challenge facing Religious Education today' in D. Lane (ed.), *Religious Education and the Future* (Dublin: Columba, 1985).

National Council for Curriculum and Assessment, *Redraft Syllabuses for Religious Education* (Dublin: NCCA, 1997).

McCourt, F., *Angela's Ashes* (London: HarperCollins, 1996).

Murray, D. 'The Role of the Catholic School' in D. Murphy and V. Rice (eds.), *Studies in Education*, Vol. 11, No. 1, 1-13.

Rahner, K., 'Foreward' in D. Fennell (ed.), *The Changing Face of Catholic Ireland* (Dublin: Geoffrey Chapman, 1968).

Sealey, J., *Religious Education: Philosophical Perspectives* (London: George Allen & Unwin, 1985).

Scottish Office Education Department, *Religious and Moral Education*, 5-14 (Edinburgh, 1992)

Scottish Office Education Department/Scottish Catholic Education Commission, *Religious and Moral Education*, 5-14 (Catholic Schools), Consultation Document (Edinburgh, 1992).

Watson, B., *The Effective Teaching of RE* (London: Longman, 1993).

Weafer, J. & Hanley, A., *Whither Religious Education?* (Dublin: Columba, 1989).

Chapter 6: Pastoral Care in a Catholic School Today

ASTI (1997), Statement on Relationships and Sexuality Education, *The Irish Times*, 20 June 1997.

Bryk, A. S., 'Lessons from Catholic High Schools on Renewing our Educational Institutions', in McLaughlin, T., O'Keefe, J. & O'Keeffe, B., *The Contemporary Catholic School: Context, Identity and Diversity* (London: Falmer, 1996).

Button, L., *Group Tutoring for the Form Teacher: 2, Upper Secondary School* (London: Hodder & Stoughton, 1986).

Congregation for Catholic Education, *The Catholic School* (London: Catholic Truth Society, 1977).

Cotterell, J., *Social Networks and Social Influences in Adolescence* (London: Routledge, 1996).

Department of Education, *List of Second Level Schools* (Dublin: Department of Education, 1995).

Doyle, P., 'Department of Education Circular re Relationships and Sexuality Education, March, 1997' (Dublin: Department of Education, 1997).

Egan, E., 'Report of the Expert Advisory Group on Relationships and Sexuality Education, July 1994' (Dublin: Department of Education, 1994).

Feheney, J. M., *Pastoral Care Workbook: Senior Cycle* (Dublin: Folens, 1994).

Feheney, J. M., *Pastoral Care – Teachers' Manual* (Dublin: Folens, 1994).

Gardner, H., *Frames of Mind: The Theory of Multiple Intelligences* (London: Heinemann, 1984).

Gardner, H., *Reflections on Multiple Intelligences: Myths and Messages* (USA: Phi Delta Kappa, 1995).

Griffiths, P. and K. Sherman, *The Form Tutor: New Approaches to Tutoring in the 1990s* (Oxford: Blackwell, 1991).

Hamblin, D., *A Pastoral Programme* (Oxford: Blackwell, 1986).

Hamblin, D., 'Pastoral Care: Past, Present and Future', in *Pastoral Care in Education*, Vol. 11, No. 4,1993.

Hume, Cardinal Basil , 'Building Bridges', in *Partners in Mission* (London: Catholic Education Service, 1997).

Leader, D. and S. Boldt, *Principals and Principalship: A Study of Principals in Voluntary Secondary Schools* (Dublin: Marino Institute of Education, 1994).

Marland, M., *Pastoral Care* (London: Heinemann, 1974).

McGahern, J., 'Schooldays: A Time of Grace' in Feheney, J. M. (ed.), *A Time of Grace* (Dublin: Veritas, 1996).

Treston, K., *Pastoral Care for Schools* (Melbourne: Creation Enterprises, 1989).

Chapter 8: Children of a Lesser God

Department of Education, Circular Letters M31/93 and M47/93 (Dublin: Department of Education, 1993).

Department of Education, *Transition Year Programmes – Guidelines for Schools* (Dublin: Government Publications Office, 1994).

Drudy, S. and Lynch, K., *Schools and Society in Ireland* (Dublin: Gill & Macmillan, 1993).

ESF, *Early School Leavers: Evaluation Report* (Dublin: European Social Fund, 1996).

Feheney, J. M., 'Memorandum Concerning Nagle-Rice Educational Project', unpublished document, 9 April 1993 (Cork: CFRC Office, 1993).

Fleischmann, A., 'Nagle-Rice Educational Project: Report', unpublished reports (Cork: CFRC Office, 1994, 1995, 1996).

Gardner, H., *Frames of Mind: The Theory of Multiple Intelligences* (London: Heinemann, 1983).

Gardner, H. (1990), 'Foreword' in Lazear, D., *Seven Ways of Knowing* (Illinois: IRI/Skylight, 1990).

Gardner, H., *Multiple Intelligences: The Theory in Practice* (New York: Basic Books, 1993).

Gardner, H., Kornhaber, M. L. and Wake, W. K., *Intelligence: Multiple Perspectives* (New York: Holt, Reinhart and Winston Inc., 1996).

Gleeson, J. and G. Granville, 'The Case of the Leaving Certificate Applied', *Irish Educational Studies*, Vol. 15, spring 1996, 113-32, 1996.

Hannon, D. and Shorthall, S., *The Quality of their Education*, ESRI, Paper No. 153 (Dublin: ESRI, 1991).

Lazear, D., *Seven Ways of Teaching* (Illinois: IRI/Skylight, 1991).

McNiff, J., *Action Research: Theory and Practice* (London: Routledge, 1992).

NCCA, 'Leaving Certificate Applied Programme' Position Paper, NCCA Steering Committee, December 1993.

OECD, 'Review of National Policies for Education' (Paris: OECD, 1991).

Shores, EF, 'Interview with Howard Gardner' in *Dimensions of Early Childhood,* vol.23, nos.4, 5-7, summer, 1995.

Chapter 9: Feminism in the Catholic Church

Butler, J., *Gender Trouble: Feminism and the Subversion of Identity* (London: Routledge, 1990).

Flax, J., *Thinking Fragments: Psychoanalysis, Feminism and Postmodernism in the Contemporary West* (Berkeley: University of California Press, 1990).

Fuss, D., *Essentially Speaking: Feminism, Nature and Difference* (London: Routledge, 1990).

Graham, E., *Making the Difference: Gender, Personhood and Theology* (London: Mowbray, 1995).

ICEL, 'The Problem of Exclusive Language With Regard to Women', printed as Liturgical Note 26 in *Liturgical Calendar* for Ireland 1992/1993 (Dublin: Veritas, 1992).

Johnson, E., *She Who Is: The Mystery of God in Feminist Theological Discourse* (New York: Crossroad, 1993).

Kaufman, G., *The Theological Imagination: Constructing the Concept of God* (Philadelphia: Westminster, 1981).

Keller, C., *From a Broken Web: Separation, Sexism and Self* (Boston: Beacon, 1986).

Kloppenborg, J., 'Isis and Sophia in the Book of Wisdom', *Harvard Theological Review* 75:57-84, 1982.

Lerner, G., *The Creation of Patriarchy* (Oxford: Oxford University Press, 1985).

Morgan, D.H.J., *Discovering Men* (London: Routledge, 1992).

Pataq-Siman, E., *L'Expérience de l'Esprit d'après la tradition Syrienne d'Antioche* (Paris: Beauchesne, 1971).

Trible, P., *God and the Rhetoric of Sexuality* (Philadelphia: Fortress, 1978).

Chapter 10: Changing Roles of Trustees and Boards of Management

CORI, *Education Bill 1997: An Analysis* (Dublin: CORI Education Commission, 1997).

CORI, *The Trusteeship of Catholic Voluntary Secondary Schools: A Handbook for the Leaders of Religious Congregations* (Dublin: CORI Education Commission, 1996).

Education Bill (Dublin: Government Stationery Office, (1997).

Education Bill (1997) First List of Amendments (Dublin: Department of Education, 1997).

Green Paper: Education for a Changing World (Dublin: Stationery Office, 1992).

Lane, D., 'Afterword – The Expanding Horizons of Catholic Education', in P. Hogan and K. Williams (eds.), *The Future of Religion in Irish Education* (Dublin: Veritas, 1997).

Tussing, A. D., *Irish Educational Expenditure – Past, Present, and Future* (Dublin: ESRI, Paper no. 92, 1978).

Vatican Congregation for Catholic Education, *The Religious Dimension of Education in a Catholic School* (Dublin: Veritas, 1988).

White Paper, *Charting our Education Future* (Dublin: Stationery Office, 1995).

Chapter 11: Staff Development as Empowering and Enabling

Adey, K. and Jones, J., 'The Professional Coordinator: Obstacles To Effective Role Performance', in *Educational Management & Administration*, Vol. 25, No. 2, pp. 133-144, 1997.

Apple, M. and Beare, J., *Democratic Schools* (Virginia: ASCD, 1995).

Aronowitz, S. and Giroux, H. A., *Education Still Under Siege* (Westport, Connecticut: Bergin and Garvey, 1993).

ASTI (1997), 'Inservice Training for Facilitators: Evaluation Report, 1996-97'; 'Minutes of the Central Executive Council (CEC) 1960-80'; Minutes of the Standing Committee, 1967-90; *The Secondary Teacher: Official Journal of the ASTI*, 1966-68; *The Secondary Teacher: Journal of the ASTI*, 1968-97.

Baccharach, S. B. and Mundell, B. (eds.), *Images of Schools: Structures and Roles in Organisational Behaviour* (California: Corwin Press, 1995).

Barber, M., *The Learning Game: Arguments for an Education Revolution* (London: Victor Gollancz, 1996).

Boyle, W., 'Building on Hidden Talent', in *Managing Schools Today*, Vol. 6, No. 3, pp. 18-24, 1996.

Calderhead, J. and Shorroch, S. B., *Understanding Teacher-Education: Case Studies in the Professional Development of Beginning Teachers* (London: Falmer, 1997).

Callan, J., *Schools for Active Learning: Final Report* (Maynooth, St Patrick's College, 1994).

Carrivick, S. E. and O'Donoghue, T. A., 'Principals' Perceptions of their Role in Enabling Teachers to Inform their Practice with Educational Research', in *Research in Education: An Interdisciplinary, International Research Journal*, Vol. 57, May, pp. 36-4, Manchester University Press, 1997.

Cavaleri, S. and Fearon, D. (eds), *Managing in Organisations that Learn* (London: Blackwell, 1996).

CCSS, Archival material, including Reports of Executive Meetings and Annual General Meetings, 1929-1988.

Charting our Education Future: White Paper on Education (Dublin: Stationery Office, 1995).

CMRS, *FIRE:* Report by the Working Party on the Future Involvement of Religious in Education (1973).

CMRS, *Report on Adult Education* (1977).

CMRS, Report of the Working Party on Religious as Employers in Secondary Schools (1978).

CORI, *The Trusteeship of Catholic Voluntary Secondary Schools: Handbook for the Leaders of Religious Congregations* (1996).

Council of Europe, Council for Cultural Co-operation (CDCC), 'The Development of Human Resources for Secondary Education in Europe: Teaching and non-Teaching Staff – Today and Tomorrow,' Report of seminar, Portugal, 1996.

Crease, M. and Bradley, H., 'Ways in which Governing Bodies Contribute to School Improvement: Findings from a Pilot Project', in *School Leadership and Management*, Vol. 17, No. 1, pp. 105-15, 1997.

Danielson, C., *Enhancing Professional Practice: A Framework for Teaching* (ASCD, 1996).

Diggins, P. B., 'Reflections on Leadership Characteristics

Necessary to Develop and Sustain Learning School Communities', Paper delivered at the Summer Institute, Uppsala University, Sweden (1996).

Diggins, P. B., Doyle, E., Herron, D., *Whole School Development* (Dublin: Drumcondra Teachers' Centre and West Dublin Teachers' Centre, 1996).

Doyle, E., *Directory of In-Service Education* (Dublin: Secretariat of Secondary Schools, 1985).

Duffy, D., 'Inservice Training and the Internal Management of Post Primary Schools', in *Irish Educational Studies,* Vol. 14, spring 1990, pp. 278-285.

Earley, P., *School Governing Bodies Making Progress?* NFER, 1994.

Education Bill (1997).

Esp, D. and Saran, R., *Effective Governors for Effective Schools* (London: Pitman, 1995).

Evans, L., 'A voice Crying in the Wilderness? The Problems and Constraints facing 'Extended' Professionals in the English Primary Education Sector', in *Teachers and Teaching: Theory and Practice,* Vol. 3, No. 1, pp. 61-83, 1997.

Farrelly, F.P., 'School-based Staff Development in a Selected Sample of Voluntary Secondary Schools in the Republic of Ireland.' Unpublished M. Ed. Dissertation, Maynooth, 1987.

Fidler, B., 'Inaugural Editorial: The Priorities of the Journal', in *School Leadership and Management,* Vol. 17, No. 1, pp. 5-8, 1997.

Fielding, M., 'Delivery, Packages and the Denial of Learning: Reversing the Language and Practice of Contemporary INSET', in Bradley, H., Conner, C. and Southworth, G. (eds.), *Developing Teachers, Developing Schools,* pp. 18-33 (London: David Fulton Publishers, 1994).

Gardner, H., *The Unschooled Mind: How Children Think and How Teachers Should Teach* (London: Fontana, 1991).

Glasser, W., *The Quality School Teacher* (New York: Harper, 1993).

Goleman, D., *Vital Lies, Simple Truths: The Psychology of Self-Deception* (London: Bloomsbury, 1997).

Goleman, D., *Emotional Intelligence: Why it can Matter more than IQ* (London: Bloomsbury, 1996).

Gregorc, A. F., 'A Systems-oriented Leader's Guide to Selecting Appropriate Services and Products', in *ASCD Curriculum Handbook*, 1995, 13.59-13.72 (1995): 'The Human Side of Models', in *ASCD Record*, Vol. 8, No. 2, pp. 38-41 (1990).

Hamblin, D., *Staff Development for Pastoral Care* (London: Basil Blackwell, 1989).

Hargreaves, D. H., 'A Road to the Learning Society', in *School Leadership and Management*, Vol. 17, No. 1, pp. 9-21, 1997.

Herron, D., Reports from the Director of the West Dublin Education Centre, 1993; 1994-95; 1996-97.

Hickey, A., 'The Professional Development of the Second Level Teacher: The Case for a Holistic Approach', in *Studies in Education: a Journal of Educational Research*, Vol .13, No. 1, spring 1997, pp. 43-52, 1997.

Hyland, A. and Hanafin, J., 'Models of Incareer Development in the Republic of Ireland: An Analysis', in *Irish Educational Studies* Vol. 16, pp. 144-71, 1997.

'Inset Service: An Activity-based Approach to Professional Development', in *Managing Schools Today*, Vol. 6, No. 6, pp. 1-4, (1997).

Institute of Guidance Counsellors, *Guidance and Counselling Service in Second-Level Schools and the Role of the Guidance Counsellor* (1996).

Ireland: CHL, Review of Professional Development in Teaching, 1991, Report commissioned by the NCCA (Dublin: Department of Education, 1992).

Ireland: *Charting Our Education Future*, White Paper on Education, Ireland (Dublin: Government Publications, 1995).

Ireland: *Operational Programme for Human Resources Development*, 1994-99. (Dublin: Stationery Office).

Irish Council of Churches' Board of Community Affairs, *The Churches' Rights in Education in Ireland* (Belfast: Inter-Church Centre, 1982).

Kogan, M., Johnson, D., Whitaker, T., Packwood, T., *School Governing Bodies* (London: Heinemann, 1984).

Kohn, A., *Punished by Rewards* (Boston: Houghton Mifflin, 1993).

Leader, D. and Boldt, S., *Principals and Principalships: A Study of*

Principals in Voluntary Secondary Schools (Dublin: Marino Institute of Education, 1994).

Leonard, D. and Dundon, P., *School Leadership Programme: Evaluation of the School Leadership and Whole-School Development Programme provided by the Secretariat of Secondary Schools* (Limerick: Centre for Studies in Gender and Education, 1996).

Lyons, J., *School 2000: Exploring the Relationships which Constitute Good Schools* (Clare Education Centre, 1997).

McGuinness, J., *Teachers, Pupils and Behaviour: A Managerial Approach* (London: Cassell, 1993);

   A Whole School Approach to Pastoral Care. (London: Kogan Page, 1989)

Mahon, O., *Negligence and the Teacher* (Clare: Ennis Teachers' Centre, 1995)

Main, A., *Educational Staff Development* (London: Croom Helm, 1985).

Martin, M., *Discipline in Schools: A Report to the Minister for Education* (1997).

Mayo, A., *Managing Careers: Strategies for Organizations* (London: Institute of Personnel Management, 1991).

Murray, Bishop Donal, 'The role of the Catholic school', in *Studies in Education: A Journal of Educational Research*, Vol. 11, No. 1, spring, pp. 1-13,. 1995.

OECD, *Review of Irish Education* (Paris: OECD, 1991), *The Oxford Dictionary* (Oxford: OUP, 1996).

Pierce, A., 'Effective Exits', in *Managing Schools Today*, Vol. 6, No. 6, March 1997, pp. 10-11 1997.

Schein, E., *Career Dynamics: Matching Organizational and Individual Need* Addison Wesley, 1978).

Secretariat for Secondary Schools: *Manual for Boards of Management of Catholic Secondary Schools; Articles of Management of Catholic Secondary Schools* (1991, revised 1996); *Handbook for Principals.*

Senge, P. M., *The Fifth Discipline: The Art and Practice of the Learning Organization* (New York: Doubleday, 1990).

Sotto, E., *When Teaching Becomes Learning: A Theory and Practice of Teaching* (London: Cassell, 1994).

Spark, D. and Hirsh, S., *A New Vision for Staff Development* (Virginia: ASCD, 1997).

Spaulding, A., 'Life in Schools – A Qualitative Study of Teacher Perspectives on the Politics of Principals: Ineffective Leadership Behaviors and their Consequences upon Teacher Thinking and Behavior', in *School Leadership and Management*, Vol. 17, no. 1, pp. 39-55, 1997.

Starratt, R. J., *Transforming Educational Administration* (New York: McGraw Hill, 1996);

   The Drama of Leadership (London: Falmer, 1993)

   'Communication as Script and as Scripting', in *Journal of Management Systems*, Vol. 5, No. 2, 1993, pp. 62-69.

Stoll, L. and Fink, D., *Changing Our Schools* (Oxford: OUP, 1996).

Sugrue, C. and Uí Thuama, C., 'Lifelong Learning for Teachers in Ireland: Policy, Provision and Vision, in *British Journal of In-service Education*, Vol. 23, No. 1, 1997, pp. 55-70.

Chapter 12: Challenges of Educational Leadership: Meaning, Community and Excellence

Coghlan, D., *Renewing Apostolic Religious Life* (Dublin: Columba, 1997).

Duignan, P. A. & Macpherson, R. J. S., *Educative Leadership: A Practical Theory for New Administrators and Managers* (London: Falmer, 1992).

Rashford, N. S. & Coghlan, D., *The Dynamics of Organisational Levels: A Change Framework for Managers and Consultants* (Reading, MA: Addison-Wesley, 1994).

Sergiovanni, T. J., 'Leadership and Excellence in Schooling', *Educational Leadership*, 41 (February 1984), 4-13 (1984).

Starratt, R.J., *Leaders with Vision: The Quest for School Renewal* (Thousand Oaks, CA: Corwin, 1995).

Starratt, R.J., *Transforming Educational Administrators – Meaning, Community and Excellence* (New York: McGraw-Hill, 1996).

Tuohy, D. 'Teacher Self-Evaluation: Discipline or Dyslexia in a Learning Organisation', *Irish Educational Studies*, 14, 64-82, 1995.

Tuohy, D. & Coghlan, D., 'Integrating Teacher and School Development through Organisational Levels', *Oideas,* 42, 83-97, 1994.

Tuohy, D. & Coghlan, D., 'Development in Schools: A Systems Approach Based on Organisational Levels', *Educational Management & Administration,* 25 (1), 65-77, 1997.

Chapter 13: Catholic Schools at the Crossroads

Bryk, A.S., Lee, V.E. and Holland, P.B. *Catholic Schools and the Common Good* (Cambridge Mass: Harvard University Press, 1993).

Coleman, J.S., T. Hoffer and S.D. Kilgore, *High School Achievement: Public Catholic and Private Schools Compared* (Chicago: University of Chicago Press, 1981).

Coleman, J.S. and T. Hofer, *Public and Private High Schools: The Impact of Communities* (New York: Basic Books, 1987).

Chapter 14: The Future of the Catholic School: An English Perspective

Arthur, J., *The Ebbing Tide: Policy and Principles in Catholic Education.* (Leominster: Gracewing, 1995).

Bryk, A. *et al., Catholic Schools and the Common Good* (Cambridge, Mass: Harvard University Press, 1993).

Catholic Bishops' Conference of England and Wales, *The Common Good in Education* (London: Catholic Education Service, 1997).

Chadwick, P., *Schools of Reconciliation: Issues in Joint Roman Catholic-Anglican Education* (London: Cassell, 1994).

Department for Catholic Education and Formation, *A Struggle for Excellence* (London: Catholic Education Service, 1997).

Grace, G., 'Education is a Public Good' in D. Bridges and T. McLaughlin (eds), *Education and the Market-Place* (London: Falmer, 1994).

Grace, G., *School Leadership: Beyond Educational Management* (London: Falmer, 1995).

Grace, G., 'Leadership in Catholic Schools' in T. McLaughlin *et al.* (eds.), *The Contemporary Catholic School: Context, Identity and Diversity* (London: Falmer, 1996).

Grace, G., 'Realising the Mission: Catholic Approaches to School Effectiveness' in R. Slee *et al.* (eds.), *Effective for Whom? School Effectiveness and the School Improvement Movement* (London: Falmer, 1997).

Groome, T., 'What Makes a School Catholic?' in T. McLaughlin *et al.* (eds.), op. cit.

Hastings, P., 'Openness and Intellectual Challenge in Catholic Schools', in T. McLaughlin *et al.* (eds.), op. cit.

Hume, B., 'The Church's Mission in Education', an address given in April 1995 and reprinted in *Partners in Mission* (London: Catholic Education Service, 1997).

Konstant, D., 'The Church and Catholic Independent Schools', an address given in January 1996 and reprinted in *Partners in Mission*, op. cit.

McClelland, V., 'The Concept of Catholic Education' in V. McClelland (ed.), *The Catholic School and the European Context* (Hull: University of Hull, 1992).

McLaren, P., *Schooling as a Ritual Performance* (London: Routledge, 1993).

McLaughlin, T., O'Keefe, J. and O'Keeffe, B. (eds.), *The Contemporary Catholic School: Context, Identity and Diversity* (London: Falmer, 1996).

Nichols, V., 'The Church's Mission in Education in a Multi-Faith Society', address given in April 1995 and reprinted in *Partners in Mission*, op. cit.,

O'Keeffe, B., 'Catholic schools in an Open Society: The English Challenge', in V. A. McClelland (ed.), *The Catholic School and the European Context* (Hull: University of Hull, 1992).

O'Keefe, J., 'No Margin: No Mission' in T. McLaughlin *et al.* (eds.), op. cit.

Pring, R., 'Markets, Education and Catholic Schools' in T. McLaughlin *et al.* (eds), op. cit.

Sacred Congregation for Catholic Education, *The Catholic School* (Homebush, NSW: St Pauls, 1988 ed.).

Wexler, P., *Holy Sparks: Social Theory, Education and Religion* (London: Macmillan, 1997).

Chapter 15: The Future of the Catholic School: An Irish Perspective

Arthur, J., *The Ebbing Tide: Policies and Principles of Catholic Education* (Herefordshire: Gracewing, 1995).

Barry, D., 'The ASTI and the Development of the Post-Primary School Structure' in *The Secondary Teacher*, Vol. 13, No. 1, winter 1984 (Dublin: ASTI, 1984).

Bishops of England and Wales, *Partners in Mission* (London: Catholic Education Service, 1997).

Bryk, Anthony S., 'Lessons from Catholic High Schools on Renewing our Educational Institutions', in McLaughlin T., J. O'Keefe SJ and B. O'Keeffe (1996), *The Contemporary Catholic School: Context, Identity and Diversity* (London: Falmer, 1996).

Bryk, Anthony S., V. E. Lee and P. B. Holland, *Catholic Schools and the Common Good* (Cambridge: Harvard University Press, 1993).

Congregation for Catholic Education, *The Catholic School* (London: Catholic Truth Society, 1977).

CORI, *The Trusteeship of Catholic Voluntary Secondary Schools* (Dublin: CORI, 1996).

Department of Education, *List of Second-Level Schools, 1995-96* (Dublin: Department of Education, 1995).

Drudy, S. & K. Lynch, *Schools and Society in Ireland* (Dublin: Gill & Macmillan, 1993).

FIRE, 'Future Involvement of Religious in Education (FIRE) Report' (Dublin: CMRS, 1973).

Flynn, Marcellin, *The Effectiveness of Catholic Schools* (Homebush, NSW: St Pauls, 1985).

Flynn, Marcellin, *The Culture of Catholic Schools* (Homebush, NSW: St Pauls, 1993).

Gallagher, M. P., *Clashing Symbols* (London: Darton, Longman & Todd, 1997).

Greeley, Andrew M., 'What Use are Catholic Schools in America?' *Doctrine and Life*, Vol. 47, No. 2, February 1997.

Hornsby-Smith, M., 'Catholic Stocktaking', *The Tablet*, 6 February 1993.

Kavanagh, A., *Secondary Education in Ireland: Aspects of a Changing Paradigm* (Carlow: Patrician Brothers, 1993).

McClelland, V. A., 'Education' in Hastings, A., *Modern Catholicism: Vatican II and After* (London: SPCK, 1991).

McLaughlin T., J. O'Keefe and B. O'Keeffe, *The Contemporary Catholic School: Context, Identity and Diversity* (London: Falmer, 1996).

O'Keeffe, T., 'The Religious Development of Male Adolescents in a Catholic Secondary School: A Comparative Study.' (Unpublished M. Ed. Dissertation, University of Hull, CLEO, Cork, 1997).

Paul VI, *Evangelii nuntiandi* (London: Catholic Truth Society, 1975).

NOTES

Chapter 3: Religion, Culture and Schooling

1. Most of the quotations used here can be found in Hyland and Milne (1992, 224- 32).
2. There is an interesting series of articles on the theme edited by Marc Coutty in *Le Monde de l'Education, de la Culture et de la Formation*, 246, March 1997.
3. The expression 'rounded persons' is taken from the former Minister for Education, Niamh Bhreathnach's John Marcus O'Sullivan Lecture, 'Towards a Coherent Philosophy of Education'. See Bhreathnach, 1994,5.

Chapter 5: Teaching Religion to Young People Today

1. 'Godless programmes' is the name given by the author to health education, values clarification and personal development programmes.
2. This symbiosis of Catholic school and Catholic community is well presented by Bishop Donal Murray in 'The Role of the Catholic School', *Studies in Education*, vol. 11, no.1, 1-12.

Chapter 11: Staff Development as Empowering and Enabling

1. This was acknowledged by the OECD (1991) and encouraged by Rule 58, *Rules for Primary Schools*, concerning 'extra personal vacation' days: four such days may be taken in lieu of an approved summer course of four days duration; five days may be taken for a three-week course; no paid substitution is available. Sugrue and Uí Thuama (1997, 58) suggest that 'many [primary teachers]… do not avail of these additional discretionary holidays', though statistical evidence for this is unavailable.
2. See *Annual General Reports* of the Education Centres, 1996 and 1997.
3. Between 1967 and 1969, when *Curaclam na Bunscoile* (1971) was in a limited pilot phase, efforts were made by some of the Primary Inspectors of the Department of Education to

involve participating teachers in team-teaching. This writer was among the pilot teachers in a large Dublin school.

4. In Ireland, the establishment of the Mater Dei Institute of Education by Archbishop John Charles McQuaid of Dublin quickly set a headline (not devoid of controversy) in teacher education. The Second Vatican Council and *Gravissimum educationis*, the publication by the Sacred Congregation for Catholic Education of *The Catholic School* (1977), and a further and more developed document, *The Religious Dimension of Education in a Catholic School* (1988), gave additional impetus to the catechetical movement.

5. Curriculum changes by the Department of Education continue to give impetus to professional development courses for teachers, though such a system of response may not be as reactive as is suggested by Hickey (1997, 43-52); the current involvement of teachers as leaders in professional development for teachers of transition-year programmes, Civic, Social and Political Education, the Leaving Certificate Vocational, the Applied Leaving Certificate, Business, Music, Health Promotion and Relationships and Sexuality Education is evidence of a type of *rapprochement* between what Hickey calls a 'reactive' and a 'pro-active' response.

6. The Minutes of the Central Executive Council (CEC) and of the Standing Committee of the ASTI from 1960 to 1980 are a tribute to the many teacher members who devoted time outside the school day in promoting curriculum and professional development courses. See also the account of the Education Committee of the ASTI, 5 January 1980. Henry Collins, as chairman, worked energetically with the Committee on the development of the Higher Diploma in Education (in conjunction with St Patrick's College, Maynooth), on in-service for teachers, pastoral care and pupil transfers.

7. In fairness to the Department of Education, it must be pointed out that the Secretariat of Secondary Schools, which is the executive arm of the Joint Managerial Body and the Association of Management of Catholic Secondary Schools, received financial assistance in the pilot and delivery phases

of the School Leadership Programme, recently evaluated by Leonard (1996) in *School Leadership Programme.*

8. The CCSS voluntarily ceased to exist in 1988 as part of a greater partnership between the Catholic managerial bodies. The Association of Management of Catholic Secondary Schools (AMCSS) is now the negotiating body for Catholic schools. It is also a constituent partner with other Church school managers in the Joint Managerial Body.

9. The author is completing doctoral research on the managerial bodies: while many schools did not facilitate professional development for either nuns or lay teachers in these years, a number of religious congregations, notably the Dominicans and the Loreto Sisters, led the way.

10. *The Secondary Teacher*, Vol. 2, No. 4, April 1967, p. 5: the editorial (by Thomas O'Dea) was commenting on the recent and first time the ASTI was addressed by a president of the Conference of Convent Secondary Schools. On this occasion, the president was Mother Jordana, OP. The editor referred to the fact that the audience 'for the most part had never heard a nun lift up her voice in public'. He added that in the 'various subject associations nuns usually form the majority of the audience … [that there was] a new reaction from them now … once silent, now they discuss, question and contribute … and even argue'.

11. The publication was an account of a six-week professional research visit by Eileen Doyle, then president, CCSS, and Br Declan Duffy, FMS, chairman of the Education Commission. The research focused on the development of adult education, including staff development in Catholic schools – see *Report on Adult Education* published by the CMRS, 1977.

12. A study of the topics of the Annual General Conferences of the CCSS, the CMRS, the Catholic Headmasters' Association and the Teaching Brothers' Association in particular is indicative of growing awareness of the importance of staff development and training.

13. Future Involvement of Religious in Education, Confidential Report commissioned by the Major Religious Superiors and the Hierarchy (1973). Paul Andrews SJ was chairman.

14. The Minutes of the CCSS meetings, the Reports of the Annual General Meetings and Conferences and the writer's personal notes give details but few statistics.

15. The Department of Education now sanctions two days annually as 'staff days', provided a minimum of eight weeks notice is given and a very detailed application form completed.

16. Hoyle (1975) suggested that professionality be viewed as a continuum, one end of which was 'professionality' or the knowledge, skills and procedures teachers use in their classrooms. This differs from professionalism or the statute-related elements of teaching. The other end of the continuum of professionality is concerned with teachers' values, pedagogy and philosophical beliefs, which contribute to a wider vision of education – Evans (1997), 'A Voice Crying in the Wilderness?', pp. 61-83.

17. The development since 1993 by Trinity College, Dublin and (initially) the Drumcondra Education Centre of modular, weekend and summer course work leading to diplomas and masters qualifications is an example of meeting individual teacher needs and aspirations. An interesting recent development is a number of staff teams who are pursuing these qualifications but with a research emphasis on whole school development planning in their schools.

18. As a lecturer/facilitator with the School Leadership Programme of the Secretariat of Secondary Schools, the writer's records of the participating *teachers'* evaluation enumerate their principal professional concerns as follows: managing learning in classrooms; mixed ability teaching with the focus on methodologies in different subjects; motivation and learning; how to deal with over-dependence on teaching.

19. According to the *Manual for Boards of Management for Catholic Secondary Schools* (revised 1996) 16, par. B, under 'The Powers of the Board of Management': 'In a pastoral context the Board of Management has to make certain provision for its staff such as devising adequate channels of communication and consultation between management and

staff and ensuring the ongoing formation of the staff through in-service training.'

The published draft of the Education Bill stated that the school plan was the responsibility of the Board of Management and was to be done in accordance with the directions of the Minister for Education – *Education Bill, 1997,* par. 52, 1 and 2; See also CORI (1996), *Guidelines on School Development Planning,* for the trustees of their schools.

20. The 'teaching principal' (for schools of less than eight teachers) in primary schools might perceive themselves as having a role, even indirectly through teamwork, 'in enabling teachers to inform their practice with educational research'; the Leader and Boldt (1994) study showed that principals of voluntary secondary schools were 'generally involved with low value tasks'. An Australian research project is of interest – cf. Cattickvick and O'Donoghue (1997).

21. A profile of sixty secondary schools with which I have been associated since 1989 shows that the majority of staff had spent their entire teaching careers in the one school: in twenty of these schools, a number of these teachers had also completed their initial teaching practice in the same school.

22. The CHL (1991) report recommended distance education for teachers. However, the human contact with colleagues in other schools during term is significant in enabling teachers to experience other ways, perhaps, and other school systems; The White Paper (1995, 127-8) criticised the fragmented approach to in-service, which was 'largely provider-driven'. Empowering teachers to make structured 'professional explorations' in places of good practice, and to adapt as appropriate within their own school, has been significant in whole school development planning.

23. The short-lived Teachers' Council of 1974 might have brought about such an agreed professional ethic. Increasing demands on teachers at the close of the century highlight the lacuna, though we must acknowledge the publication, *The Role of the Guidance Counsellor* (1996), by then Minister for Education, Niamh Bhreathnach, and the continuing work of the National Centre for Guidance Counselling.

24. Hargreaves highlights the increasing power of economic factors in influencing educational change. The 'centre' might be 'at national or state level' and would tend to see educational provision as consumer-led and results-driven.

25. For some thoughts on employers' commitment to staff development see Boyle (1996), 'Building on Hidden Talent', p.18.

26. Since 1980, the religious congregations and trustees of the largest section of second-level schools have contributed significantly to developing statements of the philosophy of their various schools in the light of an increasing awareness of the need to formalise mission statements, in the context of a changing Ireland and a changing Catholic Church. Much has been learned since the beginning of that process, which was spearheaded by the Conference of Major Religious Superiors (now CORI). Each Board of Management is charged and entrusted with managing the school in the context of the stated philosophy. It is, therefore, a vision that staff and board, together with all those who constitute the school community, are challenged to realise.

27. An Irish study of the working relationships between primary-school principals and chairpersons, and a similar study at secondary level, could yield insights into why some boards appear to be more effective than others.

28. The work of Diggins, Doyle and Herron as team and team leaders in staff development since 1992; See Herron, 'Reports', 1993-4, 1996, 1997, on whole school development planning in the primary and second-level schools with which he and his team members work; the Maynooth project, led by Jim Callan (1996), and continuing in second-level schools in the Kildare-midlands area.

29. For a thoughtful exploration of the leadership and management of schools in the context of the development of teachers and all those who work in schools, including volunteers – Fidler (1997), 'Editorial', pp. 5-8.

30. It is worth noting that a growing number of second-level schools have abandoned the formal 'morning break' because of the difficulty of providing adequate supervision. Martin

(1997) found that the 'importance of vigilant supervision and monitoring of all activities within the school areas' was significant in promoting school discipline.

Chapter 13: Catholic Schools at the Crossroads: An American Perspective
1. Coleman was not Catholic. I have no idea what Bryk's religious background or present affiliation might be.
2. This is not the time or place to discuss this decline. However, the clericalist assumption that 'it's the laity's fault' is manifestly absurd, as is the self-serving conviction that the laity will give more if only they are reminded. It's hard to see how anyone can believe such nonsense.
3. The whole issue of the JSBS is devoted to the subject.

Chapter 14: The Future of the Catholic School: An English Perspective
1. For these distinctions, see McLaughlin, T. *et al.* (1996, 6-7).
2. James Arthur (1995) notes that the Inner London Education Authority (ILEA), in evidence to the Taylor Committee in 1976, argued that 'Catholic schools did not take their fair share of really difficult children' (105) and the Association of Metropolitan Education Authorities, as late as 1989, passed a resolution which asserted that voluntary-aided schools were 'damaging' to the interests of state education in some localities (119).
3. Deep structure analysis refers to a mode of social and educational inquiry which goes beyond surface indicators of performance or 'success' to attempt in-depth assessment of culture, process and values. A fundamental concern of this approach is to evaluate the extent to which an educational institution realises in its practice what it claims in its mission statement.
4. The 'strategic subsidy' of the religious orders has been particularly crucial in urban poverty areas in the past. The

question for the future is: Will the state, or the wider Catholic community, be prepared to take over this subsidy? In both cases, the answer seems likely to be 'no'.

5. For a discussion of the commodification of education, see Grace (1994).

6. There is, of course, no shortage of accounts of pre-Conciliar Catholic schooling which assert that the anthropology of the person was based upon a different principle, i.e. capable of good but essentially evil.

7. It seems remarkable that no designated agency for research into Catholic education in England and Wales has been established in this century. The CRDCE was inaugurated in September 1996 with an initial grant from The Society of Jesus.

8. Fieldwork research for *The Ebbing Tide* was based upon a study of Catholic schools in Oxfordshire only.

9. It is not only Catholic inner-city schools which are dealing with significant numbers of 'those who are far from the faith'; it is also, at the other end of the financial spectrum, Catholic independent schools. As Bishop David Konstant noted in his address to the Conference of Catholic Independent Schools, 'roughly half of all pupils in your schools are Catholics; there is no indication as to the religious background of the other 50 per cent' (1997, 64).

10. For an account of the progress and the difficulties associated with inter-denominational schools, see Chadwick (1994).

11. For a discussion of the importance of Catholic school mission statements in guiding such research, see Grace (1997).

12. At a more general theoretical level, Philip Wexler (1997) has called for the 'resacralising' of social and educational theory and of research inquiry in education.

THE CONTRIBUTORS

Coghlan, David
Fr David Coghlan, a Jesuit priest, teaches organisational behaviour at the School of Business Studies, Trinity College, Dublin, and is author of several books and many articles on organisation development.

Doyle, Eileen
Eileen Doyle, a former school principal, is an experienced teacher at primary, vocational, secondary and third level. She has contributed to Irish education for more than thirty years through her work on a wide variety of committees, organisations and boards. She is currently engaged in doctoral research on managerial bodies in Ireland.

Feheney, J. Matthew
Brother Feheney is a Presentation Brother and director of the Catholic Leadership in Education Office (CLEO), Cork. He has published widely in education, local and family history. His recent publications include *Pastoral Care*, 3 vols (1994), *Education and the Family* (1995), *Edmund Rice Anniversary Yearbook* (1995), *A Time of Grace* (1996). His current research interest is Catholic education.

Flanagan, Bernadette
Bernadette Flanagan, a Presentation Sister, graduated in theology and mathematics from St Patrick's College, Maynooth, in 1983. After some years teaching at second level, she returned to study at Milltown Institute of Theology and Philosophy, where she completed an MA in spirituality. She currently lectures in Theology and Spirituality at Milltown Institute, where she is also completing doctoral research on 'Spirituality in Dublin's Liberties'.

Grace, Gerald

Professor Gerald Grace is currently the director of the Centre for Research and Development in Catholic Education at the University of London, Institute of Education. He has taught education at King's College, London, at the University of Cambridge (where he was a fellow of Wolfson College) and in Wellington, New Zealand, where he was head of the Department of Education. He was Professor of Education at the University of Durham (1990-96), during which time he was also head of the School of Education there. He has published widely in education, his most recent book being *School Leadership: Beyond Education Management* (Falmer Press, 1995).

Greeley, Andrew M.

Father Andrew Greeley, a priest of the Archdiocese of Chicago, is a distinguished sociologist and best-selling author. He is professor of social sciences at the University of Chicago and the University of Arizona, as well as research associate at the National Opinion Research Center at the University of Chicago. He has written scores of books and hundreds of popular and scholarly articles on a variety of issues in sociology, education and religion. His column on political, Church and social issues is carried by the New Times Religious News Service. He is also author of thirty best-selling novels and an autobiography, *Confessions of a Parish Priest*. His latest novel is *White Smoke*.

Looney, Anne

Anne Looney, a graduate of Mater Dei Institute of Education, is a catechist in a Dublin second-level school. She has also worked in the field of adult education and as a consultant with Kairos publications. She is one of the education officers for the NCCA course committee in religious education and her recent publications include an article in *The Church in a New Ireland*, edited by Seán Mac Réamoinn (Columba Press, 1996).

McCann, Joseph F.

Fr Joseph F. McCann is a Vincentian priest who teaches in the Religious Studies Department at St Patrick's College, Drumcondra, a college of Dublin City University. He taught secondary school for many years before studying for a doctorate in education at Columbia University. Subsequent work was in ecumenical theology with the Irish School of Ecumenics. He has published *Church and Organization: A Social and Theological Enquiry* (Scranton, 1993).

McCormack, Teresa

Dr Teresa McCormack is director of the Education Office at the Conference of Religious of Ireland (CORI), is the representative body for religious congregations (male and female) in Ireland. It plays an active role in influencing public policy in education, especially in relation to educational disadvantage, curriculum and assessment and adult and community education. A Presentation Sister, Dr McCormack has taught at first, second and third level, was principal of a large secondary school and worked in community development before joining CORI. She has written widely on educational issues.

O'Keeffe, Tom

Tom O'Keeffe, a post-primary teacher in Cork, was educated at Marino Institute of Education, University College Cork and the University of Hull/CLEO. His special area of research is Catholic education, on which he has also written extensively. He is closely associated with the work of the Christian Leadership in Education Office (CLEO) in Cork.

Steele, Frank J.

Frank Joseph Steele was born in Cork in 1943 and educated at Marino Institute of Education (Teacher's Diploma), University College Cork (BA, MA) and Keble College, Oxford (DPhil). He is principal of St Aidan's College, Cork, and tutor and occasional lecturer for the MEd Programme, University of Hull/CLEO (Cork). He is also an Associate of the Presentation Brothers. His recent publications include *Towards a Spirituality for Lay-Folk* (Edwin Mellen Press, 1995).

Treston, Kevin

Kevin Treston has worked as a teacher and consultant for many years in several countries. His doctoral and post-doctoral studies were completed in the US. He is author of several books, including *Pastoral Care for Schools* (1989), *Transforming Catholic Schools* (1992), *A New Vision of Religious Education* (1993). He lives in Brisbane, Australia, and works as an educational consultant.

Tuohy, David

Fr David Tuohy SJ is director of Educational Administration at University College, Dublin. He is actively involved in staff development and has worked with schools in Ireland, the UK, Africa, Australia and the US.

Williams, Kevin

Dr Kevin Williams lectures in Mater Dei Institute of Education and is president of the Educational Studies Association of Ireland. He has published and lectured widely on philosophical and educational issues, nationally and internationally, and is author/editor of several books, including *The Future of Religion in Irish Education* (Veritas, 1997), of which he is co-editor. His current research is on the role of identity and allegiance in political life.

More from J. Matthew Feheney FPM

EDUCATION AND THE FAMILY
Ed. J. Matthew Feheney FPM

In 1994 the UN celebrated the year of the family, which coincided with the celebrations of the 150th anniversary of the death of Edmund Rice. These two events combined to promote a series of discussions on education and the family in Ireland. This publication is a collection of discussion papers presented at a conference held in University College Cork. The topics include: the involvement of the family in education, the importance of self-esteem, suicide, Christian feminism and the educational needs of the Christian family. Education and the family will be of great benefit to those involved in education and of interest to those dealing with the young.

N: 1 85390 305 1   **176pp Paperback**   **£7.95**

• • • • • • • • • • • • • •

A TIME OF GRACE - SCHOOL MEMORIES
Edmund Rice and the Presentation Tradition of Education
Ed. J. Matthew Feheney FPM

Published to mark the beatification of Edmund Rice on 5 October 1996, this timely offering from J. Matthew Feheney looks retrospectively at the contribution made by the Presentation Brothers to education in Ireland. The book contains contributions from past pupils, teachers and others associated with the Brothers. The contributors are well known in media and academic circles and include Liam Nolan, Edmund Van Esbeck and John McGahern. The book also contains extracts from the late Sean O'Faolain's autobiography.

N: 1 85390 356 6   **198pp Paperback**   **£7.95**

Available from Veritas and all good Bookstores

VERITAS
7/8 Lower Abbey Street, Dublin 1 – Tel: (01) 878 8177 · Fax: (01) 878 6507
Also: Stillorgan, Cork, Ennis, Letterkenny, Sligo

UK: Lower Avenue, Leamington Spa, Warwickshire CV31 3NP
Tel: (01926) 451 730 · Fax: (01926) 451 733

Other Related Titles

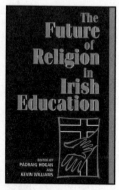

THE FUTURE OF RELIGION IN IRISH EDUCATION
Ed. Padraig Hogan And Kevin Williams

Religious influences permeate the education system at all levels
recent years, a number of significant changes have occurred wi
religious education and many young people are express
negative attitudes towards religion. This publication probes
seriousness of the problem while attempting to predict the futur
religion and education in Ireland. With a decline in the adhere
of the sacraments and a disturbing increase in cults and sects,
timing of this book could not be better. It attempts to provide
analysis of, and perspective on, these changes.

ISBN: 1-85390-322-1   **152pp Paperback**   £6.

• • • • • • • • • • • •

FAITH AND CULTURE IN THE IRISH CONTEXT
Ed. Eoin G. Cassidy

The dramatic changes in religious belief patterns set the backd
for this unique perspective on faith in Ireland. This publicat
provides an examination of the changing profile of Irish f
practice within the context of the emerging cultural changes in
developed world. Eminent scholars from both secular and religi
circles examine these changes. Contributors include Michael P
Gallagher SJ, Bishop Donal Murray, Christopher T. Warren
Marguerite Corish, in a collection of essays presented a
symposium on faith and culture held at Mater Dei Institute
Education.

ISBN: 1 85390 331 0   **176pp Paperback**   £9.

Available from Veritas and all good Bookstores

VERITAS
7/8 Lower Abbey Street, Dublin 1 – Tel: (01) 878 8177 · Fax: (01) 878 6507
Also: Stillorgan, Cork, Ennis, Letterkenny, Sligo

UK: Lower Avenue, Leamington Spa, Warwickshire CV31 3NP
Tel: (01926) 451 730 · Fax: (01926) 451 733

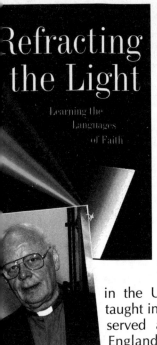

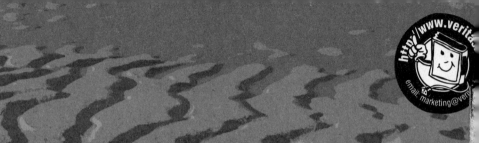

welcome to www.veritas.ie

FIND OUT more about these and any other <u>Veritas titles</u> directly **on our WEBSITE.**

Order over the **Internet** from ANY of our listed categori

You can also enquire about **ANY** book of interest to you.

Why not join in on <u>our on-line</u> discussion grou Our **CHAT GROUP** allows you to share and air your views w others.

Even if you have nothing to say, the <u>chat group</u> makes fascinating reading!!!

Contact us NOW at our website...

http://www.veritas.ie

for further information contact email: marketing@veritas.ie or phone (01) 878 81